SUPER-INFINITE

Katherine Rundell is a Fellow of All Souls College, Oxford, where she works on Renaissance literature. Her bestselling books for children have been translated into more than thirty languages and have won multiple awards. Rundell is also the author of the book for adults, *Why You Should Read Children's Books, Even Though You Are So Old and Wise*. She has written for, among others, the *London Review of Books*, the *Times Literary Supplement*, the *New York Review of Books* and the *New York Times*, largely about books, though sometimes about animals, night climbing and tightrope walking. *The Golden Mole and Other Living Treasure* was published in 2022.

Further praise for *Super-Infinite*:

'Rundell, with her own beautiful style, makes you cheerfully submit to and share her adoration of the man.' Jenny Colgan, *Spectator* Books of the Year

'Rundell's tone is conversational . . . [and] belies a staggering amount of learning. *Super-Infinite* is a refreshing biography.' Michael Delgado, *Prospect*

'This sparkling biography of the metaphysical poet turned preacher illuminates an era of plague, persecution and great existential change.' Justine Jordan, *Guardian*

'Excellent . . . Rundell tells these stories engagingly . . . What truly matters, and makes *Super-Infinite* emphatically worth reading, is that Rundell is a *writer*.' Joe Moshenska, *Literary Review*

'On reading this extraordinary biography you are left concluding that [Rundell's] talent, like that of her hero's, must somehow by super-infinite.' *Sunday Times*

'A wonderful, joyou[...] [...]rogative intelligence. I[...] [...]sterious

of men brought out into the light, for all to see. I just loved it.'
Maggie O'Farrell

'The greatest strength of Rundell's book is the way she magics this world to life, making its intricacies and insanities comprehensible.' *The Times*

'Rundell offers a fresh view of a writer living permanently at the edge of his senses.' *Catholic Herald*

'Rundell has an engagingly idiosyncratic and playful style . . . In Rundell, Donne has an authoritative and sympathetic chronicler . . . This fine book demands and rewards your fullest attention, just as its subject does.' Alexander Larman, *Observer*

'It brings the poet, his poetry, his many lives and his turbulent Elizabethan and Stuart times vividly to life.' Simon Sebag Montefiore

'Katherine Rundell's brave and detailed new biography of John Donne is just the book we need: the life, family, historical background, religious questions and – best of all – the poetry, are imaginatively researched and subtly treated. The result is worthy of its subject.' Claire Tomalin

'What a delightful book *Super-Infinite* is: companionable, astute, intimate in tone and clear-eyed in judgment, it brings Donne and his milieu to glorious life. I loved it.' Nick Laird

'Crackling with gusto and sympathetic intelligence, *Super-Infinite* places John Donne fairly and squarely in his own times, while making those times feel contiguous with our own.' Andrew Motion

'Katherine Rundell has a wonderful touch, light yet profound, which perfectly suits her extraordinary subject. Unmissable.' Simon Jenkins

'*Super-Infinite* is a stylish, scholarly and gripping account of Donne's ecstatically divided self . . . a work super-relevant to our own troubled times.' Rose Tremain

SUPER-INFINITE

*The
Transformations
of
JOHN DONNE*

KATHERINE RUNDELL

faber

To Bart van Es, whose teaching changed
the course of my life

First published in 2022
by Faber & Faber Ltd
Bloomsbury House
74–77 Great Russell Street
London WCIB 3DA
This paperback edition first published in 2023

Typeset by Faber & Faber Ltd
Printed and bound by CPI Group (UK) Ltd, Croydon, CR0 4YY

A CIP record for this book
is available from the British Library

ISBN 978–0–571–34592–2

MIX
Paper | Supporting
responsible forestry
FSC
www.fsc.org
FSC® C171272

Printed and bound in the UK on FSC® certified paper in line with our continuing
commitment to ethical business practices, sustainability and the environment.
For further information see faber.co.uk/environmental-policy

4 6 8 10 9 7 5

CONTENTS

INTRODUCTION

I

The power of John Donne's words nearly killed a man. It was the late spring of 1623, on the morning of Ascension Day, and Donne had finally secured for himself celebrity, fortune and a captive audience. He had been appointed the Dean of St Paul's Cathedral two years before: he was fifty-one, slim and amply bearded, and his preaching was famous across the whole of London. His congregation – merchants, aristocrats, actors in elaborate ruffs, the whole sweep of the city – came to his sermons carrying paper and ink, wrote down his finest passages and took them home to dissect and relish, pontificate and argue over. He often wept in the pulpit, in joy and in sorrow, and his audience would weep with him. His words, they said, could 'charm the soul'.

That morning he was not preaching in his own church, but fifteen minutes' easy walk across London at Lincoln's Inn, where a new chapel was being consecrated. Word went out: wherever he was, people came flocking, often in their thousands, to hear him speak. That morning, too many people flocked. 'There was a great concourse of noblemen and gentlemen', and in among 'the extreme press and thronging', as they pushed closer to hear his words, men in the crowd were shoved to the ground and trampled. 'Two or

1

three were endangered, and taken up dead for the time.' There's no record of Donne halting his sermon; so it's likely that he kept going in his rich, authoritative voice as the bruised men were carried off and out of sight.

Donne the preacher: engraving by Pierre Lombart,
after an unknown painting

II

Just fifteen years before that, the same man finished a book and immediately put it away. He knew as he wrote it that

2

it could be dangerous to him were it to be discovered. He was living in obscurity in Mitcham, in a cold house with thin walls and a noxious cellar that leaked 'raw vapours' to the rooms above, distracted by a handful of gamesome and clamouring children. It was a book written in illness and poverty, to be read by almost no one. The book was called *Biathanatos*; a text which has claim to being the first full-length treatise on suicide written in English. It laid out, with painstaking precision, how often its author dreamed of killing himself.

III

A decade or so before, the same man, then about twenty-three years old, sat for a portrait. The painting was of a man who knew about fashion; he wore a hat big enough to sail a cat in, a big lace collar, an exquisite moustache. He positioned the pommel of his sword to be just visible, an accessory more than a weapon. Around the edge of the canvas was painted in Latin, 'O Lady, lighten our darkness'; a not-quite-blasphemous misquotation of Psalm 17, his prayer addressed not to God but to a lover. And his beauty deserved walk-on music, rock-and-roll lute: all architectural jawline and hooked eyebrows. Those eyebrows were the author of some of the most celebratory and most lavishly sexed poetry ever written in English, shared among an intimate and loyal group of hyper-educated friends:

License my roving hands, and let them go
Behind, before, above, between, below!
O my America! My new-found land!
My kingdom, safeliest when with one man manned!

The Lothian Portrait, artist unknown, c.1595

Sometime religious outsider and social disaster, sometime celebrity preacher and establishment darling, John Donne was incapable of being just one thing. He reimagined and reinvented himself, over and over: he was a poet, lover, essayist, lawyer, pirate, recusant, preacher, satirist, politician, courtier, chaplain to the King, dean of the finest cathedral in London. It's traditional to imagine two Donnes – Jack Donne, the youthful rake, and Dr Donne, the older, wiser priest, a split Donne himself imagined in a letter to a friend – but he was infinitely more various and unpredictable than that.

Donne loved the *trans-* prefix: it's scattered everywhere across his writing – 'transpose', 'translate', 'transport', 'transubstantiate'. In this Latin preposition – 'across, to the other side of, over, beyond' – he saw both the chaos and potential of us. We are, he believed, creatures born transformable. He knew of transformation into misery: 'But O, self-traitor, I do bring/The spider love, which transubstantiates all/And can convert manna to gall' – but also the transformation achieved by beautiful women: 'Us she informed, but transubstantiates you'.

And then there was the transformation of himself: from failure and penury, to recognition within his lifetime as one of the finest minds of his age; one whose work, if allowed under your skin, can offer joy so violent it kicks the metal out of your knees, and sorrow large enough to eat you. Because amid all Donne's reinventions, there was a constant running through his life and work: he remained steadfast in his belief that we, humans, are at once a catastrophe and a miracle.

There are few writers of his time who faced greater horror. Donne's family history was one of blood and fire; a great-uncle was arrested in an anti-Catholic raid and executed: another was locked inside the Tower of London, where as a small schoolboy Donne visited him, venturing fearfully in among the men convicted to death. As a student, a young priest whom his brother had tried to shelter was captured, hanged, drawn and quartered. His brother was taken by the priest hunters at the same time, tortured and locked in a plague-ridden jail. At sea, Donne watched in horror and fascination as dozens of sailors burned to death. He married a young woman, Anne More, clandestine and hurried by love, and as a result found himself thrown in prison, spending dismayed ice-cold winter months first in a disease-ridden cell and then under house arrest. Once married, they were often poor, and at the mercy of richer friends and relations; he knew what it was to be jealous and thwarted and bitter. He was racked, over and over again, by life-threatening illnesses, with dozens of bouts of fever, aching throat, vomiting; at least three times it was believed he was dying. He lost, over the course of his life, six children: Francis at seven, Lucy at nineteen, Mary at three, an unnamed stillborn baby, Nicholas as an infant, another stillborn child. He lost Anne, at the age of thirty-three, her body destroyed by bearing twelve children. He thought often of sin, and miserable failure, and suicide. He believed us unique in our capacity to ruin ourselves: 'Nothing but man, of all envenomed things,/Doth work upon itself with inborn sting'. He was a man who walked so often in darkness that it became for him a daily commute.

But there are also few writers of his time who insisted so doggedly and determinedly on awe. His poetry is wildly delighted and captivated by the body – though broken, though doomed to decay – and by the ways in which thinking fast and hard were a sensual joy akin to sex. He kicked aside the Petrarchan traditions of idealised, sanitised desire: he joyfully brought the body to collide with the soul. He wrote: 'one might almost say her body thought.' In his sermons, he reckoned us a disaster, but the most spectacular disaster that has ever been. As he got older he grew richer, harsher, sterner and drier, yet he still asserted: 'it is too little to call Man a little world; except God, man is a diminutive to nothing. Man consists of more pieces, more parts, than the world doth, nay, than the world is.' He believed our minds could be forged into citadels against the world's chaos: he wrote in a verse letter, 'be thine own palace, or the world's thy jail.' Tap a human, he believed, and they ring with the sound of infinity.

Joy and squalor: both Donne's life and work tell that it is fundamentally impossible to have one without taking up the other. You could try, but you would be so coated in the unacknowledged fear of being forced to look, that what purchase could you get on the world? Donne saw, analysed, lived alongside, even saluted corruption and death. He was often hopeless, often despairing, and yet still he insisted at the very end: *it is an astonishment to be alive, and it behoves you to be astonished*.

¶

How much of Donne remains to us? Those who love Donne have no choice but to relish the challenge of piecing him together from a patchwork of what we do and do not know. He is there in his work, always; but there are moments in his life where we must work out from fragments and clues what it was that he was doing: there is a long gap in his childhood, another after university, more after his marriage, and in his later years he flickers in and out of sight. Time eats your paperwork, and it has eaten some of his. We have, for instance, not yet discovered any diaries, no books of household notes or accounts. There are no manuscript drafts of poems – we have only one English poem in his own handwriting – and so no evidence of him at work, building the verse from false starts and scratches. He burned all his friends' letters to him after they died; a letter was, for him, akin to an extension of the living person, and should not exist without its parent – so we have no gossipy to-and-fros in the letter archive.

But what remains is a miracle; because a colossal amount of Donne's work has been rescued from time's hunger, remarkable in the period for its variety and sweep.

There are two long prose treatises on religious questions,

one of which – an attack on the Jesuits called *Ignatius His Conclave* – is racy and explosive and delicious, and the other of which – an argument that Catholics must take the Oath of Allegiance to the King, called *Pseudo-Martyr* – is so dense it would be swifter to eat it than to read it. There are thirty-one pieces of half satirical, half serious prose writing called the Problems and Paradoxes: essays with stings in them, and the *Essays in Divinity*, which are hyper-learned disquisitions on various books of the Bible. There is *Biathanatos*, his treatise on suicide, an interrogation of sin and conscience. There are the *Devotions upon Emergent Occasions*, a collection of twenty-three meditations on humanity, written at breakneck speed during a near-fatal illness in the very teeth of what Donne believed was going to be his death. (Having published them within weeks of writing them, he went on to survive another eight years.) There are 160 sermons, dating from 1615 to 1631 – six of which were published during his lifetime, the rest collected by his son into three great luxurious folios after his death.

There are 230 letters, to his friends, patrons and employers, the majority of which were also collected and published posthumously by his son, John Donne junior. John junior had a bad habit, when editing the letters, of removing all dates and changing the names of the addressees to make his father's early acquaintance seem more high-flying and high-society, so dating and attributing them is an ongoing and gargantuan task. Anyone turning to the prose letters seeking disquisitions on politics or news of his love affairs would be disappointed; Donne lived under a state which both censored and spied on its citizens, and his letters are largely – though not solely – practicalities. Will you come for dinner? I am ill. Might you give me money? Can you find me work? (Or, more accurately, because a significant portion of the letters are outrageous pieces of flattery: you are so ravishingly exquisite, can you find me work?)

And there are the poems: about two hundred of them, totalling just over 9,100 lines. In among those lines are epithalamia – poems written to salute a marriage – and obsequies – poems written to mourn a death. There are satires, religious verse, and about forty verse letters, a tradition he loved; poems of anything from twelve to 130 lines, carrying news, musings on virtue and God, and declarations of how richly he treasures the friend to whom he is writing. The idea of writing letters in verse wasn't his own – Petrarch did it, and the tradition dates all the way back to Ovid, whose *Heroides* are imagined verse letters by the wronged heroines of Roman and Greek myths – but Donne seems to have used the form more than any other poet of his lifetime. There was something in the way a verse letter could elevate the details of the day-to-day and render it sharp-edged and memorable that he cherished. It appealed to the part of him that wanted his own brand of intense precision to suffuse everything he touched.

And then there is the work Donne is most famous for; the love poetry and the erotic verse. To call anyone the 'best' of anything is a brittle kind of game – but if you wanted to play it, Donne is the greatest writer of desire in the English language. He wrote about sex in a way that nobody ever has, before or since: he wrote sex as the great insistence on life, the salute, the bodily semaphore for the human living infinite. The word most used across his poetry, apart from 'and' and 'the', is 'love'.

This body of surviving work is enough, taken together, to make the case that Donne was one of the finest writers in English: that he belongs up alongside Shakespeare, and that to let him slowly fall out of the common consciousness would be as foolish as discarding a kidney or a lung. The work cuts through time to us: but his life also cannot be ignored – because the imagination that burns through his poetry was the same which attempted to manoeuvre through the snake pit of the Renaissance court. This book, then, hopes to do both: both to tell the story of his life, and to point to the places in his work where his words are at their most singular: where his words can be, for a modern reader, galvanic. His work still has the power to be transformative. This is both a biography of Donne and an act of evangelism.

§

You cannot claim a man is an alchemist and fail to lay out the gold. This, then, is an undated poem, probably written for Anne More, some time in his twenties, known as 'Love's Growth' –

I scarce believe my love to be so pure
As I had thought it was,
Because it doth endure
Vicissitude and season as the grass;
Methinks I lied all Winter, when I swore
My love was infinite, if Spring make't more.
But if this med'cine, love, which cures all sorrow
With more, not only be no quìntessence,
But mixed of all stuffs paining soul or sense,
And of the Sun his working vigour borrow,
Love's not so pure and abstract as they use
To say, which have no mistress but their Muse;
But, as all else being elemented too,
Love sometimes would contèmplate, sometimes do.

And yet not greater, but more eminent,
Love by the Spring is grown,
As in the firmament
Stars by the Sun are not enlarged but shown.
Gentle love-deeds, as blossoms on a bough,
From love's awakened root do bud out now.
If as in water stirred more circles be
Produced by one, love such additions take;
Those, like to many spheres, but one heaven make,
For they are all concentric unto thee;
And though each Spring do add to love new heat—
As princes do in times of action get

New taxes, and remit them not in peace—
No winter shall abate the spring's increase.

Read the opening stanza and all the oxygen in a five-mile radius rushes to greet you. It's a poem with gleeful tricks and puns in it. 'But if this med'cine, love, which cures all sorrow/With more' is a small, private gift for Anne More; no matter how many millions of other people have read it since, the poem was different for her. Donne baked time's accumulation and love's accumulation with it into the structure of the poem: twenty-four ten-syllable lines, plus four of six (equalling twenty-four): the hours in the day. Seven rhymes per stanza: the days in the week. Twenty-eight lines in the poem: the days in a lunar month, each day part of love's growth.

Love, he writes, is a mixture of elemental things: 'as all else being elemented too' – and so 'love sometimes would contemplate, sometimes do.' Donne is more daring than he sounds: the thirteenth-century theologian Thomas Aquinas's ideal was the 'Mixed Life', one of contemplation and action. Donne hijacks the Aquinian ideal for his own erotic purpose: the *do* is sex. It's the same impulse as in another poem, 'The Ecstasy', where bodies must join as well as minds, 'else a great prince in prison lies.' True sex, he insists, is soul played out in flesh.

'Love's Growth' hangs on the idea of apparently infinite love, made more – which, once you have read all that he wrote, is wholly unsurprising. John Donne was an infinity merchant; the word is everywhere in his work. More than infinity: super-infinity. A few years before his own death, Donne preached a funeral sermon for Magdalen Herbert, mother of the poet George Herbert, a woman who had been his patron and friend. Magdalen, he wrote, would 'dwell bodily with that righteousness, in these new heavens and new earth, for ever and ever and ever, and infinite and super-infinite forevers'. In a different sermon, he wrote of how we would one day be with God in 'an infinite, a super-infinite, an unimaginable space, millions of millions of unimaginable spaces in heaven'. He loved to coin formations with the *super-* prefix: super-edifications, super-exaltation, super-dying, super-universal, super-miraculous. It was part of his bid to invent a language that would reach beyond language, because infinite wasn't enough: both in heaven, but also here and now on earth, Donne wanted to know something larger than infinity. It was absurd, grandiloquent, courageous, hungry.

That version of Donne – excessive, hungry, longing – is everywhere in the love poetry. Sometimes it was worn lightly: who has yet written about nudity with more glee, more jokes? In 'To His Mistress Going to Bed', written in his twenties, the speaker attempts to coax his lover out of her clothes:

Full nakedness! All joys are due to thee:
As souls unbodied, bodies unclothed must be
To taste whole joys.

The poem could be seen as one of domineering masculinity, except that at the end of it there's a joke: only the man stands naked. 'To teach thee, I am naked first; why then/ What need'st thou have more cov'ring than a man?'

Then there is the wilder, defiantly odd Donne, typified by the poem for which most people know him, 'The Flea'. The speaker watches a flea crawl over the body of the woman he desires:

> Mark but this flea, and mark in this
> How little that which thou deny'st me is;
> Me it sucked first, and now sucks thee,
> And in this flea, our two bloods mingled be.

When the poem was first printed in 1633, the typographers used the 'long s', a letter that looks almost identical to an f, for the words 'sucked' and 'suck': which offers readers of the third line another, more extravagant rendering.

In 'Love's Progress', he summons up the outlandish edge of sex. He describes a woman's mouth:

> There in a creek, where chosen pearls do swell,
> The remora, her cleaving tongue doth dwell.

The remora is a sucking fish; it was supposed, according to Pliny the Elder, to have the ability to haul ships to a stop in the ocean. Not many women dream of having their tongues compared to semi-mythical sea creatures – but, as with his flea, it's his way of embodying the strangenesses of human fleshy desire. He allows himself to end on a major chord, a switch to bawdy lusting:

Rich Nature in women wisely made
Two purses, and their mouths aversely laid:
They, then, which to the lower tribute owe,
That way which that exchequer looks must go;
He which doth not, his error is as great
As who by clyster gives the stomach meat.

Donne seems to deserve the questionable recognition of being the first to so use 'purse' for female genitalia. The 'exchequer' implies that those who travel down the body must pay a tax: and ejaculate is the fitting tribute. (Men were believed to need a huge amount of blood to form sperm within the body: a ratio of 40:1.) A 'clyster' is an enema tube which was used to carry nutrients to the body via the rectum. The argument – that those who don't con-summate love are as mad and upside-down as those who try to nourish the body via the anus – has teeming desire in it, but very much resists the tradition of Petrarchan flowers. It refuses to be pretty, because sex is not and because Donne does not, in his love poetry, insist on sweetness: he does not play the 'my lady is a perfect dove' game beloved by those who came before him. What good is perfection to humans? It's a dead thing. The urgent, the bold, the witty, the sharp: all better than perfection.

There is the meat and madness of sex in his work – but, more: Donne's poetry believed in finding eternity through the human body of one other person. It is for him akin to sacrament. *Sacramentum* is the translation in the Latin Bible for the Greek word for mystery: and Donne knew it when he wrote, 'We die and rise the same, and prove/Mysterious by this love.' He knew awe: 'All measure, and all language, I should pass/Should I tell what a miracle she was.' And in 'The Ecstasy', love is both a mystery and its solution. He needed to invent a word, 'unperplex', to explain:

'This ecstasy doth unperplex,'
We said, 'and tell us what we love . . .'

But as all several souls contain
Mixture of things, they know not what,
Love these mixed souls doth mix again,
And makes both one, each this and that.

'Each this and that': his work suggests that we might voyage beyond the blunt realities of male and female. In 'The Undertaking', probably written around the time he met Anne, the body can take you to a grand merging:

If, as I have, you also do
Virtue attired in woman see,
And dare love that, and say so too,
And forget the 'he' and 'she' . . .

His poetry sliced through the gender binary and left it gasping on the floor. It's in 'The Relic', too: 'diff'rence of sex no more we knew/Than our guardian angels do' – for angels were believed to have no need of gender. He offered the possibility of sex as transformation: and we are more tempted to believe him when he says it, because he is the same man who acknowledges, elsewhere, feverishness, disappointment and spite in love. He is sharp, funny, mean, flippant and deadly serious. He shows us that poetry is the thing – perhaps the only thing – that can hold love in words long enough to look honestly at it. *Look: love.*

¶

He took his galvanising imagination and brought it to bear on everything he wrote: his sermons, his meditations, his religious verse. In the twenty-first century, Donne's imagination offers us a form of body armour. His work is protection against the slipshod and the half-baked, against anti-intellectualism, against those who try to sell you their money-ridden vision of sex and love. He is protection against those who would tell you to narrow yourself, to follow fashion in your mode of thought. It's not that he was a rebel: it is that he was a pure original. They do us a service, the true uncompromising originals: they show us what is possible.

To tell the story of Donne's life is to ask a question: how did he, possessed of a strange and labyrinthical mind, navigate the corresponding social and political labyrinths of

Renaissance England? What did his imagination look like when he was young, and how was it battered and burnished as he grew older? Did it protect him from sorrow and fury and resentment? (To spoil the suspense: it did not.) Did it allow him to write out the human problem in a way that we, following on four hundred years later, can still find urgent truth in? This book argues that it did. 'Dark texts', he wrote to a friend, 'need notes' – and it is possible to see his whole body of work as offering us a note on ourselves. This book aims to lay out that note as clearly as possible: how John Donne saw us with such clarity, and how he set down what he knew with such precision and flair that we can seize hold of it, and carry it with us. He knew about dread, and it is therefore that we can trust him when he tells us of its opposite, of ravishments and of love.

THE PRODIGIOUS CHILD

In one way, and one way only, it was an auspicious beginning: John Donne was born on Bread Street in central London, from one end of which you have a clear and easy view of St Paul's Cathedral. He was born in sight of both his future job and his final resting place, which must be rare. In every other way, it was a hard time to come into the world. It was 1572 – month unknown – and a Catholic plot to assassinate Queen Elizabeth I had just been foiled. The Duke of Norfolk was executed for treasonous Popish machinating, and it was a bad year in which to be an English Catholic.

Donne's mother, Elizabeth Heywood, was the great-niece of the Catholic martyr Thomas More. She sounds to have been formidable, unafraid to assert herself: a woman of whom it was whispered (erroneously) that she carried the head of Thomas More in her luggage when she travelled. Donne's father, also John Donne, was an ironmonger, though not of the horny-handed, rugged variety; he was warden of the Ironmongers' Company. The family had once owned magnificent estates, before they had been confiscated by the Crown in the various Tudor shake-downs of Catholic landowners. He married, in Elizabeth, the daughter of a musician and epigrammatist who had played for Henry

VIII; so Donne was born into a family who had known the smell and touch of a king.

What was his childhood? When London burned in 1666, a colossal chunk of history burned with it; the house in which Donne was born was reduced to cinders, along with 13,200 other homes; the cathedral he would later preach in, and eighty-seven parish churches; and, too, catastrophic amounts of paper across the city, carrying records of the details of thousands of ordinary lives. Whole libraries' worth of paper: accounts, disputes, wills, play texts and poems, postmasters' trunks, bills, love letters folded so intricately into paper locks that you couldn't open them without leaving a telltale tear; all gone. Time and fire together have laid waste to so much of the paper that might have told us about Donne. The names and lives of his siblings, for instance, are blurry; there were at least two before him, Elizabeth and Anne, then John, and after him Henry and then we aren't so sure. But to fill the gaps, we have the account written by Izaak Walton, Donne's friend and first biographer, and a man with a claim to have written the first literary biography in English.

Walton was a gentle, retiring kind of man. He was younger than Donne by two decades, and had been Donne's adoring parishioner in London. Best known in his lifetime as the author of *The Compleat Angler*, an ecstatic poetic celebration of fishing, he was at his most perceptive when talking about trout – but in taking time off fish to set out the facts of his friend's life, Walton created one of the most valuable resources we have. All Donne scholars must be profoundly grateful to him: but, equally, rarely has a man been so keen to make his subject appear a shining example to all humanity. Walton didn't subscribe to the sceptical school of biographer, who carry a pen in one hand and a knife in the other. He was eager from the very outset to reassure his readers about Donne's worth. 'Though [Donne's] own learning and other multiplied merits may justly appear sufficient to dignify both himself and his posterity; yet the reader may be pleased to know, that his father was masculinely and lineally descended from a very ancient family in Wales, where many of his name now live, that deserve, and have great reputation in that country.' Born high enough to merit some small awe, Walton wants us to know. (Donne's connection to the Welsh Dwns has never, in fact, been proven.)

Donne came of stock that valued literary flourishes. Donne's maternal grandfather John Heywood had his own line in ironical verse. In his *Play Called the Four PP*, the four Ps (a pardoner, a palmer, a 'pothecary and a pedlar) hold a competition to see who can speak the biggest lie. The palmer wins:

> I have seen women five hundred thousand
> Wives and widows, maids and married
> And oft with them have long time tarried
> Yet in all places where I have been
> Of all the women that I have seen
> I never saw nor knew, in my conscience
> Any one woman out of patience.

Years later, Donne would write with exactly the same sceptical eyebrow:

If thou beest born to strange sights,
Things invisible to see,
Ride ten thousand days and nights,
Till age snow white hairs on thee:
Thou, when thou return'st, wilt tell me,
All strange wonders that befell thee,
   And swear,
   'Nowhere
Lives a woman true, and fair.'

Donne's family prized good jokes in extremis (and, evidently, casual sexism as a comic trope). His grandfather became famous for his deathbed comedy: his confessor, repeating over and over that 'the flesh is frail', to which Heywood: 'Marry, Father . . . it will go hard but you shall prove that God should a made me a fish.'

When Donne was four, his father died and his mother married again to a John Syminges, a physician who had been several times the President of the Royal College of Physicians. It might sound a gentle, upper-middle kind of upbringing: but to be born a Catholic was to live with a constant, low-level, background thrum of terror.

England had been so shot through with religious violence in the sixteenth century that there was ample evidence to cast either side as villain. Mary I, a Catholic, had burned at least three hundred Protestants, and now with Protestant Elizabeth on the throne a concerted effort was made to channel national ire at the Catholic minority. John Foxe's *Book of Martyrs* had been published in 1563, nine years before Donne's birth, and its frontispiece illustration served well to remind those in doubt of where the country stood: on one side Catholics with bulbous noses are seized by gleeful demons, while on the other Protestants with aquiline profiles burn in the fires of persecution and rise to glory.

It was in the spring of 1574, when Donne was a toddler, that disaster first came for the family. His mother's uncle Thomas Heywood was suddenly and without warning arrested. A house on Cow Lane, close to Donne's own home, was raided; officials discovered Thomas, a priest and former monk, along with 'divers Latin books, beads, images, palms, chalices, crosses, vestments, pyxes, paxes and such like'. (A pyx was the box used for wafers: a pax was a piece of engraved wood which was kissed by Catholics during the Peace. Before the invention of the pax the congregation used to kiss each other, until it was felt this was unreasonably intimate – and plaguey – for church.)

At the time, the penalty for being a Catholic priest was to be hanged, drawn and quartered – which meant being stretched, hung until almost dead, and then having the arms and legs severed from the body while crowds looked on. One Richard Simpson was caught by a priest hunter – not unlike a bounty hunter – in 1588, and was hanged, drawn and quartered in the company of two other men. A bystander remarked that he 'suffered with great constancy, but did not evince such signs of joy and alacrity in meeting death as his two companions'. (This evokes Samuel Pepys's laconic note of 1660: 'I went out to Charing Cross to see Major General Harrison hanged, drawn, and quartered – which was done there – he looking as cheerful as any man could do in that condition.') It's unclear from the Privy Council records exactly what happened to Thomas – but tradition holds that he was executed as his family looked on.

The punishments of Catholics were designed to be as performative as they were cruel. In response, the loyalty of families like Donne's, necessarily driven underground, took on correspondingly strange and lurid shapes. The Thomas More tooth, and the head it came from, is a vivid example. After More's death, his head was put on a pike for several weeks at London Bridge; his formidable daughter, Margaret Roper, bribed the executioner, whose job it was to take down the heads and throw them into the Thames, to give it to her instead. She pickled it in spices; and when one of the teeth worked loose she gave it as a sacred relic to Jasper and Ellis Heywood, Donne's uncles, both of whom were Jesuits, a then-newish Catholic missionary order founded in 1540 by Ignatius of Loyola. There was a story that once, when the two uncles were going on separate journeys, unable to decide who got to take the tooth, it 'fell asunder and divided of it self'. Not just Catholic, then, but super-Catholic: the kind of Catholic which relishes the theatre and paraphernalia of martyrdom.

Sir Thomas More, after Hans Holbein the Younger

Donne would have been familiar with all the legends of More, the one-time Lord Chancellor of England: with his many works of hyper-learned prose, his asceticism (More liked to wear a grey goat's hair shirt next to his skin, now enshrined at Buckfast Abbey) and his insistence on educating

26

his daughters to almost unheard-of levels of female erudition. His mother's proud Catholicism meant he would have heard from his cradle about More's steadfast refusal to acknowledge Henry VIII as supreme head of the Church of England, and about his subsequent death by beheading. More's wit was inexhaustible, uncompromising, and with him to the very last breath: 'I pray you,' he was supposed to have said to the executioner as he mounted the scaffold, 'master Lieutenant, see me safe up, and for my coming down let me shift for myself.' And, once settled: 'Pluck up thy spirits, man, and be not afraid to do thine office; my neck is very short; take heed therefore thou strike not awry.' The Undersheriff of London wrote: 'I cannot tell whether I should call him a foolish wiseman, or a wise foolishman.' Donne grew up knowing you were supposed to meet death with a flourish: he never forgot it, right to the very end.

Elizabeth I had hoped to let Catholicism fade quietly away, starved to death without a public institution; but in 1570, two years before Donne's birth, a papal bull excommunicated her, calling her 'the pretended Queen of England', 'the servant of crime'. In response the English government's attitudes to the Catholic population became more anxious, more repressive, more bloody. But Catholics with living memory of Mary I were unlikely to forget that if the fate of a religion could wane, it could also wax. Donne was taken by the adults around him to witness the blood and suffering of his religion. Much later, he wrote that in the past he had seen executions of Catholic priests, and around their bodies 'some bystanders, leaving all old Saints, pray to him whose body lay there dead; as if he had more respect, and better access in heaven.' It's likely that his Catholic tutors would have shepherded him to the deaths, to show him the brutality of the world and the possibility of rising through it to the heavens; a front-row view of a dark and scarring kind of theatre.

Donne was once taken right into the heart of the fear, inside the Tower of London to visit his uncle Jasper. Jasper, another man whom Donne was brought up to honour, was an unexpected candidate for the wild adventure that his life became. His early education had taken place in the royal court, alongside Princess Elizabeth – the most useful connection of his life, and one that would save it. He should, really, have been a scholar with a quiet, paper-bound life, chewing on swan-feather quills (Elizabeth's preferred writing pen: popular at court) and disputing the finer points of religious heresy. He had been made a Fellow of All Souls College, home of the incurably bookish, where he produced three translations of plays by Seneca. But he had to leave Oxford, unable to negotiate the ever more stringent reforms against Catholics, and became a Jesuit priest. He felt the strain of it: he suffered night terrors and underwent an unsuccessful exorcism. For all that, he did not lack bravery: he attempted to convert some of the country's most powerful earls (the 'big fish', he said) to Catholicism, and in doing so caused a scandal so loud he had to make a break for France. He was almost in sight of Dieppe when a storm blew his boat, drenched and battered, all the way back to England. He was arrested, tried, indicted for treason and locked in the Tower of London.

It was there that his sister Elizabeth, Donne's mother, came to minister to him, and to secretly carry messages between Jasper and another Jesuit, William Weston. If caught, Elizabeth would not have been safe from punishment by virtue of her sex: in 1592 a Mrs Ward was hanged, drawn and quartered for helping a Catholic priest to escape his pursuers in a box; a Mrs Lynne was put to death for harbouring a priest in her home. Once, Weston disguised himself in other clothes and came with Elizabeth into the Tower, an act of astonishing bravery or stupidity or both, to go into arms' reach of the jailers. Weston was terrified: 'I accompanied her to the Tower, but with a feeling of great trepidation as I saw the vast battlements, and was led by the warder past the gates with their iron fastenings, which were closed behind me.' Donne, aged twelve or thereabouts, accompanied them, perhaps as a way of making the party seem innocent and familial; he wrote, later, that he was once at 'a Consultation of Jesuits in the Tower, in the late Queen's time'. Heywood petitioned his one-time playmate the Queen for leniency. She granted it: he was deported to France, and from there to Rome, never returning to the country of his birth, where they were so liable to cut him into four.

Self-bifurcating molars and state-endorsed torture: these were the things of Donne's early years. It was a darkly particular way to grow up; not only the terror and injustice, but the *strangeness* of it: how unhinged the world must feel, that you are persecuted for professing that which you believe to be the most powerful possible truth. Not 'strange' as in 'unfamiliar', for being killed for your religion was hardly new; strange as in unmoored from all sense, reason, sanity.

John Donne's mother almost certainly did not, in truth, carry Thomas More's head in her accoutrements: Margaret Roper had it until she died in 1544, when she left it to her husband, who was buried with it: it's unlikely that he would have loaned it out like a library book. But Donne's internal baggage was piled high with skulls: with persecuted family members, with the wounds of his mother and uncles. He felt his family had been tried beyond almost any other: 'I have been ever kept awake in a meditation of martyrdom, by being derived from such a stock and race, as, I believe, no family (which is not of far larger extent, and greater branch- es) hath endured and suffered more in their persons and fortunes, for obeying the teachers of the Roman doctrine, than it hath done.'

His family would haunt him for life: and nothing in his writing gives the impression he was surprised that it should be so. We are haunted animals: ghosts, Donne's work and life suggest, should be treated as the norm. He accepted it as such. To read him is to know that we cannot ever expect to shake off our family: only to pick up the skull, the tooth, and walk on.

THE HUNGRY SCHOLAR

Donne worked on words his entire life. It was a time in which prodigal talent among the young was common – his near contemporary, the poet Katherine Philips, claimed to have 'read the Bible thorough before she was full four years old', and his biographer Izaak Walton calls Donne 'another Picus Mirandula' – the Italian philosopher and child prodigy who was made a protonotary by the Pope at the age of ten (a protonotary was the highest grade of monsignor, entitling him to wear a lot of purple velvet). Even reckoning that Walton is beamish and over-saucing with his praise (and that Pico della Mirandola was murdered at the age of thirty-one by arsenic poisoning, and thereby provides a sad ideal), Donne was born hungry, a lifelong strainer after words and ideas. He sought to create for himself a form of language that would meet the requirements of someone who watched the world with careful and sceptical eyes.

Donne was not sent to school. He was missing very little; the schools of sixteenth- and seventeenth-century England were grim, ice cold metaphorically and literally. Eton's dormitory was full of rats; at many of the public schools at the time, the boys burned the furniture to keep warm, threw each other around in their blankets, broke each other's ribs and occasionally heads. The Merchant Taylors' school had in its rules the stipulation, 'unto their urine the scholars shall go to the places appointed them in the lane or street without the court', which, assuming the interdiction was necessary for a reason, suggests the school would have smelled strongly of youthful pee. Because smoking was believed to keep the plague at bay, at Eton they were flogged for the crime of not smoking. Discipline could be murderous. It became necessary to enforce startling legal limits: 'when a schoolmaster, in correcting his scholar, happens to occasion his death, if in such correction he is so barbarous as to exceed all bounds of moderation, he is at least guilty of manslaughter; and if he makes use of an instrument improper for correction, as an iron bar or sword . . . he is guilty of murder.'

Instead, Donne was educated at home. Walton tells us that he learned fluent Latin – as would have been requisite, for a gentleman's son – though he makes no mention of Greek; Donne learned that later, under his own tutelage, with a tenacity that is characteristic of him. In 1584 he enrolled with his younger brother Henry at Hart Hall, Oxford University; their ages were given as eleven and ten respectively, although in fact they were both a year older. All students over sixteen were required to take an oath acknowledging royal supremacy over all questions of religion: but it was thought that a child under sixteen couldn't be expected to understand the nature of the oath, and therefore the young brothers could live under the radar in Hart Hall, a place with a reputation for nurturing and protecting Catholics. There was less burning in the quiet streets of Oxford than in London (at least since Archbishop Thomas Cranmer, condemned under Mary for refusing to acknowledge papal supremacy, had met a fiery death in 1556). There were more books in Oxford, more people his own age, less dying.

Both Oxford and Cambridge were, at the time, just edging into fashionability: until shortly before Donne arrived, both places had been looked at with sceptical eyes by anyone with claim to any class. In 1549, Oxford students were 'mean men's children set to school in hope to live upon hired learning'. It was only as the century wore on that more gentry started to pass through the doors – by the time Donne came to live there, it had started to have a little cachet. There were various attempts to give it more of a gleam: when the antiquary William Camden published the *Life of King Alfred* by the medieval monk Asser, he added notes of his own, putting into the mouth of the monastic the fake claim that the University of Oxford had been founded by Alfred the Great. And the city would have been very beautiful in 1584, yellow-stoned and with the River Isis nearby. Its spires soared less ecstatically skywards than today, as most of the colleges were not yet fully formed, and the great Bodleian Library did not open until 1602, but it was still a place worth loving.

Some students at Oxford worked formidably. Donne, according to Walton, was one of them: 'in the most unsettled days of his youth his bed was not able to detain him beyond the hour of four in the morning.' If this is true, he was not wildly unusual. In 1550, a student at Christ Church sketched out his day: from 6 to 7 a.m., he studied Aristotle's *Politics*; then Roman law; then further study, dinner at 11 a.m., then studying some Cicero, then from 1 to 3 p.m. 'I exercise my pen, chiefly in writing letters, wherein as far as possible I imitate Cicero', then civil law, 'which I read aloud so as to commit them to memory'; then after supper, 'walking up and down some part of the college, we exercise ourselves in dialectical questions'. Others, almost certainly, were less impressively dedicated. Among the treasures of unstudied manuscripts in Britain's university archives, there is one from the early seventeenth century which pokes fun at the idea of hard work:

The Oxford Scholar

As I was riding on a day
One chanced to ask me by the way
How Oxford scholars pass their time
And thus I answered all in rhyme

Item for Homer poor blind poet
Oh, if our tutors did but know it
For old tobacco we make free
Till smoke makes us as blind as he.

Donne was unlikely to have been lonely. He had Henry, his familiar companion, to bicker with and protect. They had a well-off aunt, a Mrs Dawson, whose husband Robert kept the Blue Boar Inn, on the corner of what is now Blue Boar Street and St Aldate's. The Dawsons would have welcomed the boys, Catholicism and all. They may have been Catholic themselves: certainly, they were known for having as their long-term guest one Mr Henslowe, 'once of New College and expelled out of that house for popery, who lieth now at the sign of the Blue Boar'. The boys' souls, and rapacious young stomachs, would both have been catered for.

And, soon, Donne had friends: he was a contemporary, though younger, of the poet John Hoskins, who was a rebel and a wit, and would have called to those corresponding rebellious parts in Donne. Hoskins was elected to the role of *terrae filius* ('son of the soil') – a role which allowed him to be the licensed jester at the university's ceremonies, making jokes against senior officials – which would have appealed to Donne's sceptical, satirical streak. Hoskins, though, took it too far – his more personal attacks on the university's grandees were badly received, and he was abruptly expelled from Oxford. There was Richard Baker, grandson of the first ever Chancellor of the Exchequer, who arrived at Hart Hall on the same day as the Donne brothers and who wrote approvingly that as Donne grew older he was 'not dissolute, but very neat; a great visitor of ladies, a great frequenter of plays'. Above all, it was here Donne met

Henry Wotton, Baker's roommate. With his fine blue eyes and aquiline nose, Wotton was to prove a true ally: a swift talker, a natural diplomat, a great introducer of men. He was to end up an ambassador, and it showed young. It was to Wotton that Donne wrote, 'Sir, more than kisses, letters mingle souls,/ for, thus friends absent speak.'

§

During this time we know Donne was collecting his fascinations in a book: a collection of scraps and shards of knowledge known as a commonplace book. Its current whereabouts are mysterious: Donne gave it to his eldest son, who left it to Izaak Walton's son in his will, who left all his books and papers to Salisbury Cathedral. If it is ever found, it will cause great and joyful chaos among the Donne community. Because, simply, Donne wouldn't be Donne if he hadn't lived in a commonplacing era; it nurtured his collector's sensibility, hoarding images and authorities. He had a magpie mind obsessed with gathering. In his work, as Samuel Johnson said disapprovingly, you find the 'most heterogeneous ideas are yoked by violence together'. The practice of commonplacing – a way of seeking out and storing knowledge, so that you have multiple voices on a topic under a single heading – colours Donne's work; one thought reaches out to another, across the barriers of tradition, and ends up somewhere fresh and strange. It's telling that the first recorded use of the word 'commonplacer' in the *Oxford English Dictionary* is Donne's.

The commonplace book allowed readers to approach the world as a limitless resource; a kind of ever-ongoing harvesting. It was Erasmus, the Dutch scholar known as 'the prince of the humanists', who codified the practice. The compiler, he wrote, should 'make himself as full a list of place-headings as possible' to put at the top of each page: for instance, beauty, friendship, decorum, faith, hope, the vices and virtues. It was both a form of scholarship and, too, a way of reminding yourself of what, as you moved through the world, you were to look out for: a list of priorities, of sparks and spurs and personal obsessions. Donne's book must surely have had: angels, women, faith, stars, jealousy, gold, desire, dread, death. Then, Erasmus wrote

> whatever you come across in any author, particularly if it is especially striking, you will be able to note it down in its appropriate place: be it a story or a fable or an example or a new occurrence or a pithy remark or a witty saying or any other clever form of words . . . Whenever occasion demands, you will have ready to hand a supply of material for spoken or written composition.

As always with any intellectual pursuit, there were those who were anxious about achieving the ideal commonplace book, and, as it always does, the market seized on a way to monetise that anxiety. It became possible to buy ready-prepared commonplace books with the quotations already filled in: years' worth of work achieved without lifting a quill. Buying a ready-made text meant that you avoided the potential pitfalls: for instance, of making a heading and then finding either too much or not enough to fit. Sir Robert Southwell (there are many famous Robert Southwells of the period: in this case, the President of the Royal Society rather than the saint who was disembowelled) had a commonplace book in which some headings were confidently set down and then left forever blank (*Academia* and *Tedium*), while others (*Authoritas* and *Error*, *Religio* and *Passio*) left him scribbling in increasingly tiny handwriting at the foot of the page, and scoring out other headings to make space. Crucially for Donne, though, the commonplace book wasn't designed to be used for the regurgitation of memorised gobbets: it was to offer the raw material for a combinatorial, plastic process.

The ideal commonplacer is half lawyer, building up evidence in the case for and against the world, and half treasure hunter; and that's what Donne's mind was in those early days. This is a poet who in one single poem could pass through references to Aristotelian logic and Ptolemaic astronomy, to Augustine's discussion of beauty, and Pliny's theory on poisonous snakes being harmless when dead.

T. S. Eliot, a man who had in common with Donne both poetic iconoclasm and good clothes, loved his writing. He said: 'When a poet's mind is perfectly equipped for its work, it is constantly amalgamating disparate experience,' whereas 'the ordinary man's experience is chaotic, irregular, fragmentary.' For Donne, apparently unrelated scraps from the world were always forming new wholes. Commonplacing was a way to assess material for those new connections: bricks made ready for the unruly palaces he would build.

Donne's heterogeneity, which so annoyed Johnson, wasn't a game: it was a form of discipline. Commonplacing plucks ideas out of their context and allows you to put them down against other, startling ones. So, with Donne, images burst from one category into another; when he writes in ribald, joking defence of sexual inconstancy, he compares women to foxes (fairly normal in the poetry of the day) and ruminants (not normal):

Foxes and goats, all beasts change when they please:
Shall women, more hot, wily, wild then these,
Be bound to one man?

Love is a fish: a 'tyran pike, our hearts the fry'. Birds are lassoed to justify infidelity: 'Are birds divorced, or are they chidden/If they leave their mate, or lie abroad a-night?' In 'The Ecstasy', love is cemented, a balm, concoction, mixture, allay: terms stolen from alchemy. The writing is itself a kind of alchemy: a mix of unlikely ingredients which spark into gold. Images clash up against each other, and the world looks, however briefly, new.

¶

After about three years at Oxford, Walton said, Donne took his magpie mind to Cambridge; and although no record of Donne being enrolled there for a degree exists, the records are so imperfect that it's very possible. Donne would have arrived at a time when poetic war was being waged by his seniors. The poet and pamphleteer Thomas Nashe (about five years older than Donne) and the Harvey brothers Richard and Gabriel (about two decades older) swaggered over the city, feuding on literary battlefields. The Harvey brothers wanted to shake up English literary traditions, to bring the laws of Latin hexameters to English verse; Nashe mocked them for it: '[Gabriel Harvey] goes twitching and hopping in our language like a man running upon quagmires, up the hill in one syllable, and down the dale in another.' Gabriel Harvey was also an inventor of words: 'jovial', 'notoriety', 'rascality'. So the idea that language might be bent into different shapes was all around Donne in that year, as well as the idea that poetry was something you might care enough to physically fight about. Poetry for those young men was more than a way to show off the brightest sparks of their wit, or a way to pass the evenings (though of course it was that too: the evenings were long, and you couldn't be drunk all the time). It was a way to challenge political and social convention under the careful shield of metaphor; if you were going to criticise, do it in verse. (Spenser's *Mother Hubberd's Tale* was well known to be a veiled attack on

Lord Burghley, the Lord High Treasurer.) And it was part of the great humanist project: it allowed you to step into a tradition of chroniclers and visionaries, celebrants and beauty merchants. Poetry mattered more, then, than at almost any other time since.

It's possible, though, that he didn't go to Cambridge at all: some biographers have had it that he left Oxford and made a bolt for Europe – because for all its hushed libraries and broad quads, Oxford was not safe for Donne. His uncle Jasper had been made aware, via his intricate networks of those in and out of the court, that the Privy Council had resolved to start rounding up selected students as young as twelve, and make them swear the Oath of Supremacy. Any who refused risked being taken from their parents and forced to become 'school hostages', educated under 'good schoolmasters'. That this hyper-cautious surveillance was spreading to such little children was, in part, Jasper's own fault. Jasper had been attempting to recruit scholars in their teens at Oxford and Cambridge and coax them into studying at continental seminaries. He shuttled twenty students from English universities to the English seminary at Rheims in 1582, and then another fifty in 1583. From there, some went to Rome, others to France where the Duke of Guise, a luxuriously coiffed nobleman with hair down to his fourth vertebra, was planning to recruit them into a military arm: so Elizabeth's anxiety about something being afoot at the universities was entirely well founded. Heywood was suspected of gathering ranks for a full-scale

'Enterprise' – an invasion of England. Donne must have been closely watched, lest he appear to be a young accomplice to his uncle's 'perpetual aqueducts' of young people being siphoned off across the water.

Jasper was not the only one making waves of Catholic obstinacy: Donne's mother was also courting trouble. Donne's stepfather had died suddenly, and Elizabeth soon remarried, this time to Richard Rainsford, 'gentleman, dwelling in Southwark' – but grief did not seem to have muted her. In 1589 'Mistress Symones Mr Doctor Symone's wife late deceased' was brought up before the parish and fined 'for not coming to church to receive the communion'. Possibly the news of the fine, or of the death, hastened his return – or perhaps he felt himself ready for the noise and scope of the capital – but when we next see Donne he is in London, in 1591. He chose to follow in the footsteps of his magic-toothed ancestor Thomas More by enrolling at the Inns of Court.

The four Inns of Court, established in the fourteenth and fifteenth centuries, remain to this day the starting point for every barrister in England, and many more for whom the bar is just a stepping stone; through their libraries and dining halls have passed Thomas Cromwell, Francis Bacon, William Pitt the Younger, Margaret Thatcher, hordes of bishops and archbishops, enough MPs to start a war. Donne went, very briefly, to Thavie's, a feeder institution for Lincoln's Inn, into which he was duly fed. Lincoln's Inn had glamour: it had housed Francis Walsingham, Elizabeth I's spymaster.

Original thought was possible there: it had tutored John Fortescue, the Lord Chief Justice under Henry VI, who was the first to argue the then-radical principle that 'one would much rather that twenty guilty persons should escape the punishment of death, than that one innocent person should be condemned'. But the twenty-year-old Donne did not go to the Inns intending to become a lawyer; he went to be among rich, sharp-witted young men who also did not intend to become lawyers.

The Inns of Court were close to the other, royal court, and it was expected that some of the graces and smoothness of the latter would transfer to the hopeful student at the former. When Donne arrived with his ghost of an adolescent moustache and his crucifix earring, Lincoln's Inn had a membership of around 150 – of those, less than a third would be called to the bar to practise law professionally. You went to the Inns to learn the ways of the world – particularly if you had money or were expected to come into some. The Chief Secretary for Ireland declared that the study of law 'concerns noblemen and gentlemen above others, as they have great estates, and great trusts in government; in which ignorance of the laws will not well set them off'. They learned the law in order to protect their land and large houses against it, and Donne learned alongside them.

Donne seems to have joyfully erupted out of the solemn hardships of his youth and into the delight and noise of London. Though not rich, he had come into a moderate fortune from his father; enough to eat and drink and dress well. The Inns were beautiful: at Lincoln's Inn there was green space all around him, planted with elm trees with 'fair walks' among them; and he was a fifteen-minute walk from Covent Garden, back when it was truly a garden, belonging to the Earl of Bedford. The Lincoln's Inn lands included a site called Coney Garth: conies were rabbits reared with a view to eating them; in 1572, the Inns of Court decreed that 'it shall be lawful from henceforth for any man to destroy the conies' in the garden, so Donne's legal studies would have been punctuated with the occasional sight of a man and a dog in pursuit of dinner.

Technically, no women were allowed in the Inns, except for the 'laundresses' who cleaned, and who had to be under the age of twelve or over forty in order to prevent romantic entanglements. (It's tempting to find this implication – that there is no such thing as a beautiful forty-one-year-old woman – a personally provoking one.) But in fact a certain amount of mayhem seems to have been expected; in 1560, at Lincoln's Inn, a man called Dilland was 'fined 13s 4d for having a woman at night in Nugent's chamber'. Meanwhile Nugent's 'chamber fellow', Talbot, was 'fined 40s for drawing his sword and hurting Nugent', and tempers ran high over academic debate: one young man was charged with hitting one of the Benchers, a Governor of the Inn, because said Bencher had 'found fault with his study of astronomy'.

Donne learned formidably, somehow: but he didn't want his friends to know it. He was so keen not to be seen by his

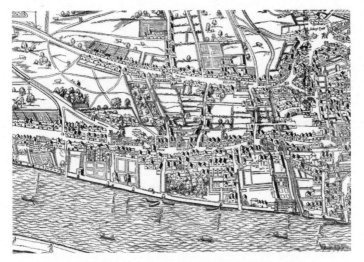

Lincoln's Inn, 1561: surrounded by fields and green spaces

peers as a future drudging middle-class man of law that he wrote to one friend, asking him to quash rumours that he intended to take the degree: 'For my purpose of proceeding in the profession of the law, so far as to a title you may be pleased to correct that imagination, wheresoever you find it.' He sounds like a boy self-conscious about his image: about his cutting the right kind of dash. Law was, he says, never more than 'my best entertainment, and pastime'; he was there for the pleasure of it. He excelled at the joyful business of frivolity: he was elected the Inn's Master of the Revels, in charge of putting on pageantry and wild parties for his fellow scholars, with raucous singing and drinking and dancing of the galliard, the finest fashion at the time. (The dance, which involved a series of enormous leaps and small hops, kicks and spins, was Elizabeth's favourite: she was said, even in her fifties, to dance 'six or seven galliards in a morning'.) But his later writing is so peppered with confident and accurate legal terminology that he must have either worked hard on the sly, or had a staggeringly retentive memory. The law's language and structures stuck with him all his life; near the end of it, he would make lawyer jokes from the pulpit: 'If any man will sue thee at law for thy coat, let him have thy cloak too . . . for if thy adversary have it not, thine advocate will.' (The pulpit Donne sounds very pleased, from where he stands, not to be a lawyer.)

The space in which Donne lived would have been small: he shared his bedroom, and probably the bed itself, with a friend, Christopher Brooke, but each had a tiny study of his own, little more than a cell, with a set of shelves for books, a stool and a table. During his time at the Inns, he began the writing of five long satirical poems, mocking with a young man's fury the corruptions of the Church, the bar, the court: and they give a good sense of what his life looked like. Satire I imagines a fellow student bursting in on him:

> Away, thou changeling, motley humorist!
> Leave me, and in this standing wooden chest,
> Consorted with these few books, let me lie
> In prison, and here be coffined when I die.

Here he reads: not just law, but philosophy, theology and poetry.

Here are God's conduits, grave divines; and here
Nature's secretary, the Philosopher;
And jolly statesmen, which teach how to tie
The sinews of a city's mystic body;
Here, gathering chroniclers, and by them stand
Giddy, fantastic poets of each land.

In comparison, the intruder, coming to lure him away, is an uncertain bet: 'Shall I leave all this constant company,/ And follow headlong, wild, uncertain thee?' In the poem, he does go, though: he heads out into the street, to seek out what the irresistible world has left out for them.

It was from that room, tiny as a 'standing wooden chest', that some of Donne's earliest poetry came. His earlier poems are often shot through with throwaway jokes, sallies against boredom which allowed him to show to his new-found friends that, though he might have less money and fewer acres than them, yet he had a faster wit. The voice is more conventional than the later verse would be, but even in the early work there is that same presence, bold and ornery and intricate, that we find later. There was already, in those early poems, the impression he was laying down what he knew about the world in the form that would be most memorable, and would seize hold of the reader most tenaciously and irreversibly.

It was a time in which blandishments were the fashion: many of the early poems are elaborate compliments to members of his coterie. He writes to Thomas Woodward, the younger brother of his friend Rowland whom he probably met through his beloved Wotton, to say how much he envies Thomas's talent in verse. It takes a lot of saying. 'All hail, sweet poet, more full of more strong fire,/Than hath or shall enkindle any spirit!' It deems all those souls unfortunate who fall into the not-Thomas-Woodward category: 'I', writes Donne, 'do thee envy;/O wouldst thou, by like reason, pity me!'

There's a joke in 'pity me'. Even in the early 1590s, Donne's verse was thought remarkable. The dramatist Ben Jonson, gossiping tipsily over dinner with the Scottish diarist William Drummond of Hawthornden, said that Donne had 'written all his best pieces ere he was 25', which would have been 1597. Donne knew that he had the seeds of something original – that what he was doing with the English language was fresh and different: in a sonnet to Samuel Brooke, his roommate Christopher's little brother, he writes, 'I sing not siren-like, to tempt, for I/Am harsh'. His voice was starting to take shape.

Donne sounded like nobody else. The majority of his fellow poets were obedient to forms and rhyme schemes inherited from the classical greats and from European traditions of courtly verse. Think of Walter Raleigh writing to Queen Elizabeth:

If love could find a quill
drawn from an angel's wing
or did the muses sing
that pretty wanton's will.

Many of Donne's readers who came after him have, for this reason, disliked his work in the way you would dislike a tooth in a basket of flowers. Samuel Taylor Coleridge, for one: 'Donne, whose muse on dromedary trots,/Wreathe iron pokers into true-love knots.' And John Dryden: 'Would not Donne's satires, which abound with so much wit, appear more charming if he had taken care of his words, and of his numbers [i.e. his scansion]? . . . I may safely say it of this present age, that if we were not so great wits as Donne, yet certainly we are better poets.'

But for Donne, divergence from the accent and peculiar breaks in form contain the very stamp of what he meant: they were never aimless. The world was harsh and he needed a harsh language.

Donne's five Satires are among the hardest to scan and read aloud: deliberately so: they sound exclamatory, darting from expostulation to fluency and back again, poetry that is quick on its feet and angry at you. Donne opened his second Satire with a joke about poets, and the way the desire to write verse catches hold of you:

Though poetry indeed be such a sin,
As I think, that brings dearths and Spaniards in;

Though, like the pest'lence or old-fashioned love
It riddlingly catch men, and doth remove
Never till it be starved out; yet their state
Is poor, disarmed, like papists, not worth hate.

A hundred and thirty years later, the poet Alexander Pope read those lines and winced. Pope believed in the moral and aesthetic superiority of poetic balance and restraint: so much so that he took Donne's Satires and 'versified' them, so that they scanned and made what he thought was nice, proper sense. In his hands Donne's line, 'Sir, though (I thank God for it) I do hate/Perfectly all this town' becomes, 'Yes; thank my stars! As early as I knew/This Town, I had the sense to hate it too.' The spike of the 'hate/Perfectly' is gone.

Pope wasn't the only one: there was also Thomas Parnell, an Anglo-Irish contemporary of Pope's, a man unafraid to rhyme 'love' and 'dove'. He was inspired by his friend's lead; he chose Donne's Satire III, an attack on all authority, a furious bark of a poem which orders us to 'doubt wisely'. Donne's eye took in the sweep of the world's corruption, and began:

Kind pity chokes my spleen; brave scorn forbids
These tears to issue which swell my eyelids;
I must not laugh nor weep sins and be wise;
Can railing, then, cure these worn maladies?

Parnell mangled it: 'Compassion checks my spleen, yet Scorn denies/The tears a passage thro' my swelling eyes.' But 'compassion' and 'kind pity' aren't the same thing, at all. Donne was perfectly capable of using the word compassion – a swift count turns up at least a dozen cases in the poetry alone – but meant exactly what he said: pity laced with kindness is still pity; harsh and generous at once, angular and vulnerable.

Parnell and Pope and their many allies were men who believed that art had rules: that poetry was a monovocal exercise; that there was one poetic voice, and we should stick to it. Years later, when Samuel Johnson compared Donne's 'false wit' with Pope's 'true wit', it wasn't a throw-away comment: it was real anxiety that Donne might be nigh-on insane. His work, for Johnson, was improper and ugly and broken – it was 'produced by a voluntary deviation from nature in pursuit of something new or strange'.

But that was exactly it. Donne did not want to sound like other poets. Human experience exceeds our capacity to either explain or express it: Donne knew it, and so he invented new words and new forms to try. He created new rhythms in poetry: Jonson said that Donne, 'for not keeping of accent, deserved hanging'. He was an inventor of words, a neologismist. He accounts for the first recorded use in the *Oxford English Dictionary* of around 340 words in the English language. Apprehensible, beauteousness, bystander, criminalist, emancipation, enripen, fecundate, horridness, imbrothelled, jig. (And, for those who bristle against the distinctive pitch of one's own heart is for each of us to build our own way of using our voice. To read Donne is to be told: kill the desire to keep the accent and tone of the time. It is necessary to shake language until it will express our own distinctive hesitations, peculiarities, our own uncertain and never-quite-successful yearning towards beauty. Donne saves his most ruthless scorn for those who chew other wits' fruit, and shit out platitudes. Language, his poetry tells us, is a set, not of rules, but of possibilities.

ANNO DNI. 1591.
ÆTATIS SVÆ 18

ANTES MVDADO
SVELTO QVE

This was for youth, Strength, Mirth, and wit that Time
Most count their golden Age; but t'was not thine.
Thine was thy later yeares, so much refind
From youths Drosse, Mirth, & wit; as thy pure mind
Thought (like the Angels) nothing but the Praise
Of thy Creator, in those last, best Dayes.
   Witnes this Booke, (thy Embleme) which begins
   With Love; but endes, with Sighes, & Teares for sins.

Will: Marshall sculpsit.

IZ: WA:

Donne aged approximately eighteen

THE EXQUISITELY CLOTHED
THEORISER ON FASHION

It was as he enrolled in the Inns of Court that Donne sat for his first painting. The portrait itself, a painted miniature probably by Nicholas Hilliard, didn't survive, but there's an engraving of it, which was deemed sufficiently handsome and lifelike to be used on the frontispiece of his collected verse after his death. In it he looks very young, and every particular of his outfit, down to the buttons, was chosen with sharp-eyed care. Clothing in sixteenth-century England was carefully regulated – a 1597 proclamation had decreed that only earls and above could wear cloth of gold, while nobody ranking below a knight could parade town in the ostentatious silk stockings known as 'netherstocks'. In addition to those laws, the Inns of Court wielded against their students a litany of sumptuary regulations, to keep the men looking as serious externally as they were presumed to be internally. All gowns were to be 'of a sad colour', and there was a formidable list of forbidden accessories and styles, including ruffs, hats, boots, spurs, swords, daggers, long hair, beards, and 'foreign fashions' generally; overall, the Inns' legislation stated that each student should ensure 'his apparel pretend no lightness, or wantonness in the wearer'.

The Donne in the 1591 engraving, in contrast, is wanton to the hilt; his hair almost reaches his shoulders, and he holds in his right hand a sword. It is the look of a man who revels in self-fashioning. He was beautiful: 'of stature moderately tall, of a strait and equally-proportioned body, to which all his words and actions gave an unexpressible addition of comeliness'. He was tall, dark, handsome, still new at the business of living.

It is possible to turn to the young Donne's work for a theory of fashion, for he understood that when we get dressed we ask something of the world. All clothes speak: they say *desire me*, or *oh ignore me*, or *endow my words with greater seriousness than you would were I not wearing this hat*. When he mocks the dress of his compatriots, he is mocking the shoddiness and lack of imagination of what they are asking for. And, he knew, the beautiful are rarely beautiful without effort. (The best-dressed people spend a secretly enormous amount of time thinking about line and shape and cloth, and imagining themselves into three dozen possible outfits before they put on their trousers.) Donne's appearance must have taken a lot of thought: it was another part of the theatricality of his work across his entire life. He understood that presentation, voice and look are not frivolities to be dismissed, but weapons to be harnessed.

The other painting of the young Donne – the one with the hat and moustache – was painted in about 1595 and is known as the Lothian portrait. (It's so named because it was in the collection of the Marquess of Lothian, mis-labelled until the 1950s as a portrait of John Duns Scotus.

Duns Scotus was a poet from the thirteenth century who, in portraits, looked as unlike Donne as it is possible to look and still be of the same species.) In both portraits, he wears a moustache so thin you could fit it under your fingernail – and it would be a mistake to assume that even the moustache came easily. Moustaches were at the time, like clothing, subject to surveillance, though by society rather than the state: Simion Grahame, a Scottish courtier, insisted in his *Anatomy of Humors* that a man should have 'his beard well brushed and always his upper lip well curled . . . For if he chance to kiss a gentlewoman, some rebellious hairs may happen to startle in her nose and make her sneeze.' He adds an interdiction against 'snotty nosed gentlemen, with their drooping moustaches covering their mouth and becoming a harbour for meldrops . . . He will drink with anybody whatsoever, and after he hath washed his filthy beard in the cup . . . he will suck the hair so heartily with his under lip.' But Donne's moustache, particularly in the Lothian portrait, is exemplary. It is careful: the moustache of a man who understands that even facial hair has to it an element of performance. To see his moustache is to know: *almost nothing is easy.*

Performance, and the clothes that accompany it, remained an interest all Donne's life. From his youth, when he posed exuberantly for images, until his death, before which he demanded that he be sketched for his statuary dressed only in his winding-sheet, Donne knew this: that to get dressed is to make both a statement and a demand. There's no such thing as neutral clothing: to attempt neutrality is itself a statement of style. Donne's poetry suggests he watched the world, a critic of dress and haircuts and behaviour. His verse from his Inns of Court period laughs at those who get it wrong, and those who care too much about getting it right: he had the world in a double bind. In 'The Anagram', he stabs at the idea of fad-fashion: 'One like none and liked of none fittest were,/For, things in fashion every man will wear.' In 'The Perfume', a satire on love poetry, the courtier, attempting to hide from his mistress's father, attempts to quieten his ridiculous fashionable clothes: 'I taught my silks their whistling to forbear;/E'en my oppressed shoes dumb and speechless were'. Some of the looks at the time would truly have been startling: a fashion for melancholia led to flowing sleeves and open shirt-necks in portraiture, while women used pads and wires to make large heart-shaped frames of hair around their heads. King Christian of Denmark had a medical condition which made his hair matt, so he wore it cropped short, but with a single rat-tail that reached down to his nipple, threaded with a pearl. The look caught on, and soon London streets were dotted with men and some women wearing a single long strand of hair, dubbed a lovelock, over the left shoulder and down over the heart.

In his Satire I, Donne conjures an imaginary companion: a vain fellow student on the make, come to tear him from his studies. The fellow student, dressed in 'motley' (the costume of a jester), is fashionable before anything else: ready to leave if someone better dressed comes along. The speaker demands,

> First swear by thy best love in earnest
> (If thou which lov'st all, canst love any best)
> Thou wilt not leave me in the middle street
> Though some more spruce companion thou do meet . . .

Donne – or at any rate, the speaker of the Satire – imagines being abandoned for some naval captain, dressed in gold-plated armour, 'bright parcel-gilt with forty dead men's pay', or a 'brisk, perfumed, pert courtier'. Donne did not admire the kind of glamour his fellow students pretended to. Glamour for Donne is a kind of neediness; one cannot be glamorous sitting alone on one's own, glamour requires witnesses: and how far can something which exists only in the presence of others really exist at all? Donne's speakers in his Satires provide witness against their will, and rail against it. He raises both eyebrows at the always-changing fashions:

> And sooner may a gulling weather-spy
> By drawing forth heav'n's scheme tell certainly
> What fashioned hats or ruffs or suits next year
> Our supple-witted, antic youths will wear.

His ire is for those who, without the protective armour that is given by wit, are easily conned into seizing on the newest hat or ruff or suit as a form of progress. Do not,

Donne's poetry would argue, buy too readily into that which the world wants to sell you. Your outward presentation has unavoidable power, and so must be engaged in with the full force of your intelligence.

There was only one time when you could escape the language of clothes: one place in which the rich pleasures of velvet and lace were superseded. He wrote in 'The Undertaking' –

> But he who loveliness within
> Hath found, all outward loathes,
> For he who colour loves and skin,
> Loves but their oldest clothes.

Their oldest clothes: the skin they were born in. Clothes had a power and a thrill to them: but they were not as good as their absence.

months.) If you fell ill, your house was boarded up with both patient and family inside for twenty days, and a paper reading 'Lord have mercy upon us' nailed to the door. The playwright Thomas Dekker wrote, 'What an unmatchable torment were it for a man to be barred up every night in a vast silent charnel-house! . . . Where all the pavements should, instead of green rushes, be strewed with blasted rosemary, withered hyacinths, fatal cypress and yew, thickly mingled with heaps of dead men's bones.' It was said that a man could 'dine with his friends and sup with his ancestors'. Dekker wrote of a man who 'felt a pricking in his arm . . . and upon this, plucking up his sleeve, he called to his wife to stay; there was no need to fetch him anything from the market; for see (quoth he) I am marked; and so showing God's Token, died a few minutes later.' The symptoms were as grim as they were swift: a racing pulse, pain in the back and stumbling was followed by agonising buboes – hard red swellings, plague sores, some cherry-size, some as large as an apple. Students who could afford it left London during the worst of it, making a dash for the countryside as cases rose in their part of the city; as far as we know, Donne, whose family were London-based, stayed. He would have seen plague rage through the schools and prisons, leaving hundreds dead and scarred, and then fall quiet again.

In 1593, cases began to grow exponentially: the theatres were closed. The bear-baiting was forced to shut, and the bears were allowed to rest easy. The brothels emptied. In the streets officials wielded three-foot-long marshal wands, to swat at people who weren't maintaining social distancing. William Shakespeare, who across the river was just beginning to make his name as a playwright, found his livelihood temporarily overturned, swiftly switched to poetry and wrote *Venus and Adonis*, an epic which abruptly made him famous at court. Donne's friend from the Inns of Court, Everard Guilpin, was a satirist whose raucous verse boasted about shunning love poetry – 'whimpring sonnets, puling elegies' – and it was to him that Donne wrote his lament for the city's swagger:

Now pleasure's dearth our city doth possess:
Our theatres are fill'd with emptiness;
As lank and thin is ev'ry street and way
As a woman delivered yesterday.

Many years later, during the outbreak of 1626, Donne preached a plague sermon which became famous for its brutality. It spares nothing. The days had an apocalyptic note to them: the ground in London was heaving with bodies, and rains occasionally brought corpses floating up to the surface of the soil. The graveyards became so full that graves had to be reopened to cram in more: 'in this lamentable calamity, the dead were buried, and thrown up again before they were resolved into dust, to make room for more.' Donne tells his audience that the ground they walk on is 'made of the bodies of Christians'. So many people have been buried and dug up again to be rearranged in tighter and tighter proximity that their bodies are in the air: 'every puff of wind within these walls, may blow the father into the son's eye, or the wife into her husband's, or his into hers, or both into their children's, or their children's into both.'

Donne was rare in that he faced the plague without offering explanation or excuse. It was as though it was only by facing it in detail, by fully delineating it, that he could stay upright. Most men offered rationalisations, the majority of which were moral rebukes: the plague, they roared, was condemnation for England's past ills, and particularly those of sordid, money-and-flesh-hungry London. One poet wrote:

Fair London that did late abound in bliss
and waste our Kingdom's great Metropolis . . .
The hand of Heaven (that only did protect thee)
thou hast provoked most justly to correct thee.

Donne rejected it: he would not blame those who died of plague. He refused to speculate. He said in his sermons that a plague could not 'give a reason how it did come'. It was 'not only incurable, uncontrollable, inexorable, but undisputable, unexaminable, unquestionable'. He laid out the scale of the tragedy like a shopkeeper lays out his wares: looked at it, turned it over and over, held it up to the light, but did not attempt the arrogance of hypothesising. He had an urgent, personal reason for his refusal to join in the clamorous condemnation of those who died of the disease; a reason which dated back to his Lincoln's Inn days.

¶

Donne had been at Lincoln's Inn for a year when his brother Henry was arrested. Henry was John's junior by a year, and had followed him after Oxford to Thavie's Inn. Given the geography of the two Inns – Thavie's just on the edge of Holborn Circus and Lincoln's Inn less than ten minutes away on Chancery Lane – they would have lived a short walk from each other: brothers who held each other close, heart-wise and geographically.

In the spring of 1593, Henry took a young priest called William Harrington into his chambers. He planned to hide him from Elizabeth's priest hunters, and feed him and care for him in secret. He was still barely more than a child, or he would have seen the impossibility of it; Henry's fellow scholars would have been all around, eating and working and gossiping. How did he expect to get food to him? How did he expect to wash Harrington's clothes, to dispose of his waste, to keep friends away, to steer clear of the laundresses? In May, without warning, Henry's chambers were raided. A man called Richard Young – close friend of the famed Richard Topcliffe, Elizabeth's chief enforcer and torturer – hunted through his rooms and found Harrington inside. Both William and Henry were arrested, but Harrington, trained to withstand pain, at first steadfastly denied being involved in the Catholic Church.

Henry betrayed him. He broke under questioning and admitted that Harrington had 'said he was a priest, and did shrive him'. Henry and Harrington were sent first to the Clink prison, and then to Newgate.

Newgate jail had been rebuilt in 1423 on a bequest from the famous Dick Whittington, Lord Mayor of London and hero, along with his cat, of many folk tales: but it had nothing of folk-tale sweetness to it. Built just inside the City of London, between Newgate Street and Old Bailey, it was notorious for its dirt and cruelty. By the time Henry was sent there, it was a grotesque place, cold and dark and humiliating. In 1500 and again in 1550, prison inspectors enquired into the conditions and issued a command that the prison be run lawfully: that it had to be told to do so was proof that it was not. Corruption and bribery were accepted as the norm; prisoners were kept in leg irons and forced to pay for their own board. The mayor himself would not set foot in it for fear of disease. The floor was said to crunch because of the carpet of lice, dead and alive. And the lice themselves could be deadly; in the city's Bill of Mortality one man has the cause of death listed as 'eaten of lice'.

It was from Newgate that Harrington was tried and found guilty of high treason, on 18 February 1594. He was subjected to the death of a traitor; he was 'drawn from Newgate to Tyborne; and there hanged, cut down alive, struggled with the hang-man, but was bowelled, and quartered'. It was recorded later that he had given 'proofs of unusual constancy and noble-mindedness in prison, at the bar, and on the scaffold'.

Henry never saw his friend leave Newgate for the scaffold. The plague was running untrammelled through the cells. A contemporary Catholic claimed that Henry was transported from the Clink to Newgate in a bid to murder him indirectly with the disease, before he could be tried; there isn't evidence to bear the rumour out, but it would have looked true to the terrified friends who saw him go in. More likely, he was moved out of institutional bloody-minded aggression: his parents lived near the Clink, in Southwark down by the river, and the commissioners for recusancy were told to move their prisoners away from any prison where they might 'have favour shown them': where relatives might have visited daily, brought food, fresh clothes, small gifts. It was explicit policy to be cruel.

Donne did not visit his brother in jail. He delayed a few days – perhaps he was afraid of the plague, or perhaps there was nobody who could tell him there was an urgency. He may not have known what was happening to the boy with whom he had gone, small and alone, to face the older, taller undergraduates of Oxford. Within days of arriving in Newgate, Henry was feverish, tortured by buboes. He died fast. He was nineteen years old.

§

Donne barely wrote about his brother's death in the letters that we have, but fever and corruption and plague got into his writing. There was the major outbreak in 1593 (more than ten thousand victims in London alone), followed by 1603 (23,045 London plague burials) and 1625, and smaller flare-ups in other years: from 1606 to 1610, plague was responsible for at least ten per cent of deaths a year. It became the constant hunter that stalked the city.

Donne was often ill in later life: his body was handsome but not strong. Henry's death must have made it more terrifying: to have lost his brother to plague would have made every one of Donne's own itches or coughs a terror. Later in life, Donne repeatedly fell ill with what's now thought to have been relapsing fever, a tick-borne infection which killed up to seventy per cent of those who contracted it. The symptoms were exactly those of the early stages of plague. Each time he felt it rise in him, there would be the question: was it the old familiar fever, or had Henry's contagion come for him?

There's a kind of imaginative ferocity to Donne's writing about death, after Henry, and it grows over time, as he loses more and more of the people he loves and their ghosts pile up around him. He becomes a pedlar of the grotesque, a forensic scholar of the entropy of the body. The word 'decay' appears a dozen times in his verse, and that Old Norse, *rot*, is scattered through his work: of an imagined love rival, he writes, 'in early and long scarceness may he rot'; in an elegy he demands of us, 'think that thy body rots'. He wrote, of death: 'Now wantonly he spoils, and eats us not,/But breaks off friends, and lets us piecemeal rot.' He invited those around him to a fleshy thought experiment: to imagine yourself as daily mouldering a little more, and see if it colours where you stand.

The body is, in its essentials, a very, very slow one-man horror show: a slowly decaying piece of meatish fallibility in clothes, over the sensations of which we have very little control. Donne looked at it, saw it, and did not blink. He walked straight at it: no explanation, justification, no cheerful sallies. There was just the clear-eyed acknowledgement of the precise anatomy and scale, the look and feel, the reality of ruin.

It was his superpower, that unflinching quality. It allowed him clarity of vision. He would, throughout his life, write to the very brink of his terror: 'I have a sin of fear, that when I've spun/My last thread, I shall perish on the shore.' But the same clarity would also allow him a fierce intensity with which to imagine himself: 'I am a little world made cunningly/Of elements and an angelic sprite.'

THE CONVERT (PERHAPS)

How much blood is too much blood to bear? Between Thomas More's execution in 1535 and Henry's death in 1593, we can count eleven members of Donne's family who died in exile or in prison for their Catholicism. There was some majesty and glory, as with Thomas More, who ended by being canonised by the Catholic Church – but also plenty of humiliation and muddy uncertainties. Donne's grandfather John Heywood had been sentenced to death over a Catholic plot, and saved himself from death at the last moment when he read a public recantation, which was then written up, extremely unflatteringly, in Foxe's *Book of Martyrs*. Donne attempts to jab back at him, much later, referring to 'the art of copying out within the compass of a penny all the truthful statements made to that end by John Foxe': a small and furious sally, not liable to wound Dr Foxe, he being dead.

Exactly when Donne turned from Catholicism to Protestantism is the central boxing ring of Donne studies: how, when and why the young man decided to turn away from the rituals and well-loved rites of his childhood. In 1593, at Henry's death, Donne was still Catholic, and when he married he was not. What happened in between? It is possible that he licked a finger and held it to the political wind, and saw that no man could advance while remaining a Catholic: it's possible there was never a change of heart, only of expedience. But if the conversion was real, there was probably no single burst of light or dark that caused it; like almost everything in our rusty-hinged, slow-moving world, it happened in pieces. There was the power of his ambition, and his understanding that promotion and success would not be compatible with open Catholicism, but there would also have been new books and new conversations, drinking with Protestants, flirtations with Protestants. There would have been the pull of other allegiances over denominational ones – to the monarch and to the idea of nationhood, which slowly took on the shape of national loyalism and led him towards the Church of England. His priorities shifted, realigned, took on new shapes. You, too, have experienced time.

And what happened to Henry must have been part of it. Donne wrote nothing that explicitly names his brother – in part because he wrote very little about any of his family. There are far more of his words to be found about eagles, dust, the suburb of Mitcham, and tax, than his own mother. But around the time of Henry's death, he wrote a verse letter to his friend Rowland Woodward, in which he confessed his heartbreak, though he never names the cause:

Grief which did drown me; and, half-quenched by it,
Are sàt'ric fires which urged me to have writ
In scorn of all.

71

In that lack of naming, you can hear the guilt that must have haunted him: he would have known that Henry was sheltering Harrington. It's been suggested Donne may even have helped shelter the man himself, although there's no evidence for it except the bond of closeness between the two brothers. The loss shaped him. It seemed to clarify his sense of the necessity of seizing control of your own self and own fate. He told a friend in a verse letter in the 1590s: 'be then thine own home, and in thyself dwell.'

There were rumours, at the time, that the Jesuits were in some way implicated in Henry's arrest. There were rifts between Jesuits and seminary priests – many Catholic priests saw the increasingly extreme positions of the Jesuits, who advocated various degrees of violence against the monarchy, from deposing to beheading, as over-much and ungodly. Harrington, the priest discovered in Henry's rooms, was one of those who had begun to feel doubts – he had written of his need to be 'answerable to my father's estate', which required loyalty to queen and country and the system into which he had been born – and when the priest hunters came crashing in through the door, whispers ran through London that Harrington had been betrayed because of his weakening stance.

It is very possible that Donne felt the Jesuits were in part to blame for the death of his brother. William Clark, a seminary priest, wrote that the Jesuits 'indirectly . . . cause Priests to be apprehended', which they did by spreading false rumours accusing the priests of being 'espialls' (spies working against the Catholics), 'sometimes termed seditious', making them vulnerable within their own community. Clark singled out Harrington as one such: a man who was driven by the Jesuits to be like a rat in a trap, unable to access the usual channels for help, and putting all those who supported him in danger. One of the most prominent seminarists of the time, Christopher Bagshaw, wrote in 1601 about the Jesuits, seemingly with Harrington in mind: 'They do not indeed directly cause Priests to be apprehended, but indirectly. That is, having spread some reports of them, whereby their good name is taken away . . . no Catholic entertaineth them, and so consequently, they are driven to poverty' – or, in Harrington's case, driven to ask the help of a teenager who proved disastrously ill equipped to provide it.

There's a poem, probably written this same year, 'The Bracelet', which reads like a coded reference to Henry. It's a poem about the loss of a mistress's gold chain, but the despair in the poem is wildly disproportionate to the loss; it is a 'bitter cost'. It's not that it's a straightforward metaphor – Henry = chain – but the outsized dread makes a poem that embodies loss. It's a veiled horror-poem. Donne issues a curse on the finder of the chain: 'But oh, thou wretched finder, whom I hate/So much that I almost pity thy state'; he leaves open the ghost of a possibility that 'finder' refers to those who found the priest in Henry's rooms. And as the speaker casts his gold 'angels' (gold coins: a pun with a lot of space for interpretation) into the fire, to make another chain:

THE (UNSUCCESSFUL)
ADVENTURER

Henry was dead, and the delight of London was dead too. By 1596, Donne was keen to get away: he was finished with the law, and with the life he had led.

At the same time, preparations for an expedition against Spain had begun. For several years, England had been in a watery conflict with its Papist enemy – Donne makes jokes about the two worst afflictions, 'dearths and Spaniards'. King Philip II of Spain had been husband to Mary I, making him *jure uxoris* ('by right of marriage') King of England, and English Protestants lived in constant fear that he might mount an attack on England and carry it off into the bosom of Rome. He had, in 1588, sent his Armada of 130 ships over the water in an attempt to overthrow Elizabeth; he was defeated by flaming English fireships laden with gunpowder, and by storms, but the English suspicion was that the passion for unthroning remained. As a result, any attempts to weaken the Spanish were seen as acts of valiant national devotion. The battle had been waged for the past years, not by armies, but by individuals: state-sponsored pirates. They were known as privateers, but it was absolutely piratical in nature: the Queen offered her subjects 'letters of reprisal', which would allow a ship's captain to loot any Spanish ships on the water, including the heavily laden trade vessels set for the Americas, and call it legal.

Now, in 1596, there were rumours that Philip was build-ing another armada, to attempt the invasion again. In London, a pre-emptive counter-strike was being planned, to take as many ships and as much of their gold as could be seized: boats were being outfitted, men being gathered. The Earl of Essex, Robert Devereux, first cousin twice removed to the Queen and generally reckoned to be the most dash-ing man in England, was at the forefront of it, seeking men. His secretary was young Henry Wotton; he may have intro-duced his employer to his friend. Donne presented himself and offered his services as a sailor – and untrained and inex-perienced though he was, they needed bodies to man the boats: he was accepted.

There's a manuscript which claims to contain 'A Journal of all the particularities that fell out in the voyage under the charge of the two Lord Generals, the Earl of Essex and the Lord Charles Howard, Lord High Admiral of England, and also the names of all the commanders and great officers with the captain and voluntary gentlemen that appertain to the army' – but alas the pages which should contain the list are blank, the compiler having had more initial enthusiasm for the task than follow-through, and so we don't know which ship he leapt aboard, so young and questing and ready for the sea.

In early June they set out, dressed in their finest clothes, silver and lace gleaming, cheered by crowds. Their weapons shone, and they were some of the best-equipped men to have departed England's docks for many years. George Carew, a captain, declared in pride that 'they are strong enough at sea to abide the proudest fleet that ever swam'. There was one brief hiccup, when the ships were blown straight back into the harbour at Plymouth the same day they sailed: but then they were on the high seas and truly away.

The first portion of the expedition was an admiral's dream; after just over two weeks, the English sailed in sight of Cadiz, where they launched a cannon attack on the Spanish ships in harbour. It was a great success, but the kind of success that was terrible to watch. Walter Raleigh wrote of the Spanish soldiers that, seeing their cause was lost, 'they all let slip and ran aground, tumbling into the sea heaps of soldiers so thick as if coals had been poured out of a sack, [from] many ports at once, some drowned, some sticking in the mud . . . many, half burnt, leapt into the water . . . if any man had a desire to see hell itself, it was there most lively figured.'

Donne wrote about the moment in his epigram '*Naue Arsa* (A Burnt Ship)', composed in the 1590s: one of the most blunt-edged of his poems, it's part lament, part fascination. It has a cruelty to it – there's pleasure in the wordplay, of men on a ship drowning in fire:

Out of a fired ship which by no way
But drowning could be rescued from the flame,
Some men leaped forth, and ever as they came
Near the foe's ships, did by their shot decay:

So all were lost which in the ship were found,
They in the sea being burnt, they in the burnt ship
    drowned.

It was here, though, that the expedition took a turn and went rogue. The British were supposed to send their own smaller ships into the harbour to capture the Spanish fleet. Instead, Essex, his blood high, went roaring ashore to sack the city and everyone followed. Cadiz fell that same day, 30 June, and the troops set about looting, taking forty-two hostages – among them the Mayor of Cadiz, several members of the council and a number of priests – for ransom. While they were busy sacking and pillaging, the Duke of Medina Sidonia ordered his own ships in the inner harbour be burned before the British could seize them. The English demanded 120,000 ducats for their hostages; when that was refused, they set fire to Cadiz and sailed home with the hostages in tow. The hostages were not freed until July 1603, when James I negotiated their return – but not before the mayor, Antonio Giron, was said to have reached English soil, lain down and died of grief. They, along with the burning soldiers, got the very worst of the enterprise.

Donne did not write about the sacking of the city; so much of war, he found, was in reality just waiting about, and he wasn't in the thick of the fighting. A contemporary wrote drily that his only achievement was 'to march into the market place with an armour on my back and a pike on my neck in an extreme hot day'.

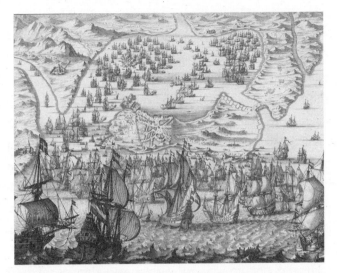

An etching of the Battle of Cadiz, 1596

The Storming of Cadiz

They arrived home to cheering crowds. It had technically been a financial failure – because they hadn't seized the Spanish ships, the Queen was able to recoup only £8,359 against her initial investment of £50,000. But it was a grand symbolic coup; it had been one of the worst Spanish defeats in the Anglo-Spanish war, a cause for bonfires and feasting. It was good enough that the Queen laid out plans for another attack, on Ferrol, where yet another fleet was being gathered by the Spanish; and Donne stepped forward to rejoin the crew. On 17 August 1597, after much waiting about in Plymouth, Donne was one of the sailors who again set out for Spain.

He did not go aboard with a straightforward heart. Nothing suggests he loved his time on the ocean, and there's an element of self-scorn in the poem 'The Calm', one of the rare poems we can easily match to a very specific moment and time in Donne's life. He wrote, of this voyage:

> Whether a rotten state and hope of gain,
> Or to disuse me from the queasy pain
> Of being beloved and loving, or the thirst
> Of honour or fair death out-pushed me first,
> I lose my end: for here as well as I
> A desperate may live and a coward die.

'Hope of gain' nods to his need, constant at the time, for money; and it is possible that there was a woman somewhere in it. War, after all, is a cure for love in Ovid.

The second expedition was, for Donne, hell. Almost immediately a violent storm broke out, and the fleet of more than a hundred ships was strewn across the ocean along the south coast. Raleigh remembered how 'we thought to yield ourself up to God, having no way to work that offered any hope.' Donne wrote, 'it rained more/than if the Sun had drunk the sea before': the sky spits out a sea's worth of water, and:

Some coffined in their cabins lie, equally
Grieved that they are not dead and yet must die.

A storm at sea, when boats were splintering and there was no possible hope of rescue until the water was calm again, was a terrifying thing. The seventeenth century produced several published collections of accounts of graphic disasters (our desire for in-depth reporting of plane crashes and our Hollywood films about ruined ocean liners are not new); one, titled 'Memorable accidents, and unheard of transactions containing an account of several strange events: as the deposing of tyrants, lamentable shipwrecks [and] dismal misfortunes', reports how the waves and noise and tearing of the ship together bring absolute certainty of death: 'It would be a hard task to represent the astonishment, terror and consternation that seized up on every heart on the ship. Nothing now was heard but cries sighs and groans: Some prostrate upon the deck implored the assistance of Heaven.' Some years later, another voyager,

William Hickey, would write of a storm, 'at this awful hour did it occur to me what I had somewhere read that death by shipwreck is the most terrible of deaths.' Donne would have known, in those hours, what the most terrible of deaths might look like.

In total chaos, they made it back to shore. Slowly, the ships were repaired. The sailors loitered about in the port, waiting to begin again, though some thought better of it, found horses and galloped home. A fellow sailor at the time noted with scorn that 'a great many of our young gentlemen (who seeing that the boisterous winds and merciless seas, had neither affinity with London delicacy, nor Court bravery) . . . secretly retired themselves home, forgetting either to bid their friends farewell, or to take leave of their General.' The smell of so many men and so little washing was awe-inspiring: a letter once ascribed to Donne, now doubted, ran, 'it is true that Jonas was in a whale's belly three days, but he came not voluntary as I did, nor was troubled with the stink of 150 land soldiers as we.' Donne was tougher than the boys who went riding home for warm fires and clean clothes, but he was undelighted by the way the days were going.

In late August the fleet prepared to set out again for Spain, but the crew was depleted, dirty and sick. Walter Raleigh's fleet, which almost certainly contained Donne, was separated from Essex's when the latter's ship started leaking, mid-sea. There were misleading reports of the position of the Spanish Armada, restless cruising in wrong directions;

and then, just before the two fleets were able to unite again, Raleigh's fleet hit a period of utter calm. 'We were very much becalmed for a day or two, and the weather extremely hot, insomuch as the wind could not bear the sails from the masts.' The finery of the ship became squalid; 'all our beauty and our trim decays.' Sailors hung their clothing from the masts and collapsed around the deck. Donne wrote: 'The fighting-place now seamen's rags supply,/And all the tackling is a frippery.'

The rest of the expedition was chaotic; the ships communicated largely by musket fire, and it's difficult to be specific with a musket. The Spanish fleet evaded the English. The English could find no viable way to attack it: they seized a few straggling ships, but failed to take several larger ones. They returned home, rocking and tipping through huge waves, to a royal reception as stormy as the weather. Nobody gathered at the dock to cheer. Sailors had foot-rot and suppurating wounds. Donne did not attempt the privateering life again.

§

Perhaps, though, voyaging had got into his blood: or perhaps it was always there. His poetry, after his sally on the sea, is shot through with images of exploration, discovery, fresh territory: 'O my America! My new-found land!' New-found lands were at the forefront of the Renaissance mind; that, and maps of lands. Maps weren't neutral objects. On the one hand they could be weapons – and on the other, they could be something very like pornography. The first accurate map of England and Wales was surprisingly late, Christopher Saxton's Atlas of 1579. It was – perhaps – created in response to the potential threat of the Belgians. Mapping could be, if not an act of aggression in itself, then one that made aggression possible: in 1564, Flemish cartographer Gerard Mercator had created the *Britanniae* map, a beautiful engraving, as large as a child's bed, made up of eight great copper plates of the British Isles. In it, the outline of Wales's coastline is significantly improved compared to any maps that had gone before – the Bay of Cardigan appears for the very first time in cartographic history – and the shape of Scotland is so much more accurate that it remained the model for subsequent maps for a hundred years. Should Catholic forces choose to invade from Europe, the new map of the coast would be invaluable.

It was unthinkable that Europe should have a better record of the coast of the British Isles than the British Isles themselves, and so the Saxton Atlas was commissioned by the Secretary of State, Lord Burghley (the same Lord Burghley who persuaded Elizabeth to execute Mary Queen of Scots: not a man who was comfortable, strategically, with leaving things open to chance). The subsequent Atlas became a kind of talisman; a revelation of the land, when for the first time people were able to trace their own familiar rivers across paper; to know that their portion of the land had been counted. Donne would have seen one, and would have known how a map could stand for life and death. Years later, near the end of his life, he would imagine himself a paper-thin chart:

> Whilst my physicians by their love are grown
> Cosmographers, and I their map, who lie
> Flat on this bed.

And just as west and east, when the map is folded, meet and touch and become the same, so West, death, becomes the East, rebirth:

> As West and East
> In all flat maps (and I am one) are one;
> So death doth touch the Resurrection.

Before that, though – before he knew about pain and fever – there was for Donne the thrill of exploration. Maps could be the sexiest paperwork. In around 1330, the Lombardian Opicinus de Canistris was making an anthropomorphic map: a scribe in the papal office of the Apostolic Penitentiary, Opicinus drew maps in which landmasses took on eyes and fingers. Opicinus used maps to transform and unfix; in one map, Spain and Italy make the leg and head of a female figure, with Avignon, the French seat of the Pope, as the heart; Corsica and Sardinia are small turds, while the top of Africa is the head of its female interlocutor. Elsewhere, Venice is a vulva alongside a sea of sperm. In one plate the female country/woman speaks an inscription, almost impossible to read; it appears to say '*venite commiscemini nobiscum*', 'come, copulate with me'. Donne knew the same thing: his verse insists, over and over, that we approach another body with the same awe with which we would step onto unknown earth. In 'The Good Morrow', from around 1602, he wrote it out, step-by-step instructions:

Let sea-discov'rers to new worlds have gone,
Let maps to others, worlds on worlds have shown,
Let us possess one world, each hath one, and is one.

THE INEXPERIENCED
EXPERT OF LOVE

Home from exploring, Donne was introduced to a man who would change his life for ever. One handshake, and the way was set to shift the whole course of his days.

(They probably didn't actually shake hands. The history of the handshake is contested: some say it dates from medieval Europe, where knights grasped each other's hands as a show that their sleeves were weaponless; others that it was part of a wider move away from the deferential hierarchical gestures of bowing and curtsying; others that it was introduced to the Tudor court by Sir Walter Raleigh, and it is for this, rather than for the potato which he absolutely did not discover, that he should be famous.)

One of the hopeful young sailors voyaging alongside Donne to the Azores was Thomas Egerton junior, a boy five years younger than Donne. They would have known each other by sight, at least, from Lincoln's Inn, that holding-pen of ambitious strivers. Thomas was himself undistinguished and barely formed, but he was the son of one of the most swiftly rising men in England. Born the Catholic illegitimate son of a minor squire, Thomas Egerton senior had risen to be a powerful lawyer, was prosecutor at the trial of Mary Queen of Scots, and, by the time Donne was introduced to him, was the Lord Keeper of the Great Seal.

Sir Thomas Egerton, 1st Viscount Brackley

The Lord Keeper was by definition one of the most influential men in the country: he sat atop the legal hierarchy of England. The holder of the post was said, in the Lord Keeper Act of 1562, to have 'like place, pre-eminence, jurisdiction, execution of laws, and all other customs . . . as the Lord Chancellor'. He was also very literally the person who had to keep the Great Seal safe, carrying it in an elaborately gold-beaded purse. James II would, years later, destroy his own Great Seal while fleeing to France in 1688, supposedly casting it into the Thames in the hope it would bring government to a halt; such was the importance of the seal's role in law-making.

Donne saw in Egerton a glittering chance; for London life, for connection, for purpose, for promotion in the world. He wrote to him: 'I had a desire to be your Lordship's servant, by the favour which your good son's love to me obtained.' Egerton, Walton tells us, 'took him to be his chief Secretary, supposing and intending it to be an introduction to some more weighty employment in the State; for which, his Lordship did often protest, he thought him very fit'. (Walton is as ever inflating Donne's importance: it's very unlikely that Donne would have been Egerton's chief secretary, for Egerton had two other, far more experienced and senior men working in the same position. But it's true that he was propelled right into the middle of Egerton's life, and that the relationship between secretary and master was an intimate one, of daily closeness and confidences.) Egerton's plan was to reform the country's legal procedures, which were in a state of such untrammelled complexity as to be incomprehensible even to the most educated lawyers. Donne, in Satire V, condemns those who 'adulterate law' and salutes Egerton's fight to 'know and weed out this enormous sin'.

The Lord Keeper was traditionally given York House for his home; a long stone pile with rear gardens opening directly onto the River Thames, from where you could leap on a boat over the water to the Globe Theatre. (These days, there are public gardens on the site, equal parts roses and cigarette butts, and nearby the Embankment tube.) Donne would have accompanied Egerton to the palace at Whitehall, where he worked: twenty-three acres and two thousand rooms, with the Privy Chamber at the very heart of it, where very few could enter in. 'The court' was not

York House, engraved after an original drawing by Wenceslaus Hollar

one single place; rather, it was a Pied Piper-like procession, in which the monarch would move between multiple palaces – from St James's Palace in London to Hampton Court, with its kitchen that could cook a thousand meals a day – and the entourage would follow: law-makers, advisers, allies, ladies in waiting, carriers of news, jesters, petitioners, hopefuls, poets. Donne would have been one of their number.

He became, in his spare time, a young man about town. There's little that remains to give us clues about his day-to-day life, but we know what kinds of entertainment the city had laid out waiting for him. Happily for a man whose verse is so peppered with animal imagery, the city was full of wild beasts. (He loved in particular 'nature's great masterpiece, an elephant/The only harmless great thing': one came to London in the 1620s.) A visiting Italian recorded how, at the Bankside, one could witness a monkey mounted upon a horse and chased by dogs around a ring: 'it is wonderful to see the horse galloping along, kicking up the ground and champing at the bit, with the monkey holding very tightly to the saddle, and crying out frequently when he is bitten by the dogs.' There was bear-baiting: one of Elizabeth's courtiers recorded how the bear would go after the dogs 'with biting, with clawing, with roaring, with tossing and tumbling', then turn to 'shake his ears twice or thrice with the blood and the slather hanging about his physiognomy'. At the Tower there was the menagerie, where you could pay to see lions so tame they kissed their keepers. Donne wrote enviously: 'Oh! Cannot we/As well as cocks and lions jocund be.'

'Nothing whereat to laugh my spleen espies/But bear-baitings or law-exercise.' – To Mr Everard Guilpin

And there were women. Lists were routinely published of the most famous and sought-after London prostitutes; one, *The Wand'ring Whore*, told of a woman, Priss Fotheringham, who would give performances known as 'chucking'. She would stand on her head, while men were encouraged to place coins in her 'commodity': 'Whereupon the sight thereof French dollars, Spanish pistols, English half-crowns are plentifully poured in . . . as she was showing tricks upon her head with naked buttocks and spread legs in a round ring.' Possibly Donne had a similar trick in mind when he wrote,

'Rich nature hath in women wisely made/Two purses, and their mouths aversely laid'; just as his work is coloured by London's plague, so too it has in it all the raucous colour and ribaldry of the city.

Donne was born into a moment in which sex was comedy and scandal, sacrosanct and commonplace: a time in which extramarital sex could be prosecuted by law, but where the law was transgressed so frequently that the consistory courts came to be known as 'bawdy courts'. Shakespeare's daughter Susanna appeared before one, bringing a furious slander case against a man who had claimed she 'had the running of the reins and had been naughty with Rafe Smith at John Palmer's'. Puritans denounced children cavorting around maypoles as frivolling in the presence of phallic symbols and 'stinking idols', but no sooner were you a boy born in the sixteenth century than the world began to plot for your sexual prowess. The French surgeon Jacques Guillemeau recorded the general belief that the length of umbilical cord left uncut on the male baby would determine the length of both his tongue and his penis.

> The navel must be tied longer or shorter, according to the difference of the sex, allowing more measure to the males: because this length doth make their tongue, and privy members the longer, whereby they may both speak the plainer and be more serviceable to ladies . . . the gossips commonly say merrily to the midwife; if it be a boy, make him good measure; but if it be a wench, tie it short.

You barely tasted air before your midwife was vexing over you like a genital sommelier. On the female side – in refutation of those who believe that female pleasure was not considered until Clark Gable cracked his first half-smile – it was widely believed that female orgasm was necessary for conception.

Was, then, the young Donne a great tumultuous lover: a conqueror of swathes of women? After so much time and so much entropy, we can only guess: but, almost certainly, not. Women of his class would have been hard to seduce – they were fiercely and carefully protected. Make a mistake, they knew, and you could be punished for life. For instance: when beautiful eighteen-year-old Mary Fitton was sent in 1595 to wait on Queen Elizabeth, she found herself captivated by William Herbert, the Earl of Pembroke. She was reported 'proved with child, and the Earl of Pembroke being examined confesseth a fact but utterly renounceth all marriage'. Mary and the earl were both threatened with the Tower; in the end Herbert was thrown in the Fleet prison and Mary banished from court. She had two further illegitimate children with a naval officer, and then married twice over, but was never forgiven by her family. It would have been better, her mother wrote to Mary's sister, if she had died at birth: 'if it had pleased god when I did bear her that she and I had been buried [together], it had saved me a great deal of sorrow . . . Write no more to me of her.'

Of course, there were those who risked it – women who calculated their fertile moments, who practised coitus interruptus or gambled on prophylactic penis baths made of ginger and vinegar. Some women tried pessaries of blanched almonds inserted into the vagina; others used castoreum (from a beaver's secretions) mixed with ground lily roots and rue – all of which sound painful and extremely likely to provoke yeast infections. There were those, moreover, who were independent and established enough for it not to destroy them. The poet Lady Mary Wroth was one, who lost her drunkard of a husband to gangrene in her late twenties and went on to have two illegitimate children with her cousin – the very same William Herbert. But by and large, the risk wasn't worth the gain.

There were, too, the brothels lining the river; in the liberties of Whitefriars to the west, and along Petticoat Lane to the east, set among the taverns and alehouses of Billingsgate and in Ave Maria Alley – now office blocks – close by St Paul's Cathedral. But that came with its own dangers, and even high prices weren't a guarantee of safety; in the pamphlet *Look on Me London* (1613) 'the young novice payeth 40 shillings or better' – a huge amount – for 'a bottle or two of wine, the embracement of a painted strumpet and the French welcome': that is, syphilis. Syphilis was rife, and could only be treated with mercury rubbed on the skin, or eaten in chunks which could cause whole mouthfuls of teeth to drop out. At its worst, the disease caused disfigurement and nasal collapse, and artificial noses – some made of plated metal, some of ivory – were marketed to replace them. A twenty-one-year-old Donne wrote with scorn and disgust about men who paid for sex: those who 'in rank, itchy lust, desire and love/The nakedness and bareness to enjoy/Of thy plump, muddy whore'.

Woodcut, artist unknown, *An Elizabethan Whore House*

The idea that Donne's poetry would give you, of a beautiful young man cutting through swathes of London's finest female population, would have been difficult – though not impossible – to pull off. It's more likely that Donne had many flirtations and dalliances (he was, after all, 'a great visitor of ladies'), and occasional intimate brushes with women – but that he wrote the early swaggering erotic poetry for which he is so famous for a small coterie of male friends, Henry Wotton and Samuel Brooke among them. Donne's early lusting verse is part of an epistolary and literary merry-go-round in which poems changed hands over and over. Donne was almost certainly an exhausted over-sexed lover in the imagination only, but he caught that voice of the libertine and exploded it, made it his own. There's a lot of poetry, from around this period, in which Donne gleefully takes on the pose of the rake. If you are looking for a masterclass in how to look and sound like a womaniser, he offers it.

For instance: you could appear to be so sated and overwhelmed by your own exploits that you are exhausted: caught somewhere between the suggestive eyebrow and the yawn. In 'Community', the poet takes on the rueful pose of the exhausted conqueror, one who has to only think of love to wither with ennui: 'changed loves are but changed sorts of meat,/And when he hath the kernel eat,/who doth not fling away the shell?' Women, strange hybrids that they were, were to be seized and then discarded:

If then at first wise Nature had,
Made women either good or bad,
Then some we might hate, and some choose,
But since she did them so create
That we may neither love nor hate
Only this rests: all all may use.

Or, alternatively, if you were seeking to appear wise in the ways of women, you might, like Donne, write about being battered by excess of love. Love, he proclaims, is only for those who are willing to be eaten alive. In 'The Broken Heart', he writes:

All other griefs allow a part
To other griefs, and ask themselves but some;
They come to us, but us Love draws;
He swallows us, and never chaws.

The man is chewed, like meat, while the heart is smashed like tableware: 'Love, alas/At one first blow did shiver it as glass.' One step further, he casts himself as so swamped in desire that he has dropped dead, a love-corpse – thirty-two of Donne's fifty-four Songs and Sonnets make some reference to death. In the opening lines of 'The Damp', he imagines that those who come to find his dead body, on seeing his lover's likeness, die too: a domino stack of lust-struck bodies:

When I am dead, and doctors know not why,
And my friends' curiosity
Will have me cut up to survey each part,
When they shall find your picture in my heart,
You think a sudden damp of love
Will thorough all their senses move,
And work on them as me, and so prefer
Your murder to the name of massacre.

Donne, ever stretching, ever extravagant, takes the pose to the furthest possible extreme: in 'The Apparition' he imagines his ghost taking revenge on a lover whose coldness tormented him into the grave. The poem, gleefully excessive, ends with a hope the woman 'bathed in a cold quicksilver sweat wilt lie/A verier ghost than I': 'since my love is spent,/ I'd rather thou should'st painfully repent.'

But, because he is Donne, even the poetry which seems straightforwardly about world-weary out-loved lovers twists out of your hands. 'Farewell to Love' begins in the well-trodden tradition of poetry about disillusionment with romantic courtly striving. It appears to end with a resolve to renounce all love:

I'll no more dote and run
To pursue things which, had, endamage me;
And when I come where moving beauties be,
As men do when the summer's sun

　　Grows great,
Though I admire their greatness, shun their heat:
Each place can afford shadows. If all fail,
'Tis but applying worm-seed to the tail.

Donne's poems have fault-lines – they slip away from you. Worm-seed was a concoction made of flower heads, an anti-aphrodisiac. The 'tail' is a Latin dick joke (because the Ciceronian Latin for 'tail' is *penis*). The lines are Donneanly ambiguous: they could mean, if all else fails, the speaker can simply apply worm-seed to the penis to cool their ardour. But it could be the opposite. Worm-seed only worked when taken orally, a fact which Donne, the stepson of a physician, would have known. The meaning could be, it's as useless to make such resolutions against love as putting worm-seed in the wrong place: passion overwhelms. Even when he is working in the same tradition as his allies, offering up imagined conquests for his friends, his verse is different. His poetry will not hold still. It tussles and shifts, the way desire does.

THE ERRATIC COLLECTOR OF
HIS OWN TALENT

Exactly what Donne did for Egerton is something of a mystery – he never says, in his letters, what precisely his job was. He calls himself 'your Lordship's secretary', but his handwriting, beautiful and erratic, didn't have the fine, regular clarity of the men trusted with copying out Chancery records. His signature appears on a bond that Egerton drew up for a man from the Inns of Court, so he may well have been a glorified clerk, dealing with legal detail. One thing we do know, though: in among his work, whether it was arduous or whether he was largely ornamental, he was still writing poetry.

It would be a mistake, though, to imagine that all this time Donne was filing his verse away, keeping it safe, copying it by candlelight into leather-bound tomes in his bedroom in the great house. Donne's early writing life was one of papery disarray. He made very little effort to keep versions of his work; he did not write with an eye to future fame, immortality. Poetry was the best possible way to set down the unwieldy human truth as he saw it, but it was for himself and his close allies. He allowed almost none of his work to go to the press in his lifetime; Izaak Walton described the poems as having been 'scattered loosely (God knows too loosely)'. When, at one point, did Donne briefly think of printing his verse, he had to cast around, writing to friends to retrieve poems of which he'd kept no copies, complaining it 'cost me more diligence to seek them than it did to write them'. He was often dismissive of his poetry; they were, he'd tell his friends, 'a rag of verses' or 'light flashes': nothing worth very much. There were poets who wrote with enduring fame in mind – Edmund Spenser was one, Milton another. Donne was different. He was the kind of man of whom George Puttenham remarked, 'I know very many notable gentlemen in the court that have written commendably, and suppressed it again, or else suffered it to be published without their own names to it: as if it were a discredit for a gentleman to seem learned, and to show himself amorous of any good art.' The thought that thousands of people from across the world would gather in hotel conference rooms to discuss poems which Donne himself had perhaps forgotten by the time he died; that hundreds of years later it would be possible to buy a mug printed with his face and the legend *let's get metaphysical*: it would have been unfathomable.

Because of this devil-may-care attitude to his own work, when you quote a Donne poem, you are in fact quoting an amalgamation, pieced together over four hundred years from an array of manuscripts of varying degrees of scrappiness. His poems were folded into small squares and passed from hand to hand, posted between friends of friends of friends: read it and pass it on. The only surviving holograph copy – which is to say, in Donne's own handwriting – of an English

Madame,

Here, where by all all Saints invoked are,
'Twere too much scisme to bee singuler,
And 'gainst a practise generall to warr;
Yett, turninge to Saints, should my Humilitee
To other Saint, then yow directed bee,
That were to make my Scisme Heresie,
Nor would I bee a Convertite so cold,
As not to tell yow, if thys bee too bold,
Pardons are in thys market cheaply sold.

When because Fayth ys in too lowe degree,
I thought it some Apostleship in mee
To speak things wch by fayth alone I see,
That ys, of yow, who are a firmament
Of vertues, where no one ys growen, nor spent,
Thay' are yor materialls, not yor Ornament.
Others, whom wee call vertuous, are not so
In thayr whole Substance, but theyr vertues grow
But in theyr Humors, and at Seasons show.

For when through tastles flatt Humilitee
In dow-bakd men, some Harmelesnes wee see,
Tis but hys flegme thats vertuous and not hee.
So ys the Blood sometymes, who euer ran
To danger vnimportund, hee was than
No better then a Sanguine vertuous man.

So Cloystrall Men who in pretence of fear
All Contributions to thys Lyfe forbear,
Haue vertu in Melancholy, and onely there.
Spirituall Cholrique Critiqs, wch in all
Religions find faults, and forgiue no fall
Haue, through thys zeale, vertu but in theyr Gall.

We' are thus but parcell-gilt; To Gold we' are growen,
When vertu ys our Soules Complexione,
Who knowes hys vertues Name or place, hath none.
Vertu ys but Aguishe when tis seuerall;
By Occasion wakd, and Circumstantiall;
True vertu ys Soule, allwayes in all deeds all.

Thys vertu, thinkinge to giue Dignitee
To yor Soule found there no Infirmitee,
For yor Soule was as good vertu, as shee.
Shee therfore wrought vpon that part of yow
wch ys Scarse lesse then Soule, as shee could doe,
And soe hath made yor Beauty, vertu too,

The only poem in Donne's handwriting: 'To the Lady Carew'

poem written by him is a verse letter 'To the honourable lady the Lady Carew' (1612): his hand is beautiful, the italic hand of a Courts-trained man, with elaborately swooping 'y's. All the other poetry we have by him was copied out by other people: some written into large vellum-bound collections with great care, fine handwriting at its most looped and elaborate, Donne nestling against the compiler's other favourites; others were scribbled into corners of a nearly-full page in a booklet, or carried in a single sheet amid bits of pocket debris until they were worn into almost nothing.

It was not only Donne's poetry that was read in this way – he was one among hundreds, at a time when it would be unusual to be an educated ambitious man and not occasionally try your hand at verse. Poetry could be made to function as entertainment, news, flirtation, insinuation, slander, religious contemplation, invoice, in-joke, thank-you note, apology, profound meditation of love, scurrilous sex dream. Like everything else, it had crazes and fashions: someone invented a joke or an image or a metrical scheme, and someone else wrote a response to it; it multiplied.

But Donne's poetry was different in one thing: once it escaped from his immediate grasp, it spread like fire. There are more than four thousand copies of his individual poems, in 260 manuscripts – and it's extremely likely there are more out there, in archives and private collections, waiting for us to discover them. Without having any way of knowing it, he became one of the most popular manuscript poets of his generation. A fair number of the copied-out poems are unattributed, so men and women didn't necessarily know who they were writing out into their books, whose poetry they were sending to a sweetheart or carrying around for luck: they only knew they loved and coveted it.

Because his poetry flew so far and so wide, Donne is one of the hardest Renaissance writers to pin down textually. Inevitably, the poems vary from copy to copy – sometimes just a letter or two, sometimes whole lines – and are often almost impossible to date. 'Slumbered' in one text will be 'snorted' in another; 'reclaimed' will be 'redeemed'. The poems we know as 'by John Donne' have in fact been constructed by editors, piecemeal, from the best of the manuscripts and the seventeenth-century print editions: the title page should, were it to be bluntly literal, read, 'Poems, by John Donne and by educated guesswork'.

On the other hand, titles of Donne's verse are plain, descriptive and uncomplicated. This is because they were largely not written by him. We know that some titles – for instance, some of the wedding-celebration epithalamia – were given by Donne, and in cases where the same title occurs in all collated manuscripts we tend to tentatively assume it's his own. 'A Nocturnal upon St Lucy's Day, Being the Shortest Day' is one. Some titles win out over rivals with greater textual authority simply because we prefer them; 'The Sun Rising' is called 'Ad Solem' in two of the three most famous manuscript groups, but was given its current title in the first printed edition of Donne's work in 1633, and will now forever be 'The Sun Rising', puzzled over by children in schools. Most, though, appear to have been added by manuscript scribes during Donne's life; there are exceptions, but by and large it looks like quicksilver Donne didn't make a habit of anything as solid as a title. His poetry left his hands unnamed, allowing it to gather up titles and edits and little flourishes from each poem's new owner. The poems were akin to living organisms, changing shape and colour as they were copied and recopied.

There is something astonishing in that: that he wore his skill so very lightly. He was willing to lose his work, perhaps because he knew there was more to come. Imagination will beget imagination, and more readily so if it is flung out instead of dragon-hoarded. At no point in his life did Donne come to an end of himself.

THE WITNESS OF
DISASTROUS INTRIGUE

Donne and his poetry would have occupied one room in the Egerton house; but there were many more, and Egerton had a household large enough to fill them all. Just before Donne was appointed, Egerton married for a second time. His wife was a woman named Elizabeth Wolley, and she had style and gloss. She had been married twice already, and had been one of the most active of the Queen's ladies of the Privy Chamber, accompanying her out on royal hawking trips to catch partridges. She brought money with her, a large household of servants and a number of striving young hangers-on. She also had a son, Francis, from a previous marriage – but not wanting her son to be in her new husband's way while he was educated, she and her brother performed a swap. She would send Francis to live with his uncle, Sir George More – an MP and owner of the beautiful Loseley Park, a manor house built with stone heisted from an abbey. George More had a reputation for munificence ('he kept 50 liveries, spent every week an ox and 12 sheep') and for a sharp temper. In return for taking Francis, he would send his third daughter to live at York House and learn the ways of the city and the court. She was fourteen, or thereabouts: her name was Anne More, and something in her face or manner bludgeoned John Donne in the heart.

She was said to be beautiful. (Although, they said the same of Anne Boleyn, a woman who in paintings looks like an unimpressed headmistress.) There is a portrait which goes by the name *An Unknown Woman*, by Nicholas Hilliard, dating from 1602, which might, or perhaps more likely might not, be of her: if it is, she is round-faced, matronly, sweet-smiling, a little exhausted. We have portraits of her father, who has a long strong nose, good space between the eye and eyebrow, and a small mouth; if that resemblance passed down to the girls, she would have looked like the profile on a Roman coin.

An Unknown Woman, attributed to Nicholas Hilliard

Donne, in and out of York House all day, would have met Anne often at the dinner table. Even though he was a paid employee, Walton tells us, 'nor did his Lordship in this time of Master Donne's attendance upon him, account him to be so much his servant, as to forget he was his friend; and, to testify it, did always use him with much courtesy, appointing him a place at his own table, to which he esteemed his company and discourse to be a great ornament.' Anne was learning the ways of London for the first time; he, to her eyes, must have seemed endlessly glamorous, with his reputation for brilliance, his swiftly summoned eloquence and his fine-crafted face.

If you were out courting, you gave gifts. In 1641, one courtship was laid out: 'he perhaps giveth her a ten-shilling piece of gold, or a ring of that price . . . then the next time, or the next time after that, each other time, some conceited toy or novelty of less value.' If you weren't rich, you could give a corset stay, carved by hand and inscribed with a message. If he gave her anything, it would perhaps have been poetry. In 'A Valediction: Of My Name in a Window', written in 1599, Donne imagines etching his name with a diamond ring on a window and his lover seeing her own reflection and his name intermingled:

'Tis much, that glass should be
As all-confessing and through-shine as I;
'Tis more, that it shows thee to thee,
And clear reflects thee to thine eye.

But all such rules love's magic can undo:
Here you see me, and I am you.

'You this entireness better may fulfil,' he wrote, 'Who have the pattern with you still' – a sly numerological joke. Using the then-popular Latin and Hebrew process of *gematria*, in which numbers are assigned to letters, 'my name', 'John Donne', and 'Anne More' all add up to sixty-four. It was the kind of coincidence that Donne – always seeking connections between things not obviously connected, always hunting out symmetries and unexpected felicities – would have relished.

But Anne was not the only exciting member of the household. There was also, at the table, the man Donne had admiringly dubbed in his poetry 'our Earl' – the Earl of Essex. He was there under duress.

¶

The Earl of Essex had been manoeuvring to become one of the most powerful men in England. The Queen loved his company and his flair for talk and games – when the two sat down together to talk, they were in for the night: 'my lord is at cards or one game or another with her, that he commeth not to his own lodging till the birds singe in the morning.' He was beautiful, book-hungry, martial-minded and extravagantly well dressed (he spent £40 on two suits of clothes for his sister's wedding: for comparison, the house Shakespeare bought in 1597 cost £60). But he couldn't

Robert Devereux, Earl of Essex, with a map of Cadiz,
the Azores and Ireland in the background

afford to be complacent – for all Essex was Elizabeth's
current favourite, Walter Raleigh was always waiting in the
wings, hoping he might slip up. Raleigh knew the chances
were good: Essex was quick-tempered, vain and liable to
explode in tantrums. Once before he had quarrelled with
the Queen over her fondness for Raleigh, storming out in
a fury that his affections were 'so much thrown down, and
such a wretch as Raleigh highly esteemed'. The Queen liked

his bumptiousness enough to laugh at him and summon him back, but nobody knew how long it would last. More, despite the fact that his seafaring had made him the adored darling of the public, his determination to continue to wage war on Spain was beginning to be distasteful in court, where the talk was of peace. His insistence on a consistently aggressive foreign policy was losing ground with the Queen – and the only person who seemed not to know how thin was the ice on which he skated was Essex himself.

In 1598, the Privy Council held a debate about Irish policy; the Great Earl Hugh O'Neill was leading a rebellion against English rule. Essex urged the necessity of war, while the Queen's principal secretary argued for peace. The Queen dismissed one of Essex's arguments and, insulted, he deliberately turned his back on her. Exasperated, she slapped him round the head and told him to go and be hanged; Essex half-drew his sword, and had to be held back by a Lord Admiral. He roared to the Queen that 'he neither could nor would put up so great an affront and indignity, neither would he have taken it at King Henry the Eighth his hands.' Legend – and the gossiping Earl of Clarendon – suggests he said to Elizabeth's face that 'she was as crooked in her disposition as in her carcass', which wouldn't have been particularly winning. He stormed out, refusing to return. Thomas Egerton was there to witness it, so Donne would have had a first-hand account.

Egerton, fearing chaos, sent a letter to Essex begging him to see his foolishness and impudence, his 'unseasonable discontentment', and to think of his employees who risked being ruined by his behaviour; Essex sent back a letter made up almost entirely of irate rhetorical questions: 'cannot princes err? And cannot subjects receive wrong? Is an earthly power or authority infinite?'

Donne, frequently called to Whitehall with Egerton, saw the gossip that ran through the rooms, where word could pass between dozens of courtiers in a single day. He was unimpressed. He wrote a verse letter 'To Mr Henry Wotton', who as Essex's man would have been urgently keen to hear the gossip. The poet was uninspired by the scandals: 'here's not more news, than virtue':

> here no-one is from th' extremity
> Of vice by any other reason free
> But that the next to'him still is worse than he . . .

The people of court, he wrote, could dish out slander but not take it:

> Suspicious boldness to this place belongs,
> And to'have as many ears as all have tongues;
> Tender to know, tough to acknowledge wrongs.

Despite the acrimony and the insults, the Council and the Queen could not fully function without Essex. In March 1599, he was sent to Ireland to quell the rebels, taking with him more than a thousand horses and sixteen thousand troops;

the largest expeditionary force ever sent across that stretch of water. Among his young men went Thomas Egerton junior and Henry Wotton, leaving Donne behind to write notes edged with discontent at his own stay-at-home days.

His envy would have grown during the start of the campaign. Wotton wrote home to Donne, enamoured of his earl, 'for our wars, I can only say we have a good cause and the worthiest gentleman of the world to lead it.' Essex knew the power that comes with knighting your allies, and he tapped people with abandon; young Egerton became young Sir Thomas. The Irish rebels mocked that 'he never drew sword but to make knights' – and Elizabeth later was so annoyed by the sea of Sirs he was creating that she threatened to demote some of them.

But despite a strong beginning, the Irish resistance was unexpectedly tenacious. Essex's men struggled to seize the upper hand; two key battles were lost, and amid the blood and confusion and waning optimism, young Thomas Egerton was wounded. Thomas was taken to Dublin Castle, for what rough and ready care was possible. It wasn't enough, and he died there, far from home. His body was sent back home, a long, disintegrating kind of journey for a corpse, for a funeral at Chester Cathedral. Donne travelled to Chester to carry his sword in procession before the coffin. The edge of envy for the excitement of the field disappeared from his letters to Wotton.

In September 1599 Essex, in direct defiance of the Queen's orders, made an uneasy truce with O'Neill. Wotton helped draft the articles of peace, working as one of two chief negotiators: a thrilling kind of task for so young a man – but when Essex returned home it was to a stony welcome. Rumour said that he ran, covered in mud from his ride, straight into the Queen's bedchamber before she had her wig on, bursting in on her wisps of hair and unpainted, ravaged face. Elizabeth, livid, ordered that Essex was to be banished from court and held captive somewhere safe until she could decide what she would do with him. As for Wotton, word reached him that the Queen was displeased with him, too, for those peace articles: pragmatically, he fled the country and headed towards Europe to watch and wait.

Elizabeth chose York House for Essex's house arrest – much to Egerton's disgust – and so in the autumn he became part of the Egerton household. He was confined to its walls; Donne would have encountered him often, full of angry plans for how to recover his footing. Very swiftly, though, the earl's health began to falter; by December 1599, he was very ill. His family asked the Queen if he might be 'removed to a better air, for he is somewhat straitly lodged in respect the Lord Keeper's household is not great'. Elizabeth, her amusement at her old unruly charmer finally exhausted, refused.

Christmas came, and Essex seemed certain to die. Donne was shocked by how jaunty everyone was, as if nothing was amiss. He wrote to a friend that the court was 'as merry as if it were not sick': the Queen came forth every night, to see 'the ladies dance the old and new country dances'. Each day was, Donne said, 'full of jollity and revels and plays' – and among them was the first performance of Shakespeare's *Twelfth Night*.

§

(It's often asked – did Donne know Shakespeare? The response, as with so much of the period, is a seesaw of maybes: probably not, but it's possible, but there is no proof, but perhaps. There's a chance they could have encountered each other this Christmas, at court; both there, both watching with careful eyes. Donne could easily have seen Shakespeare on the stage throughout his London years. Donne enjoyed the theatre, and Shakespeare was an actor in both his own and others' work; in 1610 Donne's friend John Davies wrote that 'Good Will' played upon the stage in 'kingly parts' – and they had a mutual acquaintance in Ben Jonson, who relished opining about both men at regular, waspish intervals. On the one hand, Donne was class-conscious: in 'Love's Alchemy' he took pains to refer to the fact that he kept a manservant – 'my man' – something hard to find in any other poet's work; and he may well have dismissed any notion of knowing Shakespeare, who was then a mere player. On the other, there is the ghost of a book which might link them together. For a fee of about sixpence, a publisher could register his right to a work in the Stationers' Register, an early and slightly haphazard form of copyright law; and in January 1600 was entered: 'A book called Amours by J.D., with certain other Sonnets by W.S.' by one Eleazar Edgar. Many have hoped that it might be John Donne and William Shakespeare, yoked in print. It's possible: Donne had an acquaintance called Berkeley, an ally from Cadiz, who might have passed some of Donne's poetry along to his half-brother Thomas Russell, who was a friend of Shakespeare's and later the executor of his will. Russell might, in turn, have planned to parcel up the verse and turn a swift pound on it: perhaps. But the book, if it was ever printed, no longer exists, and the W.S. could just as readily have been William Smith, a sonneteer and disciple of Edmund Spenser's, while the J.D. could have been John Davies, or indeed a misprint for M.D., Michael Drayton, whose sonnets had been published under the subtitle 'Amours' in their first edition in 1594: it's tantalisingly impossible to know.)

¶

All the while that Christmas the earl languished. If he comforted himself with the thought that the Queen missed him and that his absence was a ghost at her feast, he was wrong. 'My Lord Essex', Donne writes, 'and his train are no more missed here than the angels which were cast down from heaven, nor (for anything I can see) likelier to return.' Donne writes about his former martial leader with compassion and pity, but also a new strain of exasperation: he 'withers still in sickness . . . that which was said of Cato, that his age understood him not, I fear may be averted of your lord, that he understood not his age . . . such men want [i.e. lack] locks for themselves and keys for others.' Some, though, still loved him: some churches within earshot of York House rang their bells for him, to the Queen and Egerton's distaste.

In the early days of 1600, there was a sudden loss at York House, but not Essex: Lady Egerton died, wholly unexpectedly. It hit Egerton hard: harder than was thought seemly at the time. A looker-on wrote, 'my Lord Keeper sorrows more than so great a man ought. He is discontented that his house is made a prison of so long continuance.' Egerton's household was immediately broken up, and Anne was sent back home to Loseley Park, away from Donne and their clandestine romance.

Loseley Park, Anne's home

That spring, letters spilled out of York House. Donne wrote surreptitiously to Anne, declarations in the grand style: 'I will have leave to speak like a lover,' he said, for 'I love more than any yet.' Essex's letter, in contrast, was to the Queen, full of lamb-like submission – and he was at last allowed to leave Egerton's household for his own home, Essex House. The whole of London, though, was still uncertain as to whether the Queen planned to reinstate him in his former place of glory. He needed her to renew his grant on sweet wines, which earned him thousands of pounds, without which his extravagant living – the banquets, the music, the trousers that cost the same as a cottage – would be impossible, and he'd be ruined. But Elizabeth's patience was dead; in October 1600, she announced she wouldn't renew the grant: and abruptly Essex became a man with nothing left to lose.

As the autumn turned to winter, a furious Essex filled Essex House with dissatisfied minor aristocrats and army officers with time on their hands, and began to plan unlikely schemes to gain back his old place in court. On 3 February 1601, Essex packed Drury House in London – a house Donne would later come to know intimately – with his allies, conspiring to overthrow his enemies and re-establish himself where he felt he belonged, at the Queen's right hand. On the 7th, it became clear to the Queen that he was planning something drastic. She called a council: twice Essex was summoned, and twice he refused.

A sub-group of Essex supporters hastened to the Globe to see Shakespeare's *Richard II*, to hear the clash of (real) swords and see (fake) blood – usually made out of vinegar and sheep's blood – in a bid to make themselves feel suitably warlike. On the 8th, Thomas Egerton, along with three other nobles and their entourages, appeared at Essex House, demanding parley in the name of the Queen: it's conceivable that Donne, having lived so close alongside the earl for so long, was in tow – if not, he would later have had a full and furious telling of the day from Egerton.

Essex let the four nobles in, but left the minor figures to loiter outside. He ushered the four men into his study, shut the door on them and locked them in. Then, with fanfare but with very few firearms, Essex led his three hundred followers, including numerous other earls, into the City, heading for Whitehall. His hope was that people in the street would rally to his side: there would be a joyful uprising, and together they would seize control of the capital.

It was a disaster. The Lord Mayor shut the gates against them: the expected support did not flood the streets. Forces loyal to the Queen surrounded them, and Essex fought his way home that same afternoon with less than a hundred of his men, followed and besieged by the Lord Admiral's troops. That evening he surrendered and was taken to the Tower of London.

The Sunday after his insurrection, all the preachers in London were required by order of the Queen to give sermons condemning him; Elizabeth knew that he was still held dear by many, and that it wouldn't pay to have a beloved man beheaded. His trial was followed by thousands, with word passed by gossip, letters and dozens of manuscript copies of the prosecution and defence: Donne would have had access to every word spoken. Essex, worn out, and counselled by his own chaplain to abase himself, gave up on his swash-buckling stance of battered heroism and became a penitent. He was found guilty of treason, and went to his death with a piety so impressive that it was reported across the country. On 25 February 1601, the Queen's former favourite was beheaded in the courtyard of the Tower, watched by a small crowd. The witnesses' names were not recorded, but years later, Donne wrote a poem featuring a beheading in which he dwelt, hard, on the blood: and on the way the dying cling feverishly to life.

> Or as sometimes in a beheaded man,
> Though at those two red seas which freely ran,
> One from the trunk, another from the head,
> His soul be sailed to her eternal bed,
> His eyes will twinkle, and his tongue will roll
> As though he beckoned and called back his soul,
> He grasps his hands, and he pulls up his feet,
> And seems to reach and to step forth to meet
> His soul . . .

Donne was ideally placed to assess fallout from Essex's death, as later that same year he was suddenly made an MP. Egerton had the borough of Brackley, Northamptonshire sewn up, and he made Donne the gift of the parliamentary seat. Donne wasn't naïve; he would have known that the power that came with being a Member of Parliament was not his to wield according to his own desire; he was there as Egerton's man, to pick up information and glean snippets of news. Parliament sat for only a brief time, from October to December 1601, just enough to grant, among stormy mutterings, a new injection of supplies for the war in Ireland. There is no evidence that the young Donne, still not yet thirty, took part in any debates, spoke in public, sat on a committee or indeed participated in any way at all in the process of government; but he would have been able to gather gossip in the aftermath of the rebellion; he would have seen how deeply it had shaken the men who ruled England.

It was probably around this time that Donne wrote one of his longest, strangest poems, 'Metempsychosis'. It is so peculiar and arduous that almost nobody has read it, including some professors of John Donne: it's a semi-epic about a soul which migrates from body to body, starting with the forbidden apple in Eden, to a mandrake, several assorted fish, a sparrow, a mouse, a wolf, and finally Eve's daughter. 'I sing the progress of a deathless soul'. It was theologically risky: according to gossipy Ben Jonson, Donne's original plan with the poem 'was to have brought in all the bodies of the heretics from the soul of Cain, and at last left it in the body of Calvin. Of this he never wrote but one sheet, and now, since he was made Doctor, repenteth highly.' Some have argued that the poem is a kind of guilty metaphor, an account of Donne's shifting and mutating sympathies

Parliament in session in the reign of King James I

away from Essex. But to find the most in 'Metempsychosis',
it is best read as a poem that embodies tumult: Donne's
understanding of the order of things was in chaos, and he
wrote a poem not to explain, but to capture it. To read it
offers some of the feeling of trying to wrestle with a world
that was shifting and raw and unhinged. The body and
soul, which he spent so much time longing to bind together,
refuse to merge: instead, fish transmigrate into wolves who

transmigrate into women. You can read it as a verdict on those who expected him to behave as though the world was sane.

The whole Essex affair was a powerful lesson for Donne, of how intricate and dangerous it was to play with power, and how swiftly the men you trusted could turn on you. If he began to fall out of love with courtly things, then it perhaps started here, with that spurt of the earl's blood. His admiration for Essex had steadily waned, but the man had been his commander and the idol of the age. He would never forget him: his sermons, years later, would be full of warnings about how easy it is to fall. There is no such thing as safety, while you are alive.

THE PARADOXICAL QUIBBLER,
TAKING AIM AT WOMEN

Anne returned to London in October of 1601; her father brought her with him, to continue her education in becoming an elegant young woman. If she and her father visited York House, Donne would not have been there to greet her. Egerton, letting very little grass grow under his feet, had married for a third time, a woman of a great fortune and blueish blood named Alice Spencer. Alice – a distant cousin of the poet Edmund Spenser, and related by marriage to the Queen – brought with her three daughters and a substantial household. Donne was ousted from the newly bustling York House and moved to lodgings in the Savoy. He perhaps wouldn't have minded much: the marriage was a miserable one, and the house was soon a furious battleground. Egerton wrote later, 'I thank God I never desired long life, nor ever had less cause to desire it than since this, my last marriage, for before I was never acquainted with such tempests and storms.' In his new, sparer home, Donne would at least have had peace, in which to work and write.

It's probable, though, that Donne and Anne had been corresponding all along. There are four unattributed and undated love letters copied out into a large collection of letters, poems and accounts of table-talk known as the Burley manuscript. The manuscript, which was thought lost to fire for many decades, seems to be in the hand of Henry Wotton's secretary, William Pankhurst. The four love letters could be Donne's letters to Anne: he writes 'in all that part of this summer I spent in your presence you doubled the heat and I lived under the rage of the hot sun and your eyes'. Their correspondence was risky, and in one the man accuses the woman of depriving him of 'the happiness I was wont to have in your letters'. In another, he describes the weather's turn to cold and ice – 'the sun forsakes us' – but, he says, the heart which she melted in the summer, 'no winter shall freeze'. It does sound very like him, at his most earnest; it's the twin of his promise, in 'Love's Growth', that 'no winter shall abate the spring's increase'.

But – before the finest love poet in the English language could kneel before his love – there is the question: what had Donne, by this time, written explicitly about women? What would Anne have been able to read, had she had the inclination and ability to seek it out, that he had written about the group to which she belonged?

¶

Hope not for mind in women: at their best
Sweetness and wit, they're but mummy, possessed.
'Love's Alchemy'

The German physicist Johann Schroeder, famous primarily for his study of arsenic, was also convinced of the panacea-like properties of 'mummy'. In 1656, his *Pharmacopoeia Medico-Chymica* suggested that, while the best mummy was of course Egyptian, when it couldn't be found home-made alternatives were also workable:

Take the fresh unspotted cadaver of a red-headed man (because in them the blood is thinner and the flesh hence more excellent) aged about 24, who has been executed and died a violent death. Cut the flesh in pieces and sprinkle it with myrrh and a little aloe. Then soak it in spirits of wine for several days, hang it . . . let the pieces dry in a shady spot. Thus they will be similar to smoked meat and will not stink.

It was a cure for almost anything. It is to this medicinal powdered corpse that Donne compares women in his 'Love's Alchemy': 'they're but mummy possessed.' Useful, but hardly romantic.

It would be absurd to try Donne anachronistically as a misogynist; but alongside the poems which glorify and sing the female body and heart, there are those that very potently don't. This is the man who wrote, 'Like sun-parched quarters on the city gate/Such is thy tanned skin's lamentable state': 'quarters' means the bodies hung and quartered at the entrance to the city, particularly nasty coming from someone who had known people who had swung. Donne's delineation of love – his work that encompasses its hunger, evasion, fear, stoicism, joy – is a staggering thing, but he never was an uncomplicated lover of women.

'The Comparison', written in the 1590s, is a good example of how eye-wateringly extreme Donne's anti-female verse could be. Even if we decide that Donne's stance in relation to the voice of the poem is ironical and sceptical, the poem is shot through with disgust. The speaker compares his own mistress with that of a rival, and the text aligns itself loosely to the tradition of what is known as a 'counter-blazon'. A blazon was a courtly poem of the kind that people imagine when they think of ruffs and cross-gartered men with huge lutes: poems that catalogued the physical qualities of an adored figure, like Sir Philip Sidney's excessive praise in his verse 'What Tongue Can Her Perfections Tell':

And thence those arms derived are;
The phoenix's wings be not so rare
For faultless length and stainless hue.

Sidney's woman's hair is gold, her shoulders 'be like two white doves' and her whole person 'out-beauties' beauty itself. Donne's counter-blazon takes that tradition and knifes it in a dark alley. He writes how the sweat of his own mistress's brow is 'no sweat drops, but pearl carcanets', while on his companion's mistress:

Rank sweaty froth thy mistress' brow defiles,
Like spèrm'tic issue of ripe menstr'ous boils,
Or like the scum, which, by need's lawless law

Enforced, Sanserra's starvèd men did draw
From parboiled shoes and boots, and all the rest
Which were with any sovereign fatness blest.

A couple of decades earlier, beginning in 1572, the year
Donne was born, the Protestant Huguenots in Sancerre in
France had been under siege by the Catholic forces of the
King. The citizens ate any hides they possessed; hundred-
year-old parchment documents, horses' harnesses, shoes –
anything that had once been an animal was made into stew.
Children, the historian Jean de Léry wrote, ate their own
belts as if they were tripe. It was very common, in counter-
blazon verse, to suggest your rival's mistress was sweaty; it
was less common to suggest that the mistress's sweat was
like the fat eked out of the boiled shoes of the starving.

Then there is the prose. It's sometimes said that the
more you read Donne's verse, the more you love him, and
the more you read Donne's prose, the less you can bear
him. This is particularly true, for modern readers, with the
nineteen Problems and twelve Paradoxes he wrote: short
essays, written perhaps at the Inns of Court or possibly
a little later. They were never printed in his lifetime, but
they were sent out to his friends and from there rippled
outwards to eager readers and transcribers: there are 429
copies of the individual essays, in at least twenty-six different manuscripts.

Paradoxes were high fashion at the time; short pieces
of writing in which opposites were brought to co-exist,

earnestly or facetiously, with the sideways unspoken implication that such a clash of ideas might have a kind of
unhinged logic somewhere in it. Donne's had titles like
'That Nature is our worst guide'; 'That only cowards dare
die'; 'That the gifts of the body are better than those of
the mind'. They were in enormous vogue across Europe:
in Italy, the philosopher Ortensio Lando was writing neat
little pieces, *contra opinionem omnium* – 'against received
opinion' – in which he argued, for instance, that it was better to be ugly than beautiful, drunk than sober, ignorant
than wise. As Erasmus wrote to Thomas More, about his
own mock-encomium *The Praise of Folly*, paradoxes were
ancient: 'As for those who are offended by the levity and
playfulness of the subject matter, they should consider that I
am not setting any precedent but following one set long ago
by great writers: . . . Glauco praised injustice . . . Synesius,
baldness; Lucian, the fly and the art of the parasite.'

They were a controversial craze; for anyone wanting to
write anything politically inflammatory, phrasing it in a
paradox allowed for plausible deniability, but it could also
leave room for misinterpretation, for being thought more
radical than you were. The playwright Anthony Munday
wrote to his patron to apologise for not handing in his
promised 'Paradox Apology' because the 'misinterpretation of the work by some in authority', he wrote, made
it too dangerous. George Puttenham, the author of the
core Early Modern text on rhetoric and poetry, *The Arte
of English Poesie*, hated them. 'Oftentimes,' he wrote, 'we

will seem to cast perils, and make doubt of things when by a plain manner of speech we might affirm or deny him.' (Although Puttenham was himself a vile man, whose moral judgement was not worth much: he was regularly sued and counter-sued, imprisoned at least six times, excommunicated four times, and was said by his enemies to have kidnapped a seventeen-year-old girl and kept her locked up in his farmhouse for three years.)

All this is to say that Donne's Paradoxes and Problems can't be taken as straight opinion pieces. Nobody in Donne scholarship agrees on the question: what did Donne *mean* by them? Is there seriousness in them? Did he mean his misogyny to be so wild as to be an attack on those who would believe it?

The wittiest of Donne's Paradoxes was headed, 'That women ought to paint themselves'. Make-up was popular in Elizabeth's court: powders made from white lead mixed with vinegar, vermilion on the lips. Hairlines were tweezered. Blonde hair was coveted, and Donne would have seen dyes for sale made of yellow celandine flowers, honey and cumin, or of quicklime and tobacco. You left them in for a day, then rinsed off with a wash made of cabbage stalks, ashes and barley straw. Donne's Paradox, light-hearted and insouciant, takes the side of paint: 'Foulness is loathsome; can that be so too which helps it? . . . If in kissing or breathing upon her, the painting falls off, thou art angry: wilt thou be so, if it stick on? Thou didst love her: if thou begins to hate her then it is because she is not painted.'

Another of the Paradoxes, 'A Defence of Women's Inconstancy', rides to the defence of a woman's right to sleep around:

That women are inconstant, I with any man confess, but that inconstancy is a bad quality, I against any man will maintain . . . [Women] cannot be immutable like stocks, like stones, like the Earth's dull centre; gold that lieth still, rusteth; water, corrupteth; air that moveth not, poisoneth; then why should that which is the perfection of other things, be imputed to women as greatest imperfection? Because they deceive men?

It's so tempting to read it as a paean to female sexual liberation – except of course that it's a paradox: the model that allows the writer to both posit and ridicule simultaneously: and it goes on, rampantly uncharmingly, 'Women are like flies which feed amongst us at our table, or fleas sucking our very blood.'

Alongside the Paradoxes, though, there are the Problems; very similar in form – short essays, rarely more than a page – but sadder, heavier, and harder to dismiss entirely as ironical intellectual games. One asks 'Why have bastards best fortunes?' – from a man who was poor and struggling. Another, 'Why did the Devil reserve Jesuits till the latter day?' – from a man who had seen a hidden Jesuit priest bring about his brother's death.

Donne used his Problems to ask this question: 'Why hath

the common opinion afforded women souls?' It's unlikely that Donne had any doubt about the besouledness of his sisters and mother and female acquaintances; but the essay is dark. There's an anger in it: women, he writes, have 'so many advantages and means to hurt us (for even their loving destroys us) that we dare not displease them'. Women, he writes, are only superior to apes because they can talk: 'we deny souls to others equal to them in all but in speech for which they are beholding only to their bodily instruments: for perchance an ape's heart, or a goat's or a fox's or a serpent's would speak just so if it were in the breast and could move the tongue and jaws.'

The question of whether women had souls had, it was widely believed, been hotly debated in the year 585 by a council of bishops at Mâcon in Burgundy. Of course, it hadn't: it was just a historical misunderstanding based on a mean little pun, in which homo means both 'human' and 'adult male'. Towards the end of the sixteenth century, Valens Acidalius, a poverty-stricken young scholar, wrote a pamphlet in which he used the double meaning of homo to 'prove' that the Bible said only adult men had souls; it gained popularity, was eventually banned by the Pope. It was into this debate that Donne waded, with this parting shot: 'Perchance because the Devil (who is all soul) doth most mischief, and for convenience and proportion, because they would come nearer him, we allow them some souls.' He ends – 'so we have given women souls only to make them capable of Damnation.'

But Donne rarely gives anyone the last word on a topic: and that very much included his own self. Years later in a sermon Donne returned to the same question. He poured scorn on anyone who would dare cast doubt on whether women have a soul: 'Some men out of a petulancy and wantonness of wit, and out of the extravagancy of paradoxes' have called the 'abilities of women in question, even in the root thereof, in the reasonable and immortal soul'. Donne glares out from the pulpit: 'No author of gravity, of piety, of conversation in the Scriptures, could admit that doubt.' He is writing about himself.

'The extravagancy of paradoxes' was the pleasure and the point of them – the possibilities that lie inside pointing out absurdity. Donne discovered that if you force together the two Venn diagram circles of reason and the absurd, in the overlap there is a weapon. He chose to level that weapon at women – or possibly at those who would be credulous enough to believe his prose – or at both. He wrote in a letter, about his Paradoxes and Problems, that 'if they make you to find better reasons against them, they do their office: for they are but swaggerers, quiet enough if you resist them.' Life among lawyers had taught him to argue; but logic, Donne's writing declares, can be brought to defend illogic. Donne knew that the more bold and extravagant your stance, the easier it is to argue you actually meant the diametric opposite. Careful sobriety is dangerous, but surrealism, ribaldry, insouciance – these have a defence mechanism built in, and he seized on them with both hands.

They're cruel, too: no amount of irony or hyperbole cuts that away. They point to something anarchic and furious in his intellectual make-up. It was mostly kept down out of sight, but that hyperbolic streak was part of his strange, remarkable intellect, with its courageous munificence and its angry, bitter corners. Just as he saw, so clearly, both marvels and corruption in the state of humanity as a whole, so Donne very much embodied those extremes. He was capable of being such a joy, and such a fount of satirical, mean snide: he was both celebrant and assassin, ever shifting between the two.

ANNE

Who was she – the very young woman with whom the complicated, furious, funny author of the Paradoxes was so in love? We know very little; we do not even know how she preferred to spell her own name, as with the capriciousness typical of the period, she is spelled both Ann and Anne. It was her second name, though, that Donne played on, over and over: 'as much more loving, as more sad'. She was likely to have been fashionable, given her father's wealth, and her clothes would have been good. Stitching elaborate needle lace was the rage – geometrical patterns and flower designs, especially – and necklines were having a moment of extremes, either rising high to the chin or scooped so low they skated close to the nipple. But his poetry never describes her clothes, or her body. Donne's metaphors are vivid, wild, evocative and potent, but they're strikingly unspecific. It never occurred to him to tell us if she curved at the hip, or jutted at the collar bone, or was taller than him: presumably it was not what was important. The hunger, and the body itself, were what mattered. Perhaps to look for Anne in Donne's verse is to misunderstand what the poems are doing: they're not representations of her, but representations of him: him watching her, needing her, inventing for her. They are trumpet blasts across a hard land, more than they are portraits.

She was almost certainly a reader: he would put it on her epitaph, and Henry Wotton once in a letter referred to 'that fair and learned hand of your mistress, than whom the world doth possess nothing more virtuous'. Female literacy, though, wouldn't be something she could have taken for granted: if she was book-hungry, it would have made her stand out. There had been moments in which female education took high priority, but the stance on educating women changed as often as the fashions for coloured garters, and Anne just missed a wave; so she was unlikely to have been surrounded in her domestic sphere by female friends who valued learning or talked with her about fashions in poetry. Anne was born too late for the burst of enthusiasm for female learning that erupted between 1523 and 1538, inspired by Catherine of Aragon: there were at least seven passionate treatises published on the theme of female classical education between those years. In 1581 – three years before Anne's birth – Richard Mulcaster, the headmaster of St Paul's, wrote, 'Do we not see in our country, some of that sex so excellently well trained' that they could be compared 'even to the best Roman or Greekish paragons be they never so much praised?' But Mulcaster was lauding a dying breed. In 1561, a translation by Thomas Hoby (a scholar married to one of the most learned women of the age) of Castiglione's *The Courtier* put forward a different vision of womanhood. Women, in Castiglione's world, should have their letters, but that was less important than their grace: their painting, dancing, ability to sew a fine

in the tranches of society where there was most property and social status at stake: you might get away with a lot if you were poor, but barely a handful of upper-class children resisted their parents' dictation, and their rebellions were rarely much of a success. In the mid-fifteenth century, a young woman called Elizabeth, a daughter of one Agnes Paston, declared that she would choose her own husband. In response, she was put under effective house arrest, forbidden to talk to visitors or male servants, and was 'beaten once in the week or twice, and sometimes twice on a day, and her head broke in two or three places'. Anne would have known that Sir George More would have expected something far more impressive and gilt-edged for his daughter. So she was in a small and fiery minority when she decided to love him anyway.

She took vast risks for him: larger than he took for her. Spurred on by desire, or perhaps by Donne's urgent importuning, or by the wild optimism of youth, she risked gossip, scandal – and perhaps, at the very end, pregnancy. There are some who believe that by the winter of 1601, they would have become adept at finding brief snatched moments alone. They may well have been lovers in the weeks before they wed, hiding behind insouciant faces and very careful timing. She gave a great, recklessly romantic leap into the dark. The landing was not to be a soft one.

THE DARING OF THE LOVER,
AND THE IMPRISONED GROOM

Was he worth the sacrifice she made, when she forswore the thousand easier futures that surrounded her? The alternatives would have been right in front of her: she could have aimed for a life more like that of her cousin by marriage Elizabeth (uncle Egerton's third wife's daughter) who had that year been married off to Baron Hastings, with all the castles and gardens and wall hangings embroidered with unicorns that that involved. What was Donne, that she decided to risk her father's wrath in order to share his days, his small income, his bed?

If he took her to bed like he wrote – if he knew how to render bodily his poetry – then he was worth sacrificing all the wall hangings in England for. To read him – to read all of his love poems together – is to feel yourself change, for his is a passion which acknowledges the strangeness you are born with.

His best poetry is a triumphant call of desire, sincerity, joke, all bound into one. It's there, for instance, in 'A Valediction, Forbidding Mourning': the lovers are imagined as the two feet of a pair of mathematical compasses, joined eternally at the base.

If they be two, they are two so

As stiff twin compasses are two:
Thy soul, the fixed foot, makes no show
To move, but doth, if th'other do;

And though it in the centre sit,
Yet when the other far doth roam,
It leans, and hearkens after it,
And grows erect as it comes home.

It is so extravagantly witty, and so riotously plays only
by its own rules. It needed to be clever, because he demands
that sex be intelligent: it's the poem of a man who has the
temerity and invention to see the human condition in a piece
of metal. It loves the body, because Donne, unlike so many
of the highbrow poets who went before him, never pretended not to have a body – 'grows erect as it comes home' is a
pun so obvious it might as well be a little sketch of a penis.
Yeats wrote, 'Donne could be as metaphysical as he pleased,
and yet never seemed inhuman or hysterical as Shelley often
does, because he could be as physical as he pleased.'

But it is fundamental to his love poetry that the body
Donne imagines isn't just a body. It transforms, and becomes
simultaneously other things: a world, a state, a city, a planet-
ary sweep. The lover looks at the woman in 'The Good
Morrow' and sees a world atlas: 'Where can we find two
fitter hemispheres/Without sharp North, without declining
West?' In 'To His Mistress Going to Bed', the woman's girdle
becomes a constellation of stars, and her body is the entire

world. 'Off with that girdle, like Heav'n's zone glist'ring,/ But a far fairer world encompassing.' And, again, 'My king-dom, safeliest when with one man manned!' And the man in 'The Sun Rising' chides the rising sun, declares, 'She all states, and all Princes I'. She becomes the world:

> since thy duties be
> To warm the world, that's done in warming us.
> Shine here to us, and thou art everywhere:
> This bed thy centre is, these walls, thy sphere.

Of course, some of that woman-as-state, woman-as-world is Donne working in a tradition. He was not anywhere close to the first poet to claim to find in woman an everything. Pierre de Ronsard, fifty years older than Donne and France's 'Prince of Poets', tells the sun, '*va te cacher*', and asks it if it has seen, in its orbiting of the world, a thing more whole than the woman of the poem.

But some of it was personal. Donne's mind was caco-phonous. His relentless imagination was his single most constant feature; he wrote about his 'worst voluptuousness, which is an hydroptique immoderate desire of humane learning'. In his darker moments, it tortured him. His mind had ceaselessness built into it. It was to be, throughout his life, a site of new images, new theology, new doubts: even those who disliked his work acknowledged that he was a writer who had erupted through the old into the new. A contemporary wrote that, with him, it was 'the lazy seeds/of servile imitation thrown away/and fresh invention planted'.

But the *always* of that imagination must have been exhausting. For a mind like that, sex – real sex, true sex – would allow a singleness to hush the multitudinous mind. It's why so much of Donne's imagery around sex is so totalising: the man and woman become one, the woman becomes a state, a country, a planet. Sex, for Donne and those like him: permission, for those who watch the world with such feverish care, to turn one person into the world and to watch only them. It was a transforming of his constant seeking for knowledge. To adore and to devour and to be devoured is its own kind of focus: a gasp of a different kind of oxygen.

§

And so they married.

The wedding took place 'about three weeks before Christmas', in 1601, according to Donne. It was very small: no more than five guests. The fashion for brides swathed in white, popularised by Queen Victoria, had not yet begun; burgundy was popular in Italy, gold in Austria. Elizabeth's sumptuary clothing laws, still in place until James I swept them all away, would have forbidden that Anne wore tinselled satin or silk, or velvet in crimson, scarlet or blue; but it's likely, given its clandestine nature, she only wore the best of what she already had.

The couple were probably married at the Savoy. First a thirteenth-century crenellated palace belonging to Peter,

Count of Savoy, it had been rebuilt as a hospital with a chapel for the needy under Henry VII, and by the time Donne reached London part of it was let to fashionable people who had enough money to dress themselves in sweeping hats and cloaks but no need for an actual town house. With the Earls of Huntingdon, Cumberland and Northampton registered among its tenants, it had a glamour to it. But it was also, legally speaking, decreed a 'liberty', which meant it was free from the ordinary jurisdiction of the city; later it became an infamous spot for secret marriages.

Samuel Brooke – the same loved S.B. to whom Donne wrote one of his very earliest poems – performed the ceremony. He had been ordained two years before and was chaplain of his Cambridge college. The couple would have spoken almost precisely the same words that couples married in the Church of England speak today, taking their words from the 1559 Book of Common Prayer: 'I John take thee Anne to my wedded wife.' To answer the moment where Samuel asked, 'Who giveth this woman to be married unto this man?' there was Samuel's brother Christopher Brooke, who had known Donne at the Inns and had agreed to stand in. 'And the Minister receiving the woman at her father or friend's hands, shall cause the man to take the woman by the right hand, and so either to give their troth to the other.' The service takes less than half an hour, if you go fast: they wouldn't have needed much of either of the Brooke boys' time.

Nonetheless: both brothers were to have good reason to regret their generosity very soon.

After the wedding Anne returned to Loseley in the countryside with her oblivious father as if nothing had happened, and Donne went back to his lodgings, to wait and hope. To hope for what, beyond a good moment to break the news, is hard to say. The moment didn't come, so in the end, on 2 February, almost two months after the wedding day, he wrote a letter, and sent it to his father-in-law via the 9th Earl of Northumberland, Henry Percy.

It wasn't, by any reckoning, a good letter. Donne was aiming for both humility and authority; he instead succeeded in sounding at once over-confident and mildly unhinged:

> I knew my present estate less than fit for her; I knew, (yet I knew not why) that I stood not right in your opinion; I knew that to have given any intimation of it, had been to impossibilitate the whole matter. And then having these honest purposes in our hearts, and those fetters in our consciences, me thinks we should be pardoned, if our fault be but this, that we did not, by fore-revealing of it, consent to our hindrance and torment.

It is a wonderful word, 'impossibilitate'. The first date currently given for it in the *OED* comes thirty years later, so it was possibly Donne's own invention: an inauspicious beginning for a word. His aside, 'I knew, (yet I knew not why) that I stood not right in your opinion' is comically unplacatory – asking 'why don't you like me?' rarely endears the asker. He continues,

I know this letter shall find you full of passion; but I
know no passion can alter your reason and wisdom; to
which I adventure to commend these particulars: that it
is irremediably done [he spells it 'donne': a fantastically
inappropriate pun on his own name]; that if you incense
my Lord you destroy her and me; that it is easy to give
us happiness; and that my endeavours and industry,
if it please you to prosper them, may soon make me
somewhat worthier of her.

It's multiple requests rolled up in one: daughter, and a job,
and forgiveness. What Donne did not add, though, was that
he had already, in January, prepared and brought his suit
to the ecclesiastical Court of Audience. He had employed
lawyers representing him and Anne to argue before the
judge, Richard Swale, that the marriage was valid; he had,
essentially, stolen a march on his father-in-law, but had no
intention of telling him so.

From the point of view of George More, with his notoriously
quick temper and his aspirations to nobility, it was a disaster.
Anne might have formed a great alliance, have given him
titled in-laws with whom to socially machinate: now she had
bound herself to a scribbling reprobate, without property
and with a dead religious traitor for brother. Moreover,
not only was Donne, having spent most of his inheritance,
not rich – and Donne wrote that 'some uncharitable malice
hath presented my debts double at least' – but rumours had
reached Sir George that he was as sexually promiscuous as

his poetry implied: 'that fault which was laid to me, of having deceived some gentlewomen before.' Donne was also out of favour with Sir Thomas Egerton for routinely tampering with (as Egerton saw it) or improving (as Donne saw it) the letters that Egerton gave Donne to copy. The essayist Francis Osborne, looking on from a distance, used Donne's example as a warning to his son: 'it is not safe for a secretary to mend

Sir George More, whose face Anne may or
may not have inherited

the copy his master hath set him . . . lest he should grow jealous, that you valued your conceptions before his.' So to Sir George he was a glorified servant, and not even a very obedient one.

Sir George went immediately to Egerton. Anne was still a minor, so Donne had broken canon law. Donne was summarily dismissed from Egerton's household. The shock and betrayal of it would have felt colossal: the bond between master and secretary was supposed to be as strong as that between man and wife. Donne would have been even more bewildered immediately afterwards: he was thrown into the Fleet prison to await further investigation. Egerton did nothing to prevent it. The two Brooke brothers meanwhile were tracked down, arrested and locked up in prison; Christopher in the Marshalsea, and Samuel, seemingly, in Newgate. As a lawyer and a minister, they had potentially committed more serious crimes than Donne. Given they didn't even get a marriage out of it, the loyal brothers undoubtedly proved the losers of the day: they tried to be the heralds of love, and got only rats in return.

The Fleet prison was simultaneously disgusting and expensive: a debtor's prison, it didn't have even the dignity and royal tinge of the Tower. It stood on the banks of the River Fleet in east London – the same river that gave its name to Fleet Street – and had a grille looking onto the street through which prisoners could beg for alms. Prisons were profit-making enterprises: you paid for each turn of the key, paid to have your irons removed, paid for your food and lodging. The rooms were cramped and dank, fourteen and a half feet by twelve, and ceilings low enough to touch. The treatment was cruel to the point of deadly; in 1593 a bill had been sent to Parliament accusing the deputy warden of murder.

The Fleet prison

Donne's brother had died in one prison: now he was in another, and, like Henry, he was growing increasingly desperately unwell. On 11 February, locked in his cell, he got hold of ink and paper and wrote a more desperate plea to Sir George. He no longer stood upon his pride.

And though perchance you intend not utter destruction, yet the way through which I fall towards it is so headlong, that, being thus pushed, I shall soon be at bottom, for it pleaseth God, from whom I acknowledge the punishment to be just, to accompany my other ills with so much sickness as I have no refuge but that of mercy, which I beg of Him, my Lord, and you.

This new, humbler letter asked More to think of Anne: 'all my endeavours and the whole course of my life shall be bent to make myself worthy of your favour and her love, whose peace of conscience and quiet I know must be much wounded and violenced if your displeasure sever us.' Donne's fall from nuptial rebellion to obeisance was very swift: fast enough to overturn his whole understanding of what you could and couldn't talk your way around.

Sir George sent word in return that he would leave the matter up to Egerton. It was then to Egerton that Donne wrote, in full obeisance: More, 'whom I leave no humble way unsought to regain', he said, 'refers all to your Lordship'. He was, he said, now cognisant of how he had sinned: 'your justice hath been merciful in making me know my offence, and it hath much profited me that I am dejected.' But since the accumulation of pain had worked upon him, he begged that Egerton might 'be pleased to lessen that correction which your just wisdom hath destined for me'. Egerton unhardened his heart a little and ordered that Donne should be allowed to return to his lodgings. He stayed there, under house arrest in dark midwinter, while the legality of his marriage to Anne was decided by the city's Commissioners.

Donne's health began to improve as soon as he was out of the jail, but his life was still in chaos. While the High Commission deliberated, he continued to send out flocks of letters. Some were to Sir George – in one, he reiterated his passion for Anne, and begged permission to send a note to her:

My conscience, and such affection as in my conscience becomes an honest man, emboldens me to make one request more, which is that by some kind and comfortable message you would be pleased to give some ease of the afflictions which I know your daughter in her mind suffers; and that (if it be not against your other purposes) I may with your leave write to her; for without your leave I will never attempt any thing concerning her.

'Without your leave I will never attempt any thing concerning her' – a bold statement, it must have sounded to Sir George, all things considered. If he was permitted to write to his newly made wife, the letters alas don't survive. But there was also the question of the Brooke brothers. Walton says he 'neither gave rest to his body or brain, nor to any friend in whom he might hope to have an interest, until he had procured an enlargement for his two imprisoned friends'. He lobbied Egerton. In the end, Christopher Brooke – who would go on, eventually, to live down his brief stint in jail and become an MP for multiple constituencies

– marshalled all his lawyerly ability and wrote to Egerton himself. He was good at it: he apologised, and pleaded a need to be in York, where he had a legal practice and court session had begun four days ago. His love for Donne is strong in the letter – he ends it, 'and pardon me a word for him [Donne], my lord; were it not now best that every one whom he any way concerns, should become his favourer or his friend, who wants (my good lord) but fortune's hands and tongue to rear him up and set him out.' The letter, coupled with Donne's own importuning, worked, and the brothers were at last allowed to leave their prison cells and dust down their briefly halted lives.

Very slowly, George More began to come round. Walton puts his eventual change of heart down to Donne's transformative charm, the kind of personality that could heat a cold room by force of will – Donne, Walton says, when he worked to 'entice, had a strange kind of elegant irresistible art'. It's equally probable, though, that it was looking increasingly certain that the marriage would be a legal fait accompli, and so Sir George was grudgingly accepting the inevitable. By the time the court decision was to be made, he was mollified enough to agree to try to help Donne recover his position with Egerton.

Donne wrote a letter to his former employer, full of a kind of hopeful despair: 'I was four years your Lordship's secretary, not dishonest nor greedy. The sickness of which I died is that I began in your Lordship's house this love. Where I shall be buried I know not.' The urgency of his position was not just in the immediate need for money, but also that if Egerton wouldn't have him back, it would be taken as a sign that he was completely unemployable. 'To seek preferment here with any but your Lordship were a madness. Every great man to whom I shall address any such suit, will silently dispute the case, and say, would my Lord Keeper so disgraciously have imprisoned him, and flung him away, if he had not done some other great fault, of which we hear not.'

Egerton – perhaps remembering the hints that had been given him, during Donne's imprisonment, of Donne's difficult Catholic family, perhaps remembering his secretary's inability to stop correcting his grammar – would not be persuaded. According to Walton, Egerton felt 'unfeignedly sorry for what he had done, yet it was inconsistent with his place and credit, to discharge and re-admit servants at the request of passionate petitioners'. Donne remained fired.

On 27 April 1602, Donne's marriage was declared good and sufficient. Richard Swale, the judge to whom Donne's lawyers had so swiftly hurried to make their case, issued a decree from the Court of Audience of the most emphatic kind. Donne's case, Swale decreed, was 'reliable and from top to bottom to be pronounced well-founded and proved', and, nothing could be 'excepted, argued, proposed, alleged or proved that would negate the accusation of the said John Donne in this case, or in any way weaken it': it was a very unambiguous victory. 'A true and pure marriage', he declared, had been contracted 'between the said Anne

Moore alias Donne and John Donne'. Donne was allowed to take up his wife.

§

One of the things most people know about Donne, along with 'no man is an island', is the pun: 'John Donne, Anne Donne, Undone.' It's supposed to come from these dark days, just after his marriage. But it is characteristic of everything to do with Donne that it isn't at all straightforward: it's very possible the pun was never Donne's, or, if it was, it wasn't meant to mean what we think it means. The primary source for it is slippery Walton: 'Immediately after his dismission from [Egerton's] service, he sent a sad letter to his wife, to acquaint her with it: and, after the subscription of his name, writ, *John Donne, Anne Done, Un-done.* And God knows it proved too true.' Walton calls the wedding 'the remarkable error of his life' and this version of the story is the one that fits best with his version of what Donne was.

The pun appears before that, though, in several other places: one, the anonymous 1658 collection *Witty Apophthegms*, suggests, wildly improbably, that Donne wrote the words to his father-in-law: he 'took his pen and writ (and sent it to the old man) in this manner, John Donne, Anne Donne, undone, which wrought good effects on the old man'. Another version, William Winstanley's *England's Worthies*, has Donne scratching the words into the window of his jail: 'In the time of Master Donne's melancholy imprisonment, how true I know not, only I have heard it often discoursed, that he writ on the window with the point of his Diamond, reflecting the then present affliction of his Marriage with these words, John Donne, done and undone.'

These all agree at least in this: that Donne, miserable and alone, made his pun in the midst of his sorrow. There is, though, an entirely different rendering of the pun, in *A Choice Banquet*, a jest book written by Archibald Armstrong in 1660, which has just as much claim on the truth as any of the others: 'Doctor Donne after he was married to a maid, whose name was Anne, in a frolic (on his Wedding day) chalked this on the back-side of his kitchen door, *John Donne, Anne Donne, Un-done.*' In this version, the un-done refers not to the dramatic overturning of his hopes and the loss of his job and position, but something gladder, a sexual undoing. It's kinder, and has in it a kind of carnival spirit of new discovery. It's traditional, and probably more likely, to believe the sadder, more despairing version – but this book chooses to believe in the possibility, too, of a man floored and upended by desire.

THE ANTICLIMACTICALLY
MARRIED MAN

He had his teenaged bride in his arms – but where exactly to go with her was the difficulty. His prison debts for himself and the two Brooke brothers now reached to £40 – a huge sum, at a time when a schoolmaster might be paid £20 a year. Anne had a dead aunt who had left her £100, but beyond that they had very little bar their clothes and their wits.

At the last moment they had sudden, rich luck: a young cousin of Anne's, Francis Wolley, a godson of the Queen, offered a place in his manor house at Pyrford. Francis was about nineteen and a gifted gambler – it was said that he once won £800 in a single night, betting with royalty and earls. His house was eight miles out of Guildford, more than twenty miles from London, handsomely set in large grounds, and amply 'adorned with paintings of fowl and huntings, etc.' Whether Anne and Donne liked the hearty decor or not, they gladly moved in. It was here, as guests of a charming boy gamester, that they spent the first three years of their married life.

It was probably at Pyrford that Donne wrote 'The Sun Rising'. While it's a love poem you would eat your own heart for, it's also not entirely what it seems. First of all, there's a hidden spike in it, levelled at Donne's father-in-law. In 1597, George More had published a little treatise called *A Demonstration of God in His Works*, an attempt to prove unequivocally the existence of God. In it he, like his son-in-law, writes about the sun rising, a mixture of Psalm 19 and his own muscular enthusiasm: 'who seeth not the glorious arising of the sun his coming forth as a bridegroom out of his chamber, and his rejoicing like a mighty man to run his race?'

Donne refuses to rejoice like a mighty man; instead he heckles it:

Busy old fool, unruly Sun,
Why dost thou thus
Through windows, and through curtains call on us?

He appears to be laughing at his father-in-law's more conventional efforts; and by extension, at George More's text more widely, which is not a piece of rhetorical wizardry: it argues that an atheist is akin to a stone, or a monster not fully human. It doesn't sound dull, but does manage to be; it opens with a preface addressed 'England, my dear country give me leave, out of love and duty, a dutiful and loving servant to speak unto thee.' (England chose not to listen. It wasn't by any stretch a bestseller.)

There's also a joke and an equivocation in it which is often missed: at the end of the poem the sun does rise, of course, because suns do. But then Donne could claim that he wanted it to rise all along:

Shine here to us, and thou art everywhere:
This bed thy centre is, these walls, thy sphere.

It's not a straightforward adoration poem – it's also a poem about bravado; about a young man visibly conjuring good out of necessity. If you are battered and thwarted in your day-to-day life, still in your poetry you can pretend the sun only rises because you allow it. The poem knows the speaker is being absurd, but it also knows that he shines.

¶

'We can die by it,' he wrote, 'if not live by love'. There had been the great leap of desire and hope: and then there was reality. Pyrford, on the banks of the River Wey just outside Woking, in Surrey, was a long ride from London and the theatres and bear pits: a good thirty miles on hard roads. When Donne looked back at these days, at the prison and the time that followed, he wrote: 'I died at a blow then, when my courses were diverted.' He discovered very swiftly – as many men and far, far more women have discovered before and since – that domesticity had neither the outside witnesses necessary for glamour nor the drill-down intensity of private study.

Worse, every day he was away from London, a friend wrote, his chances of making something grand of himself grew smaller. 'Your friends are sorry that you make yourself so great a stranger, but you best know your own occasions.

Howbeit, if you have any designs towards the Court, it were good you did prevent the loss of any more time . . . the places of attendance . . . grow daily dearer.'

Donne had no obvious employment in these years. He studied and read widely, but there was very little money. Meanwhile, his friends were moving into the fast stream of Renaissance politics. Henry Wotton, who had retreated so prudently to Europe to wait out the Queen's fury (or her life, whichever ended first), was in Tuscany in 1602 when he was given a mission. The Grand Duke of Tuscany had intercepted letters detailing a plot to poison King James VI of Scotland. The King had to be warned, and Wotton – quick-witted, eager to please and fluent in Italian – was chosen to go, carrying letters to James and vials of antidotes prepared by the Italians. In order to evade the suspicion of the would-be regicides, Wotton travelled under the name Ottavio (or Octavio) Baldi.

Izaak Walton, who came to know and love Wotton in later life through Donne, told the story of his arrival at James's Scottish court: 'When Octavio Baldi came to the Presence-chamber door, he was requested to lay aside his long rapier – which, Italian-like, he then wore.' Wotton delivered his message to the King, who was in the company of a handful of his courtiers, officially and in Italian: then 'after a little pause, Octavio Baldi steps to the table, and whispers to the King in his own language, that he was an Englishman, beseeching him for a more private conference with his Majesty, and that he might be concealed during his stay in that nation.' Wotton stayed with the King, living as Baldi, for three months, after which 'he departed as true an Italian as he came thither.' For Donne, living amid someone else's horse portraiture, surviving on the charity of a man a decade younger, the difference between their two lives must have been hard. His letters to Wotton were remarkably unjealous, but they were full of yearning. The love was constant: when Wotton was about to depart on another journey, as ambassador to Venice, Donne wrote asking if he would be long enough in London for him to dash down to town so that 'such a one as I may yet kiss your hands'. But in the same letter, he included a verse, stoic and wry and mournful –

For me (if there be such a thing as I)
Fortune (if there be such a thing as she)
Spies that I bear so well her tyranny
That she thinks nothing else so fit for me.

Another friend of Donne's, Sir Henry Goodere, sent weekly news of life amid the jostle and plotting of the court. Goodere was the son of a well-off landowner and had been knighted, like young Egerton, in Ireland. Sweet-natured and profligate, he was intent on cutting a figure at court, and throughout his life spent far more money than he had. They were an unlikely pairing, and it's not clear how they met – but if Donne had a best friend, it was Goodere. His letters to Donne didn't survive – Donne carefully burned

Sir Henry Wotton

them after Goodere's death, as was his custom – but at least forty-eight of Donne's to him are extant: letters in which Donne is, by turns, sympathetic, loving, wry and full of exasperated advice. Several times during their lifelong friendship he would stay up late after an already long day, rewriting Goodere's formal letters for him, to save him from embarrassing himself in his work. Goodere's weekly letters would have been full of news: he took part in court masques, attempted business deals that went haywire, was a keen hawker.

In return for Goodere's news, Donne had nothing to send but poetry, which he dismissed even as he packed it into the packet of paper:

> I accompany [this letter] with another rag of verses,
> worthy of that name for the smallness and age, for it hath
> long lain among my other papers, and laughs at them
> that have adventured to you: for I think till now you saw
> it not, and neither you nor it should repent it. Sir, if I were
> any thing, my love to you might multiply it, and dignify
> it: but infinite nothings are but one such.

They were hard years for Donne and Anne. There were many moments in which the flashes of his old relishing self flared up again – some of the love poetry certainly dates from this period, though it's impossible to say how much. There were days with glee in them, but also days in which his new, unfamiliar work of marriage and consistency and obligation felt as onerous as any job he had ever done. A letter written a few years later to Goodere catches exactly the up-and-down sweep of Donne's mood:

> Sometimes when I find my self transported with jollity, and love of company, I hang leads at my heels; and reduce to my thoughts my fortunes, my years, the duties of a man, of a friend, of a husband, of a father, and all the incumbencies of a family: when sadness dejects me, either I countermine it with another sadness, or I kindle squibs [fireworks] about me again, and fly into sportfulness and company.

It was a difficult, emotionally volatile task; Donne was attempting, still young and stumbling, to find his footing in a world which was not welcoming him with open arms.

THE AMBIVALENT FATHER

Donne very swiftly became a father. His daughter Constance was born in the beginning of 1603, in the dark depths of the Surrey winter. In London, the Queen was growing frail, and another wave of plague was rising.

As far as we can tell, Donne was not an exemplary parent; or at least, he wasn't a father who seemed to garner much joy from his children. Renaissance filial relations among the upper classes were carefully choreographed affairs: all lifted hats and hinging knees. The great biographer and antiquary John Aubrey, author of a collection of biographies called *Brief Lives*, wrote, disapproving:

> Gentlemen of thirty and forty years old were to stand like mutes and fools bareheaded before their parents; and the daughters (grown women) were to stand at the cupboard-side during the whole time of their proud mother's visit, unless (as the fashion was) leave was desired, forsooth, that a cushion should be given them to kneel upon, brought them by the serving man after they had done sufficient penance in standing.

Donne, in contrast, relished that theatrical element of the status quo: 'children', he noted with approbation in a sermon,

'kneel to ask blessing of parents in England; but where else?'
Everything that made him so spectacular a poet made him
ill-suited to being a father: having a parent whose mind is
riddling, intense and recalcitrant of easy comfort is rarely
what a child dreams of.

In those early days of marriage, Donne found himself
almost housebound: he wrote to Goodere, 'I have not been
out of my house since I received your packet. As I have much
quenched my senses, and disused my body from pleasure,
and so tried how I can endure to be mine own grave, so I
try now how I can suffer a prison.' The monotony of home
life chipped away at his ability to rouse himself: 'if I ask
myself what I have done in this last watch, or could do in
the next, I can say nothing.' He describes his domesticity as
stagnant water: 'When I must shipwreck, I would do it in
a sea, where mine impotency might have some excuse; not
in a sullen weedy lake, where I could not have so much as
exercise for my swimming.'

He did at least have the grace to be guilty that he was
dissatisfied. Donne's letters very rarely painted domestic
scenes – but there is one letter, to Goodere, which does.

I write not to you out of my poor library, where to
cast mine eye upon good authors kindles or refreshes,
sometimes, meditations not unfit to communicate to near
friends; nor from the highway, where I am contracted,
and inverted into my self, which are my two ordinary
forges of letters to you. But I write from the fire side in

my parlour, and in the noise of three gamesome children; and by the side of her, whom because I have transplanted into a wretched fortune, I must labour to disguise that from her by all such honest devices, as giving her my company and discourse; therefore I steal from her all the time which I give this letter, and it is therefore that I . . . gallop so fast over it.

There's affection in it, but heavily laden with exasperation: it's one of the moments in his letters in which Donne is most suddenly human.

He does not seem, though, to have gone hunting for other sexual partners. For all the monotony, and all the drudgery, Donne was – if we believe him – faithful to Anne. He wrote, in an undated essay: 'Thou hast delivered me, O God . . . from the Egypt of lust, by confining my affections, and from the monstrous and unnatural Egypt of painful and wearisome idleness, by the necessities of domestic and familiar cares and duties.' In 'confining my affections', Donne claims fidelity to Anne. It could just be a piece of showy rhetoric – or even a way of staring down guilt – but Donne was addressing God: perhaps unlikely to lie. Anne wouldn't necessarily have thanked him for it, given her whole adult life became the bearing and mourning of children – but the poet who found ten dozen ways to write the joy and sorrow of sex, once hers was – if we take him at his word – hers alone.

That's not to say, though, that there weren't flirtations;

most particularly, with a woman of substance, intelligence and high style, Magdalen Herbert. Magdalen was five years older than Donne, the mother of a brood of poets and philosophers. They first established a relationship over a chance meeting in around 1599, but in the early years of the new century the acquaintance kindled into a more intimate friendship. It's often suggested, by Walton among others, that Donne wrote his 'Autumnal' for Magdalen. The poem begins beguilingly: 'No spring, nor summer beauty hath such grace,/ As I have seen in one autumnal face.' It goes on, though, less flatteringly: 'But name not winter faces, whose skin's slack,/ Lank as an unthrift's purse, but a soul's sack.' Donne would have to have been spectacularly off in his assessment of what he could venture (which, given his miscalculation of his wedding, is not completely impossible) to have thought the poem would charm an older woman. It's more likely that Donne kept to letters and verse epistles: she was, he wrote in his most courtly mode, 'a world alone', he was 'your servant extraordinary'. What sets it apart from his other friendships was that Walton thought it necessary to state outright that though Donne was struck with 'the beauties of her body, and mind', yet it 'was not an amity that polluted their souls'; the need to say it suggests there might, perhaps, have been rumours. Donne's fidelity may possibly have been absolute, but he certainly allowed himself space, in his relationship with his patronesses, for a certain linguistic leeway. What Anne thought, of his vaunting praise of other women, we can't know; she would have been worldly enough to know

Riding, I had you though you still stayed there,
And in these thoughts, although you never stir,
You came with me to Mitcham and are here.

The days would have been a little easier for the whole
family, despite the chill and the thinness of the walls. Two
of Anne's sisters lived a carriage ride away from the new
house, one at Peckham and one in Beddington, so family
visiting was more possible. Donne, though, spent as much
time as he could escaping his brood. From 1607 to 1611,
he took lodgings in the Strand, riding often to London and
not returning for days: in London, he could be a dashing
youngish man again, dining and gossiping, and not a stuck-
at-home parent.

For a man so emphatic, and capable of such fervent
enthusiasm, he never did manage to enthuse very emphatically about his offspring while they were alive. The closest
he ever gets to writing enthusiastically about them as a
group is in one riotously uneffusive note to Henry Wotton:
'I am a Father as well as you, and of children (I humbly
thank God) of as good dispositions.' He heralds the birth of
his daughter Margaret (his fifth daughter, and tenth child)
with an unflattering note to a friend, three days before she
was baptised: 'I must beg of you to christen a child, which
is but a daughter.' There is, on the one hand, real joy in
the announcement of his son Nicholas in 1613: 'The newest
thing that I know in the world, is my new son'. Everything
with a fresh-born baby becomes re-possible. But he writes

in the same letter, 'I stand like a tree, which once a year bears, though no fruit, yet this mast of children.' 'Mast' is a weight, but is also a fruit from forest trees that is inedible to humans but was used as food for swine. So his children, in this mood, are unwholesome and burdensome produce. Few warm details of Donne's children pepper his letters; he wrote, as far as we know, no poetry for or about them. Queen Elizabeth's court astronomer John Dee noted his child's first word in his diary, but Donne mentions them when they are born and then for three reasons: when they are ill; when they are loud, 'gamesome', or expensive; and when they are dead.

Death marched in and out of the house for the whole of his and Anne's life together. Three of their children died before their tenth birthday; another two were stillborn – and it is in recording their deaths that his love of them flares into life. He wrote, in the winter of 1614, of Anne, who has just miscarried: 'I have already lost half a child, and with that mischance of hers, my wife [has] fallen into an indisposition, which would afflict her much, but that the sickness of all her other children stupefies her.' Donne is readying himself for another loss: 'of one of which [children], in good faith, I have not much hope . . . if God should ease us with burials, I know not how to perform even that: but I flatter myself with this hope, that I am dying too; for I cannot waste faster than by such griefs.' He lost no children to that epidemic: but, in March 1614, wrote:

Perchance others may have told you that I am relapsed into my fever; but that which I must entreat you to condole with me, is, that I am relapsed into good degrees of health; your cause of sorrow for that, is, that you are likely to be the more troubled with such an impertinency as I am; and mine is, that I am fallen from fair hopes of ending all; yet I have 'scaped no better cheap, than that I have paid death one of my children for my ransom.

It is a strange mix of half-achieved comedy ('your cause for sorrow', he says, that he is alive) and misery: the baby was his Mary, just over three years old. 'Because I loved it well, I make account that I dignify the memory of it, by mentioning of it to you.'

How did Donne take such deaths? Infant mortality was a blunt fact of life – depending on the region, anything from one hundred to four hundred out of a thousand live-born babies did not live to their first year, and children could be taken at any time by dysentery – known as 'bloody flux' – whooping cough, smallpox, 'scarlatina' (scarlet fever) and myriad other unidentified fevers. The death of children was so much more common that today there's often an assumption that the loss of each child was less strongly felt. But that seems implausible – even though it was very differently expressed. In the early seventeenth century, stone effigies of lost babies began appearing on the tombs of the families. Donne's contemporary Ben Jonson lost his eldest son, Benjamin, at the age of seven. He wrote, in the poem 'On

My First Son': 'Rest in soft peace, and, asked, say, "Here doth lie/Ben Jonson his best piece of poetry."'

And there are other, vivid accounts of loss. Lady Mary Carey wrote a prose dialogue on the loss of her boy that has at its heart a keening cry: 'the Lord hath taken from me a Son, a beloved Son, an only son, an only Child, the last of three, and it must needs affect me; can a woman forget her suckling child?' Gertrude Aston Thimelby's poem 'On the Death of Her Only Child' summons up the blame, embraces it:

Dear infant, 'twas thy mother's fault
So soon inclosed thee in a vault
And father's good, that in such hast
Has my sweet child in heaven placed.

The poems that are saddest have a tooth-gritted hope in them: the effort involved in attempting to turn misery into possibility is so palpable and so unconvincing. Elizabeth Egerton's epitaph 'On My Boy Henry' begins, 'Nor can I think of any thought, but grieve/For joy or pleasure could not me relieve.' It ends, though: 'But you art happy, sweet'st on high/I mourn not for thy birth, nor cry.' Marcel Proust – a man whose love for provocative metaphors has much in common with Donne's – said: 'people of bygone ages seem infinitely remote from us. We do not feel justified in ascribing to them any underlying intentions beyond those they formally express: we are amazed when we come across an emotion more or less like we feel today in a Homeric hero.'

The details of grief are different across time, and the places where the suffering laid their blame and guilt were different, and suppression and expression were different, and the attempts at comfort were different. But rage and sorrow and loss are rage and sorrow and loss.

Donne knew what it was to be haunted by that sorrow. Several years later, in 1612, under very different circumstances, he would go to Paris, leaving his wife in London. She was by then pregnant with their eighth child. Walton writes about this moment in his biography far more vividly than any other:

Two days after their arrival there, Mr Donne was left alone, in that room in which Sir Robert [Drury], and he, and some other friends had dined together. To this place Sir Robert returned within half an hour; and, as he left, so he found Mr Donne alone; but, in such ecstasy, and so altered as to his looks, as amazed Sir Robert to behold him: insomuch that he earnestly desired Mr Donne to declare what had befallen him in the short time of his absence? To which, Mr Donne was not able to make a present answer: but, after a long and perplexed pause, did at last say, I have seen a dreadful vision since I saw you: I have seen my dear wife pass twice by me through this room, with her hair hanging about her shoulders, and a dead child in her arms: this, I have seen since I saw you. To which, Sir Robert replied; Sure Sir, you have slept since I saw you; and, this is the result of some melancholy dream, which I desire you to forget, for you are now awake. To which Mr Donne's reply was: I cannot be surer that I now live, then that I have not slept since I saw you: and am as sure, that at her second appearing, she stopped, and looked me in the face, and vanished.

Donne never managed to show much effervescence about his children, but they were shot through his nerves and sinews. He sent a messenger to London the next morning; the man returned twelve days later. Anne, he said, had borne a stillborn child 'the same day, and about the very hour that Mr Donne affirmed he saw her pass by him in his Chamber'. For all his bluntness about his children, the thought of them literally haunted him. To read Walton's account is to be reminded that it is not only the effusive who feel the heavy weight of love.

HOW TO PRETEND TO HAVE READ
MORE THAN YOU HAVE

Queen Elizabeth died, aged sixty-nine, in the spring of
1603. Quick-witted and quick-tempered to the very grave,
she refused to go to bed; when Robert Cecil told her she
must, she was said to have slapped him back: 'Must! Is *must*
a word to be addressed to princes? Little man, little man!'
London put on black and unleashed a funeral procession
of splendid sorrow and extravagant dolour. The historian
William Camden sketched a drawing of her funeral procession, labelling the groups like a map: 'children of the
chapel', 'poor women to the number of 266', 'countesses
and viscountesses' in one group, 'Earls' daughters and bar-
onesses' in another, and at the end, the Queen's effigy on a
canopied four-horse chariot, flanked by six barons. All of
the women have the same nose, as does Sir Walter Raleigh.
Donne would write about her, much later: 'In the death of
that Queen, unmatchable, inimitable in her sex; that Queen,
worthy, I will not say of Nestor's years, I will not say of
Methusalem's, but worthy of Adam's years, if Adam had
never fallen; in her death we were all under one common
flood, and depth of tears.'

King James I – previously James VI of Scotland, son of
Mary Queen of Scots, thin legs but broad shoulders, quick-
witted but poor table manners – took the throne. Poets

The funeral procession of Queen Elizabeth.

poured forth their praise. (The verse produced for new monarchs is traditionally known as Ascension Literature, and James inspired some of the most remarkably boring poetry of the period. If Donne joined in, his offering has not survived.) Precisely what kind of monarch James was is still, four hundred years later, up for debate; in the nineteenth century he was said to be 'indeed made up of two men – a witty, well-read scholar, who wrote, disputed and harangued, and a nervous drivelling idiot who acted'. Within months of his coronation a letter had gone out to the Venetian Doge from a secretary: 'The new king . . . seems to have forgotten that he is a king except in his kingly pursuit of stags, to which he is quite foolishly devoted.' Donne jokes about it in 'The Sun Rising', 'go tell court huntsmen that the king will ride.' More recently, his reputation has been reassessed; he treasured peace, and learning – known as the 'Scholar King', he wrote at just eighteen a literary manual, 'Some Rules and Cautions to be Observed and Eschewed in Scottish Prosody', and published two books of not-awful poetry while King

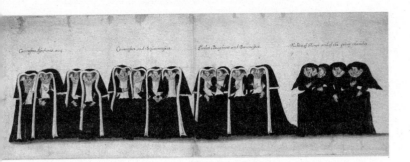

of Scotland. Married with seven children, James also loved men, and had intense, probably sexual relationships with a small number of beautiful and accomplished courtiers who rose to power under him.

A new king was a cause for optimism among England's finest under-employed; Donne would have hoped that he might yet find his way to the stipend and the favour-swapping, quid-pro-quo lucrativity that the best court jobs allowed for. There was a great spate of knightings: Egerton became Baron Ellesmere, Anne's brother Robert was knighted along with other friends of Donne's – Francis Bacon and Richard Baker from the university days – and Henry Goodere was made a Gentleman of the Privy Chamber. James, coming upon Wotton for the first time since their Ottavio Baldi days, seized him in his arms with a roar of delight, declared 'he was the most honest, and therefore the best dissembler that he ever met with', and knighted him apparently on the spot.

Nothing, though, was forthcoming for Donne. James had heard via court gossip about the marriage and the prison spell; he doesn't seem to have been inclined to risk polluting his beginning by associating with a recently fired ex-Catholic jailbird. So Donne kept writing: letters, some poems, tracts – and a text which showed how forensically and beadily he was watching and judging the world.

Donne knew intimately the power of books. Both their real power, and the easier, less arduous power that comes with putting on the language of scholarship like a disguise. Reading – even just the appearance of it – can be wielded as a weapon, and in 1604 Donne wrote an entire text that imagines that wielding and takes it to its absurd end point. In 2016, the Keeper of the Muniments at Westminster Abbey was sorting through a tin trunk of scrappy bits of manuscripts, and found that he held in his hands, entirely without warning, a new version of one of Donne's works: 'The Courtier's Library'. The new text allows us to date the work to the moment in his life when Donne was casting about for what he should become. He knew, though, what he should not be: a pretender. Its full Latin name translates to 'Catalogue of incomparable courtly books, not for sale', but Donne referred to it in his letters as his *Catalogus*: a satirical list of books that the striving courtier can introduce into conversation to make himself seem wiser, keener, sexier. The advantage is that, because none of the books exist, the courtier can't be cross-examined on them: the only way to be a true, unassailable authority on a text is for it not to exist.

The titles of the books add up to an assassin's hit list: of intellectual sloppiness, of two-faced hypocrisy and ethical ugliness in religious debate, of the pliancy of the law and of lazy humanist scholarship of the time: the misuse of something that should be treated as terrifyingly precious. The text tells us a colossal amount about Donne: which human foibles he found funny, which he found more serious. For instance, he lists an imaginary book by Sir Edward Hoby, a non-imaginary diplomat and courtier known for having liquid lunches and laying down the law at them: 'Sir Edward Hoby's Afternoon Belchings: or, a Treatise of Univocals, as of the King's Prerogative, and Imaginary Monsters, such as the King's Evil and the French Disease'.

Elsewhere its jibes are more seriously derogatory. For instance, Matthew Sutcliffe, Dean of Exeter, is treated thus: '32. *What Not? or, a Refutation of all the errors, past, present and future, not only in Theology but in the other branches of knowledge, and the technical Arts, of all men dead, living and as yet unborn*: put together in a single night after supper, by Doctor Sutcliffe.' Sutcliffe was technically an ally, in that by the time Donne was writing the *Catalogus* both he and Sutcliffe ostensibly shared a religiously conformist stance, but Sutcliffe's confident dogmatism goes against the grain of Donne's suppler mind. It gives a key to understanding Donne: the emphasis in his work on the need for rigorous attention to the world around you. The desire for totalitarian certainty, in a refutation of all the mistakes 'of all men dead, living and as yet unborn', is from a man like Donne a damning accusation.

The structure of the *Catalogus* is itself a joke. Donne

is laughing at the ability of scholarly erudition to expand into infinity; there are 141 volumes, 60,047 authors, editors, translators, amanuenses, patrons – and an unspecified horde of servants, who help the great scholarly drive by providing soiled toilet paper to use as copy-texts. Donne goes after multiple targets at once: those who enjoy religious persecution, those whose zeal blinds them to religious nuance, the pretensions of the courtier, and the power that scholarly bloviating and stupid writing has to expand upon itself, like paper rabbits.

But the book was more than a witticism – it was also a sideways political jab at the new king. Soon after he wrote his *Catalogus*, Donne panicked. In a Latin letter to Goodere (the only Latin letter we have of his), he asks for the return of his 'rag', and says he is desperately trying to recall any 'others of them have crept out into the world without my knowledge'. The book, he knew, risked being read as he intended it: a criticism of the new order. It had become very quickly obvious to Donne that the new 'Scholar King', though he stood officially on the side of learning and scholarship, was not over-fond of dissent or discussion. In 1604 (the year of the *Catalogus*) James summoned the Hampton Court Conference, ostensibly as a moment for consultation with his new subjects. Rather than nurturing free speech, though, James had crushed any theological positions which might threaten his absolute power. The King, Donne saw, was swiftly surrounding himself with those who would offer elaborate scholarly justifications for whatever political moves he had already decided on. The *Catalogus* was a how-to for those who wanted to thrive under James: if you wanted to get ahead in the new system, Donne implied, you would need to disguise your sycophancy in the most learned jargon you could invent: talk like a 141-volume book, but don't say anything at all. Scholarship itself, he feared, would have to bend before the will of the King; reduced to the value of Book 23 in the *Catalogus*, 'On the Nothingness of a Fart'.

The *Catalogus*, then, is not a dismissal of learning: it's a ferocious sally in its defence. Read, the spoof catalogue tells us, carefully, sceptically, with all your wits worn like armour against those who care more for the look of knowledge than the meat of it. Donne read prodigiously. We still have some of his own books, and the marks he made in them. They might look, the little pencil jabs along the margins, like respectful acts of attention, but to read the *Catalogus* is to know that they could just as well have been marks of condemnation or irony: little jabs of disapprobation.

Donne's scepticism was more than a wit's pose; it was a fundamental ordering principle, faced with a world in which erudition could be faked by snake oil men who smelled of ink, and charlatans would sell you false certainties between hardback covers. He valued the pursuit of knowledge too highly to watch it being bastardised without lashing out.

THE SUICIDAL MAN

I begin to be past hope of dying . . . Death came so fast
towards me that the over-joy of that recovered me.
  Letter to Robert Ker

The years between 1607 and 1610 are biographically murky.
The letters are hard to date and hard to decipher, and the
best historical records we have are of jobs that didn't happen. He failed to get a position in the Queen's household in
1607, and there are references in the letters to his application to jobs in Ireland or, even more remotely, Virginia, but
neither came to anything, if they were ever serious prospects
to begin with. It's equally likely that they were an attempt
on his part to look industrious, both to his friends and to
himself; neither Ireland nor Virginia were at all desirable
places at the time.

We do have, though, some of his weekly letters to
Henry Goodere, letters filled with attempts at counsel and
spiritual comfort, ironical gripings at Donne's own days,
money worries, and a great deal of letter-writing about
letter-writing: frequent apologies for the scrappiness of
the letter itself and of the exigencies of the carrier. This
was before Charles I's 1635 postal reforms, so his letters
crossed the city and country, haphazard and often lost, in

hands of merchants, personal servants, friends, and messenger boys who seemed always to be hovering at Donne's shoulder, ready to snatch the paper away. As the years went on, more and more letters carried accounts of sickness and pain – he grew ill, and each illness refused to fade entirely. One spring, he wrote, bluntly, 'The pleasantness of the season displeases me. Everything refreshes, and I wither, and I grow older and not better.'

As his pain grew, so too did his dream of being dead and rid of it all. In one particular undated letter, the pain was greater than normal:

> I have contracted a sickness which I cannot name nor describe. For it hath so much of a continual cramp, that it wrests the sinews . . . but it will not kill me yet; I shall be in this world, like a porter in a great house, ever nearest the door, but seldomest abroad: I shall have many things to make me weary, and yet not get leave to be gone.

In the same letter, he writes:

> The day before I lay down, I was at London where I delivered your letter for Sir Ed. Conway, and received another for you, with the copy of my book, of which it is impossible for me to give you a copy so soon, for it is not of much less than 300 pages. If I die, it shall come to you in that fashion that your letter desires it. If I warm again . . . you and I shall speak together of that . . . At

this time I only assure you, that I have not appointed it upon any person, nor ever purposed to print it.

The book he referred to was *Biathanatos*. Its title is taken from the Greek for 'violent death': it was, the title page announced when it was published years after his death, a 'Paradox, or thesis, that self-homicide is not so naturally sin, that it may never be otherwise'. In it, Donne lays out a startling argument. The majority of suicides, he writes, are committed from positions of fear, pain, self-protection or spiritual despair: those are sinful, and failures of the soul. But there is an exception: suicides which stem from a single-minded desire to advance God's glory. Donne digs from the Bible to argue that it's not against nature, but along its grain, to lean towards self-slaughter: that there is in all of us a keening towards it. He quotes Paul's letter to the Corinthians: 'Though I give my body that I be burned, and have not love, it profiteth nothing' – from it, he argues, you can conclude two things: 'first, that in a general notion and common reputation, it was esteemed a high degree of perfection to die so, and therefore not against the law of nature; and secondly, by this exception, "without charity", it appears that with charity it might well and profitably be done.'

To write *Biathanatos* was an extraordinary decision. It was dangerous, and potentially illegal, because to attempt suicide in England was a sin punishable by death. This relationship between crime and punishment always sounds like a wry and self-defeating irony, but it was darker than that: doctrine and fear together leaking out in the form of state violence. Successful suicides were buried at a cross-roads, pinned through the chest with a stake to stop the spirit escaping. In France under Louis XVI, they were dragged through town face down in the dust. In the same century, there were cases of adults murdering young children as a roundabout form of suicide. The theory was that if you murdered a baby, the child would go to heaven and, once you were arrested, you would have time to repent in the presence of a priest before your execution and therefore reach heaven too: it was a cultural and legal interdiction of such strength that it created murderers.

Donne conjured up examples from the most theatrically vivid stories in Church history – the ones with dramatic reversals, sudden sweeps of bravery and drama. There's the tale, for instance, of Nicephorus of Antioch. Nicephorus, in Donne's telling, knew a church elder named Sapritius, who was to be executed for his Christian faith. At the last minute, faced with the executioners, Sapritius lost confidence, recanted and was saved: 'And Nicephorus, standing by, stepped in to his room and cried, "I am also a Christian!" and so provoked the magistrate to execute him, lest from the faintness of Sapritius the cause might have received a wound or a scorn.' This, Donne reasoned, was 'giving of his body': a form of suicide. This free-jazz interpretation of the Nicephorus hagiography wouldn't have seemed, really, terrifyingly radical, but it was only preparation for his central, inflammatory premise: that Christ's death was a suicide.

Christ could have struck down those who crucified him, but instead he sped up his last breath on the cross; 'many martyrs having hanged upon crosses many days alive', and yet Christ died swiftly, while the thieves either side of him were still breathing. '[He] said, "No man can take away my soul, and I have power to lay it down."' Therefore the cause of Christ's death, Donne writes, was no 'other than His own will'.

There are many astonishments in it: things which sound startlingly modern. For instance, Donne argues that the fact we are very sure of something is not proof that we are right. Aristotle, he writes, was certain about the immutability of the stars; certainty which is now 'utterly defeated'. If we can be wrong about the stars in the sky, we can be wrong about anything, including the ethics of suicide. Even more astonishing, though, was Donne's radical boldness in his willingness to offer up his own horrors: because he writes personally and urgently about his own death wish. There was nobody else who had written anything like it, only him.

He lays it out, his terror and dread, like a filleted body. He probes his own suicidal desires. Perhaps, he wrote, his own questing towards death was down to his early years amid the furtive, death-haunted Catholic community: 'because I had my first breeding and conversation with men of a suppressed and afflicted religion, accustomed to the despite of death, and hungry of imagined martyrdom'. But then he goes on to offer other suggestions, spilling them out in a tumble; perhaps he was just somehow born less well protected – 'the common enemy find that door worst locked against him in me'. He is only sure of the strength of the pull within towards his own oblivion: 'whensoever any affliction assails me, me thinks I have the keys of my prison in mine own hand, and no remedy presents it self so soon to my heart as mine own sword.'

As soon as he had written *Biathanatos*, Donne began to worry about it. It was an inflammatory thing, the kind of book that might burn your career right in front of you. He did not want it read; but nor did he want it destroyed. Many years later, about to embark on a voyage, he sent a copy to his friend Robert Ker, a sophisticated and well-connected courtier, asking him to keep it safe.

It was written by me many years since, and because it is upon a misinterpretable subject, I have always gone so near suppressing it, as that it is only not burnt: no hand hath passed upon it to copy it, nor many eyes to read it . . . It is a book written by Jack Donne, and not by Doctor Donne: Reserve it for me, if I live, and if I die, I only forbid it the press, and the fire: publish it not, but yet burn it not; and between those, do what you will with it.

The book was not published until after Donne's death, when he was out of reach of the possible whispers and exclamations, of both the condemnations and the potential over-enthusiasms.

¶

How, then, did he stay alive: this man whose pain urged his thoughts towards self-slaughter? His letters show the way. On the one hand, they are a laundry list of his agonies: he demanded of his friends a high tolerance for vomit-talk. He complains of 'a stomach colic as kept me in a continual vomiting, so that I know not what I should have been able to do to dispatch this wind, but that an honest fever came and was my physic'. And, another time, sick alongside Anne, 'it hath pleased God to add thus much to my affliction, that my wife hath now confessed her self to be extremely sick; she hath held out thus long to assist me, but is now overturn'd, and here we be in two beds, or graves; so that God hath marked out a great many of us, but taken none yet.' Still, though, he attempts to joke: 'I have passed ten days without taking [i.e. eating] any thing; so that I think no man can live more thriftily.'

Elsewhere, his uvula swells in his throat and he is rendered dumb; his eyes falter. He shudders with coughs; his teeth plague him. The latter was a common enough affliction – made worse by the most popular recipes to remove tooth stains, which included the powder from a burned rabbit's head, or an abrasion made from ground brick, egg shells and myrrh. (The rich suffered it most, having eaten the most sugar; so much so that there was a brief fashion among the poor for colouring one's own teeth black in order to look glamorously prosperous.)

But in answer to his pain, Donne's letters also show him seizing hold of it and re-conceiving of it as a kind of travel. He writes to a friend: 'this advantage you and my other friends have by my frequent fevers, that I am so much the oftener at the gates of heaven, and this advantage by the solitude and close imprisonment that they reduce me to after, that I am thereby the oftener at my prayers; in which, I shall never leave out your happiness.' To be ill, then, is to journey closer to the reality of death, to be closer to the ear of God in order to importune him. And the closer to death, the more clearly you see the richness of living; Donne used his illness to demand from God's ear happiness for his friends.

More than that, though: for Donne, to be so deathly ill so frequently was to be accelerated into readiness for the world that might be to come. He wrote to a close female friend:

I am not alive because I have not had enough upon me to kill me, but because it pleases God to pass me through many infirmities before he take me either by those particular remembrances, to bring me to particular repentances, or by them to give me hope of his particular mercies in heaven . . . All this mellows me for heaven, and so ferments me in this world, as I shall need no long concoction in the grave, but hasten to the resurrection.

Ferment. To be alive is to stew in readiness: illness is a clarifying marinade, through which he might forestall the pause of the grave and leap into eternity.

They were heavy metal, Donne's letters: there is little romance in them, and a great deal of twisting and hammering at his pain to force it to take on the shape of some meaning. It is one more kind of *making*. It's a furious kind of focus, an instance of feverish, counter-intuitive seeking for good; an insistence that it must show you the truth of mortality, and allow you to see more clearly: to see the hopeless, transitory, pained soul, suffused in glories. It says a great deal about him, that he was the kind of man who demanded of pain that it shunt you closer to infinity.

§

Donne's anxieties about *Biathanatos* turned out to be true. Perhaps. In the 1650s, twenty years after Donne's death, the Regius Professor of Divinity at Cambridge, Anthony Tuckney, declared that he believed Donne's book had led a convicted criminal to attempt to poison himself. It was also said that the classical translator Thomas Creech used to hold and twist in his hands a rope while reading Donne's text: and eventually hanged himself. Correlation, of course, is not causation. But the philosopher Charles Blount wrote approvingly of *Biathanatos* in 1680: 'wherein, with no weak arguments, he endeavours to justify out of scripture, the legality of self-homicide'; then, later, he killed himself. His friends seemed to think the very possibility of suicide was first sparked by his reading of Donne, who had overturned seemingly perpetual truth and, one of Blount's friends wrote, 'found that self-preservation was not so general a precept, but it met with various limitations and exceptions'. This was possibly less significant than the fact that thirteen years had passed since his reading, and Blount had just been forbidden to marry the sister of his dead wife; but, still, it has been laid at Donne's door. To write about death in the way he did – to send a suction pump down into the gap between what we know and what we fear – was to risk chaos. Donne knew it and did it anyway.

And perhaps he never really meant to kill himself. Do those who plan to do it write so extensively about it? Or is the writing a form of exorcism? If you write down the desire, if you forensically dissect it, it cannot take you by surprise. Perhaps it is a way of stopping it from creeping up on you: perhaps it was a way of staying alive.

THE FLATTERER

And they who write to lords rewards to get –
Are they not like boys singing at doors for meat?
   Satire II

It was in around 1607 that Donne was first asked if he would turn towards the Church. Thomas Morton, former chaplain to the Earl of Rutland and now the Dean of Gloucester, offered Donne a job on the spot, if he would take holy orders. He said no. He wrote, we are told: 'I may not accept of your offer: but, sir, my refusal is not for that I think myself too good for that calling, for which kings, if they think so, are not good enough.' He must have known, even then, that his imagination would be suited to the discipline and invention of sermon writing; but, he wrote, his past dogged him. He had not yet managed to exorcise, in the public imagination, the ghost of his youthful reckless marriage and his Catholicism:

> Some irregularities of my life have been so visible to some
> men, that though I have, I thank God, made my peace
> with him by penitential resolutions against them, and by
> the assistance of his grace banished them my affections;
> yet this, which God knows to be so, is not so visible to

man as to free me from their censures, and it may be that
sacred calling from a dishonour.

And, of course, there was still the question of money.
The difficulty of history is that we must, to some extent
at least, take men at their word; we must assume that they
planned to do what they said they planned to do, and for
roughly the reasons they said they did. We cannot read
disingenuousness into every single speech, or the whole of
history would be eaten alive by scepticism. But equally, the
specific job Morton was offering was not a lucrative one –
more than half of the country's clergymen earned less than
£10 a year – and Donne had a family to feed, and good hats
and ruffs to buy.

Donne urgently needed other work. The route to preferment in Early Modern England – the route to jobs and
elite posts which put you in the same room as power – was
byzantine, labyrinthine, often unpredictable, and luck and
strategy and talent all played a part: but the one element
you couldn't do without was contacts. It was imperative,
therefore, if you weren't born at the top of the ladder of
power, to be as universally charming as you had it in you
to be, and many writers' letters of this period are peppered
with protestations of the recipients' unquenchable glories.

Donne's letters though are extraordinary, even in a time
in which compliments were core currency, for the high-
flown grandiloquence of their blandishments. Some of the
letters were carefully politic: addressed to wealthy women,

who could be sources of both gifts of money and work, such as Lady Kingsmill, doyenne of Sydmonton Court (currently owned by Andrew Lloyd Webber): 'your going away hath made London a dead carcass . . . when you have a desire to work a miracle, you will return hither and raise the place from the dead.' Similarly, in a verse epistle to the Countess of Huntingdon, wife of the fifth earl, he writes, 'from you all virtues flow'; 'To some you are revealèd as a friend,/And as a virtuous prince far off to me.' One anonymous critic of Donne wrote of his verse letters, in 1823, that 'they are disfigured . . . by an extravagance of hyperbole in the way of compliment that often amounts to the ridiculous – and by an evident want of sincerity that is worse than all.'

But Donne's flattery was more than just politically savvy ground-laying – because it wasn't only to the rich and famous that he wrote his mad fountains of praise. He saved some of his greatest encomiums for the least important. He wrote, for instance, to Martha Garrard, the wholly insignificant sister of his friend George: 'I am not come out of England if I remain in the noblest part of it, your mind, yet I confess it is too much diminution to call your mind any part of England or of this world, since every part even of your body deserves titles of higher dignity.' The Garrards were a family of London merchants, and Martha was a woman of no power or influence; she could give him nothing in return but her pleased laughter.

It's there so often with Donne, that doubleness: there was his canny, cautious, political side, planting his sycophantic adjectives in the hope they would seed money; and then there was also something else: pleasure in extravagance. There must have been real satisfaction for him somewhere in lavishing compliments. Perhaps because it was something he could offer: he could not host fine dinners, but he could send fine idioms. Or, you could read it as a wariness of the world (tame it with lavishments, before it bites you) – or you could read it as an enthusiasm for admiration itself: that he valued the hyperbole of praise and the game it set in motion. There is some of that old delight, in the extravagance of desire, in the courtly letters he sent out, heavily freighted with his praise.

One of the key targets for his charm was Lucy, Countess of Bedford. Lucy had been born the daughter of a knight, and was married off at just thirteen to the Earl of Bedford. She grew up canny and witty, and knowing the court like her own territory: on the coming of James to the throne she took daring measures, at the age of twenty-four, to secure a position in his consort's retinue. She skipped Queen Elizabeth's funeral and galloped several horses – some said to death – in order to be the first lady to greet James's bride, Anna of Denmark, as she came down from Scotland. Anna made her Lady of the Bedchamber on the spot, and she became at a stroke one of the most powerful women in England. Donne met her through his friend Goodere, and she became his most important patron, passing sums of money to him throughout his life. In exchange, multiple verse letters proclaim Lucy's beauty: 'I had never known/

Lucy Russell, Countess of Bedford

virtue or beauty but as they are grown/In you'. (Lucy was indeed very beautiful: although in the most famous portrait, she has a look of scepticism powerful enough to burn rubber.) He named his newborn Lucy after her in 1608: he wrote of 'that favour which my Lady Bedford hath afforded me, of giving her name to my daughter'.

Despite the enormous imbalance of wealth and power when it began, their friendship seems to have been both a real and a productive one. They exchanged poems, and without the countess we wouldn't have his 'Twickenham Garden', named for the garden she had had laid out on the blueprint of the Ptolemaic universe: concentric rows of trees, walks mirroring the orbits of the planets. Mixed in with his verse, though, came the begging letters, particularly after she had inherited property on her brother Lord Harington's death. Donne sent her a long memorial verse, 'Obsequies to the Lord Harington', and with it, riding pillion on his poetry, a begging letter. Faced with the problem of asking for money without appearing to, he attempted a sort of elaborate sideways pointing, to indicate-by-denying his neediness. It wasn't even slightly convincing: 'I have learned by those laws wherein I am a little conversant, that he which bestows any cost upon the dead, obliges him which is dead, but not the heir; I do not therefore send this paper to your Ladyship that you should thank me for it, or think that I thank you in it.' Lucy offered in response to pay his debts, but then – perhaps annoyed by the limited praise her dead brother garnered in the poem, perhaps because her own debts were mounting – offered up only £30, which Donne took badly. He wrote to Goodere, 'I confess to you, her former fashion towards me had given a better confidence.' A coolness began to enter in, which he, dismayed, tried to melt with another, escalatingly sycophantic, poem: in 'To the Countess of Bedford', a poem which appears at first reading to go on for ever, she is 'virtue's temple', and 'a new world doth rise here from your light'. But then, after sixty lines, Donne pauses, to say his words 'Taste of poetic rage, or flattery,/And need not where all hearts one truth profess.'

That, he knew, was the best form of flattery: the flattery of denying the need for flattery. (Shakespeare's Decius, plotting to murder Julius Caesar, reminds us: 'when I tell him he hates flatterers,/He says he does, being then most flattered.') Donne writes to Lady Bedford – quoted here in full, for the convolutions of compliment it bends through:

[I] tell you truly (for from me it sucked no leaven of flattery) with what height or rather lowness of devotion I reverence you: who besides the commandment of noble birth, and your persuasive eloquence of beauty, have the advantage of the furniture of arts and languages, and such other virtues as might serve to justify a reprobate fortune and the lowest condition: so that if these things whereby some few other are named are made worthy, are to you but ornaments such might be left without leaving you unperfect.

It could read as ironic, then, that years later in the pulpit Donne came down so hard and so often on flattery. Some of his finest thunder was reserved for sycophants:

A man may flatter the best man; if he do not believe himself, when he speaks well of another, and when he praises him, though that which he says of him be true yet he flatters; so an atheist, that temporizes, and serves the company, and seems to assent, flatters. A man may flatter the saints in heaven, if he attribute to them that which is not theirs; and so a papist flatters.

The most foolish, he said, attempt to flatter God. Flattery, he told his listeners, done often enough, created an opacity of oneself to oneself: it skewed your inner compass dial.

This, given Donne's letters, would seem a little rich: but, in the Renaissance, not all flattery was the same. Some of it was the custom – a tradition of air and sugar in prefaces and in commendatory verse: a ritual, designed to produce patrons of the arts sufficiently well fed on compliments to keep the literary world afloat. Some of it was, like a few of Donne's letters, a blatant attempt at money-whispering. But some was the way you situated yourself politically, or gave hints to the rich and powerful who if met with face-on criticism might cut your head off. Donne knew it – and in 1610 and 1611, just as his cause was starting to look desperate, he set about writing two books. *Pseudo-Martyr*, dedicated to King James, is an obsessively detailed tome, setting out the thesis that the Catholic recusants who risked their lives by refusing to take James's new Oath of Allegiance, instigated in the crackdown following the Gunpowder Plot, were committing suicide. They were deluded pseudo-martyrs, who didn't deserve a true martyr's crown. (Walton claims it took Donne six weeks to write – which should be taken with a pinch of salt, in part because it is a work of minutely detailed scholarship citing hundreds of authorities, of more than four hundred pages, and in part because such a number of writers through history have lied about how long their books took to write.)

It begins with a dedication of white-hot ingratiation:

The influence of those your Majesty's books, as the sun which penetrates all corners, hath wrought upon me, and drawn up and exhaled from my poor meditations these discourses: which, with all reverence and devotion, I present to your Majesty, who in this also have the power and office of the Sun, that those things which you exhale, you may at your pleasure dissipate, and annul; or suffer them to fall down again, as a wholesome and fruitful dew, upon your Church & Commonwealth.

This, though, wasn't purposeless fawning: it was a way Donne could signal unambiguously his allegiance to James's religious policies, and flag his devotion to serving the King. Though the wariness of the King's intellectual integrity that Donne had shown in his *Catalogus* still remained, time, expediency and experience had modified it. Before *Pseudo-Martyr*, the best-known treatise defending the oath was by James himself: it was the flattery of imitation and nuance, flattery as political allegiance – and it was a success. Donne had written a book so dry and relentless that it has a dust-storm quality to it – as one great Donne scholar said, 'who but a monomaniac would read *Pseudo-Martyr* through?' – but James loved it. He made Donne an honorary MA of Oxford, and this time (according to Walton) it was the King himself who suggested that he should consider taking religious orders. Donne again refused, 'apprehending it', Walton tells us, 'such was his mistaken modesty' to be still 'too weighty for his abilities'; but the book had set him, for the first time, squarely under James's approving eye.

The year following, Donne wrote a book in which he sets out a defence of flattery: *Ignatius His Conclave* – a text of brilliant and rampant oddnesses. Appearing anonymously first in Latin as *Conclave Ignati* in 1611, and then in Donne's own English translation, it's as though all the explosive energy in his religious thinking has been allowed to burst free in a one-man jousting match levelled at the Jesuits. In the book, Ignatius of Loyola, founder of the Jesuits, finds himself in hell and in dialogue with Lucifer. Ignatius is a fawner and flatterer: 'Ignatius rushed out, threw himself down at Lucifer's feet, and grovelling on the ground adored him.' Ignatius takes a dual stance on flattery. On the one hand, it can be a kind of backwards one-upmanship: 'whosoever flatters any man, and presents him those praises which in his own opinion are not due to him, thinks him inferior to himself and makes account that he hath taken him prisoner, and triumphs over him.' But, on the other hand: whoever flatters '(at the best) instructs. For there may be, even in flattery, an honest kind of teaching, if Princes, by being told that they are already endued with all virtues necessary for their functions, be thereby taught what those virtues are, and by facile exhortation excited to endeavour to gain them.'

Ben Jonson made a similar claim in his verse: that sometimes the only way to instruct might be through ascribing to someone good qualities which they don't possess, in the hope that it might spur them to acquire them. 'Whoe'er is rais'd/For worth he has not, he is tax'd, not prais'd.' Jonson was himself notorious for sycophancy and occasional bouts of delicious backbiting: he wrote a gushing epigram about the writer Francis Beaumont – casting himself as 'not worth/ The least indulgent thought thy pen drops forth' – and then complained to a friend that Beaumont 'loved too much himself and his own verses'.

But if you take what Donne and Jonson are saying seriously, it was something that mattered: that those who read high-flown praise as *only* flattery were not approaching the written word with the care it demanded – that sycophancy should always be examined to see if it had in it a prescription. Language makes demands. It is an excavatory skill; each word needs to have its surface dusted, to see if below there is gold or snakes. Those who did not understand that language was multi-layered and subtle – those who read it lazily, who failed to imagine the demands it daily makes – deserved very little in return.

§

The thing about Donne's flattery was that it *worked*. Perhaps Donne's greatest tour de force in adulation were his two poems in elegy for a young woman, Elizabeth Drury, the 'First' and 'Second Anniversary', written in the two immediate years after *Ignatius*. We do not know precisely how Donne met Sir Robert Drury – Gentleman of the Privy Chamber, a former ally of the Earl of Essex, and one of the Drurys of Drury Lane. It may well have been via Donne's sister's husband, William Lyly, who had been one of Drury's many protégés until his sudden death. (Lyly was virulently anti-Roman, and had been instrumental in catching Catholic agents of Mary Queen of Scots, which, given Donne's mother was still Catholic, would have made family gatherings awkward.) Donne's relationship with the Drurys was to be a life-shaping and real-estate-shaping boon to him.

In 1611, Robert Drury's daughter Elizabeth died in her fifteenth year, and Donne was employed by her father to write two funeral elegies. Her cause of death was rumoured and disputed. It was said she was grief-stricken after the death of a lover; elsewhere it was said she had had her ears boxed too hard and died on the spot. Donne may have heard tell of her from his sister, but had almost certainly never met Elizabeth; the girl he conjured in his elegies was one of his own invention.

They are strange, excessive, convoluted poems – often beautiful, though rarely very sad, for poems about death – and full of mad statements of the lost young woman's glory: Donne proclaims that the earth could 'have better spared the Sun or Man'. The riotous praise of them raised some eyebrows across literary London. Donne wrote that 'I hear from England of many censures of my book of Mistress Drury'; embarrassed and defensive, he regretted, he said, that he had 'descend[ed] to print anything in verse'. Ben Jonson said, eyebrows high, that 'if he had written it of the Virgin Mary it had been something.' Donne defended himself: in writing his 'Anniversary' poems, he had held up the '*Idea* of a woman'. Besides, he added waspishly, 'if any of those ladies think that Mistress Drury was not so, let that lady make herself fit for all those praises in the book, and it shall be hers.' (It's much, much less polite than it sounds: the implication being that, firstly, the women complaining aren't virtuous enough to merit his praise and, secondly, let them fuck off and die, as Elizabeth had so recently done, thereby 'making themselves fit'.)

It was not, for him, so much about the girl as it was about language: about what poetry can do in the art of praising. How far could he force poetry to *embody* the most extreme ideas that can be conceived of? 'For since I never saw the gentlewoman, I cannot be understood to have bound myself to have spoken just truths.'

It wasn't an exercise in truth: it was an exercise in testing how far he could extend his imagination of what perfection might look like. He wrote:

Her pure and eloquent blood
Spoke in her cheeks, and so distinctly wrought
That one might almost say, her body thought.

It was the same old desire that had resounded through his youth, before the complexities and compromises of marriage and family, and it was still there: the thinking body. A completed meshing of body and imagination: that would be the thing most worth having. The Donne of the 'Anniversaries' is still the same Donne as the young man in 'The Ecstasy' who declared 'love's mysteries in souls do grow,/ But yet the body is his book.' When the mind can be made to infuse every inch of the body; that is when living becomes most possible. It hadn't, Donne implied, yet been achieved, but its achievement would transform the experience of moving through the world: it would cut back at the chaos.

The poems also paid off financially. Robert Drury belonged to a once wealthy, still fairly powerful family who claimed to have come over from France with William the Conqueror (in their case, this was probably even true: although to accommodate every English family who makes this claim, the Conqueror would have had to come over with a fleet the size of Belgium). Robert Drury asked Donne – who, as a more experienced and fluent linguist, would be helpful – to join him and his family on a journey to Europe. In Paris they witnessed the engagement of Louis XIII, amid enormous pomp and French poetry; in Frankfurt, they saw the election of the new Holy Roman Emperor, amid enormous pomp and Latin poetry. On their return in 1612, the Drurys installed the Donnes in a house close to their own on Drury Lane at very reasonable rent. Donne's capacity for imaginative excess and his extravagance in linguistic pyrotechnics had, finally, secured him a home.

He had solid, comfortable ground beneath his feet – no more noxious cellars – and Westminster School a walk away for his boys. All that he lacked was clarity, about what exactly he should be doing with his life, as the time ran through his hands.

Donne was now in the very heart of London, no longer having to make the long journey on horseback to and from his
family, and it was alive with bite and noise and possibility.
Dekker wrote of the roiling city:

> at every corner men, women and children meet in such
> shoals, that posts are set up on purpose to strengthen the
> houses lest with jostling one another they should shoulder
> them down . . . Here are porters sweating under burden,
> there merchants' men bearing bags of money. Chapmen
> (as if they were at leap frog) skip out of one shop into
> another. Tradesmen (as if they were dancing galliards) are
> lusty at leg and never stand still.

Donne, best dressed among the poets, would have been
passing good outfits daily. A German visitor to London,
Frederick of Mompelgard, wrote:

> The inhabitants are magnificently appareled, and are
> extremely proud and overbearing . . . the women have
> much more liberty than perhaps in any other place . . .
> they also know well how to make use of it, for they
> go dressed . . . in exceedingly fine clothes, and give all

attention to their ruffs and stuffs . . . whilst at home perhaps they have not a piece of dry bread.

(Mompelgard was not, overall, a fan of the English and our tradition of jauntily violent xenophobia: 'they care little for foreigners, but scoff and laugh at them; and . . . one dare not oppose them, else the street-boys and apprentices collect together . . . and strike . . . unmercifully without regard to person; and because they are the strongest, one is obliged to put up with the insult as well as the injury.')

More children came: little Nicholas arrived in 1613. Money grew tighter. Donne had to give up his horse, and beg or borrow one whenever he needed a mount. Walton paints Donne in these days as caught between two desires: he had been living for so long in 'expectation of a state-employment' that the hope was engrained; but in him other, different desires were growing strong; a pull at him to work for 'God's glory' in 'holy orders'. Donne was urgently aware, always, of the fleeing time, and the question of how to pass his days almost crippled him. From 1607 to 1615, he hesitated. In 1608 he had written a letter to Goodere:

I would fain do something; but that I cannot tell what is no wonder. For to choose, is to do: but to be no part of any body, is to be nothing. At most, the greatest persons are but great wens and excrescences [lumps and protuberances on the skin]; men of wit and delightful conversation, but as moles for ornament, except they be so incorporated into the body of the world, that they contribute something to the sustentation of the whole.

Donne knew himself to be a man of 'wit and delightful conversation', and knew that it would, by itself, ultimately be worth no more than a drawn-on beauty spot: it had no real purchase on the world.

This I made account that I begun early, when I understood the study of our laws: but was diverted by the worst voluptuousness, which is an hydroptique immoderate desire of humane learning and languages: beautiful ornaments to great fortunes; but mine needed an occupation, and a course which I thought I entered well into, when I submitted my self to such a service [i.e. Egerton's service], as I thought might [have] employed those poor advantages, which I had. And there I stumbled too [he is referring to his marriage], yet I would try again: for to this hour I am nothing, or so little, that I am scarce subject and argument good enough for one of mine own letter.

That need to 'try again', and start afresh, became more pressing in London. He had known both loss and gain – the ghosts of his dead children stood alongside his swiftly-growing living ones, as his family grew older and more expensive in their needs. In the city he found himself amid the whirl of so many purposeful people; his hairline began to recede and he knew himself to be stepping into middle age; a decision had to be made. Slowly, in both doubt and hope, Donne's eyes turned towards the Church.

One reading of Donne's turn to the priesthood is that it was an expediency: a second-best. Many people, looking over his life, have believed that his heart and ambition lay always with the court, which, Virginia Woolf's father Leslie Stephen wrote, 'still charm[ed] and fascinat[ed] the strong accomplished flatterer'. The Church was a compromise: a road to public respectability and reliable money, and a way to finally scrub out the stain of what Walton called the 'remarkable error' of his marriage. And there must have been some truth in that; he had always known himself to be rare, and he wanted his talents to be recognised. The court had been the most obvious place to go, for any youth who hankered to have a sharp and remunerative spotlight shone on his intelligence.

But Donne had been hunting for God since his thirties. In around 1604 he had written 'The Cross', which is the poem of a man profoundly engaged in a project of reading the world like a book, seeking in the smallest things clues about the nature of the divine:

Look down, thou spy'st out crosses in small things;
Look up, thou seest birds raised on crossèd wings;
All the globe's frame, and sphere's, is nothing else
But the meridians crossing parallels.

The physical world was made up of symbolic meaning, and could, through relentless attention, be decoded. Your own body, stretched out in the water, could become a reminder of the crucifixion. He wrote:

Who can deny me power and liberty
To stretch mine arms, and mine own cross to be?
Swim, and at every stroke thou art thy cross.

(It's hard to picture exactly what stroke he's doing here, to mimic the cross. The first English treatise on swimming, in 1587 by Everard Digby, describes something akin to breaststroke with intervals of doggy-paddle: presumably not that.) The point, though, holds: the whole world could be mined for knowledge of the God he sought everywhere.

The idea that Donne chose the Church only because his ambition had failed elsewhere elides one fact: Donne had to fight to get there. In the last decade, a new reading of Donne's journey to the priesthood has emerged, based on new information surrounding five letters that he wrote to the man who became his patron: the most notorious courtier in London – Robert Carr, Viscount Rochester, Earl of Somerset.

Carr was the great shining star of the Jacobean court: beautiful, flaxen-haired and delicate-featured. A few years before, he had been riding in a tournament in London at which the King was present when, galloping at full tilt, he tumbled off his horse and broke his leg. James ran to him: it was said he knelt and cradled Carr in his arms until help was found. A contemporary wrote, 'if any mischance be to be wished, 'tis breaking a leg in the King's presence, for this fellow [Carr] owes all his favour to that bout.' From that happy accident, Carr had been made a Gentleman of the Bedchamber, where his intimacy with the King allowed him to grow rich. They may have been lovers – an epigram went round London, '*Rex fuit Elizabeth: nunc est regina Jacobus*' – 'Elizabeth was King: now James is Queen.' One man wrote at the time: '[James] constantly leaneth on his arm, pinches his cheek, and smoothes his ruffled garment . . . I tell you, this fellow is straight-limbed, well-favoured, strong-shoul-dered, and smooth-faced, with some sort of cunning and show of modesty; though God wot, he well knoweth when to show his impudence.'

Despite some muttering from the wider court, James appointed Carr a Knight of the Garter and granted him a place on the Privy Council. The difficulty was that Carr doesn't seem to have been an intellect suited to paperwork. He had no head for the detail of politics, so he appointed a close friend – Sir Thomas Overbury, a poet, essayist and man of letters – to be his secretary.

At the time Donne first collided with him, Carr was pulling strings in a bid to wed the dazzling young Frances Howard, who was herself married to the Earl of Essex (son of the beheaded) but was seeking an annulment. Essex had retaliated by accusing Frances of witchcraft – specifically, of cursing his penis. (Jacobean England feared witchcraft, and the fear was remarkably genital-centric. One writer, Reginald Scot, in *The Discovery of Witchcraft*, recorded

The portraiture of Robert Car Earle of Somerset Vicount Rochester, Knight of the most noble order of the Garter &c. And of the Ladie Francis his wife

Robert Carr, 1st Earl of Somerset, and Frances, Countess of Somerset

the belief that witches could magic away a man's entire groin: 'that men had had their genitals taken from them by witches, and by the same means again restored.') London society, both high and low, was agog; equal parts scandalised and delighted. James's court was already seen by those who stood outside it as a hotbed of bed-hopping: Lady

Anne Clifford, of whom Donne said she 'knew well how to discourse of all things, from Predestination to slea-silk', declared that 'all the ladies about the Court had gotten such ill names that it was grown a scandalous place.' But even in the context of a place in which gossip was rife – in which the 3rd Earl of Pembroke was said to be 'immoderately given up to women', the 3rd Earl of Dorset 'much given to women', and the Earl of Cambridge to be 'more subject to his pleasures and company of women than priests', and in which the King of Denmark had gone rogue and called the Countess of Nottingham a whore – the Carr–Howard match was still by far the most exciting and shocking. Carr's erstwhile best friend Thomas Overbury was particularly vocal against the match.

It made Carr a complicated figure for a potential patron: especially for Donne, given the history of his own marriage and his blotted romantic copybook. But Carr simply could not be bypassed. For any who sought a court-centred religious position – any Church position that did not mean being ejected to the far reaches of rural England – Carr was the route: he had come to dominate the system of ecclesiastical appointments. On a good day he could achieve almost anything, and so, in the spring of 1613, Donne wrote to Carr.

He had made his decision, he said. He had fought within himself for clarity, for many years, and the time had come to seize hold of what certainty there was before it fled.

For, having obeyed at last, after much debatement within me, the inspirations (as I hope) of the Spirit of God, and resolved to make my profession divinity: I make account that I do but tell your Lordship what God hath told me, which is, that it is in this course, if in any, that my service may be of use to this church and state.

Carr's side of the correspondence hasn't survived, but he must have responded with some warmth, because Donne either offered, or was asked, to compose a wedding poem for Carr's prospective wedding to Frances Howard. (Frances's previous marriage, it had been decreed with the King's help, was to be annulled.) Donne offered, too, to level all his legal training into writing a justification of the annulment: 'perchance this business may produce occasions wherein I may express my opinions of it in a more serious manner . . . out of a general readiness and alacrity to be serviceable and grateful in any kind.' There's an implication in Donne's letter of quid pro quo: that Carr would help him find a position in the Church, in return for Donne acting as his pen for hire.

Carr, though, had other plans. It's very likely that he wanted to make use of Donne himself; his relationship with Thomas Overbury was increasingly strained (exactly how strained would become vividly clear soon after), and he had space for a sharper, swifter counsel by his side. He sent money – thereby placing Donne in his debt – and suggested Donne apply for a handful of secular posts, for which

Donne was wholly unsuited and inexperienced. He stead-fastly failed to help Donne into the Church.

Meanwhile, preparations for the wedding continued. The ceremony was slated to take place in December 1613; and Thomas Overbury died, very conveniently, just before the grand day, thereby silencing the loudest opponent to the union. But Donne's promised poem became a problem. Opinion was slowly curdling against the bride: the words 'witch' and 'whore' were beginning to attach themselves to Frances. In mid-January 1614, the poem still hadn't been completed, and he wrote to Goodere, in reference to the promised epithalamion: 'by my troth, I think I shall not scape.' In the end he could see no way out, and he sent the poem to Carr at the end of January, a month late. It was framed as a conversation between two rustic figures, as if Donne was hiding anxiously behind his two speakers: duck-ing out of sight of any public hiss and spittle that might come his way. It condemned 'unjust opinion' and asked, 'should chance or Envy's art/Divide these two, whom nature scarce did part?' Whether or not the bride wanted the world's gos-sip rehearsed in her wedding song is unrecorded by history: poets' subjects rarely get a say in the matter.

Carr accepted the poem, but continued to block Donne's way to ordination and preferment. As the year went on, Donne wrote to Carr, difficult, circular letters, expressing thanks for 'benefits already received' from Carr but pain that Carr had put 'distractions, or diversions, in the ways of my hopes'. In 1614, the post of ambassador to Venice came up, and Donne wrote to ask if his name might be put forward. Donne knew, though, that he was not remotely qualified (he had no experience in diplomacy) and his tone shows he knew it – 'I humbly beseech your Lordship to pardon my boldness of asking you, whether I may not be sent thither?' – the implication in his letter to Carr is: if you forestall my journey to the Church, then what?

In the spring of 1614, Donne had a brief sally back into the world of politics, when he was again installed as an MP, this time for Taunton; older and wiser than his first outing in 1601, he was put on four committees. But we have no record of his ever participating in debates, and if he was biding his time for a chance, it would never come: King James dissolved Parliament after just eight weeks, in disgust that they would not allow him to raise taxes: he was 'surprised that my ancestors should have allowed such an institution to come into existence'. James ruled the next seven years without summoning Parliament. Any lingering dream Donne may have harboured of politics, left over from his first abortive foray into government in his twenties, fell dead.

It may have been the abrupt folding of Parliament that provoked Donne to speak his exasperation more bluntly to Carr: 'It is now somewhat more than a year, since I took the boldness to make my purpose of professing Divinity known to your Lordship.' He demanded that Carr either help him with some other, plausible employment, if that was what Carr was so set on, or allow him to 'pursue my first purpose' of divinity, or leave him to 'abandon all'. This letter, now dated to September 1614, means it had been a full sixteen months in which Donne, taking what bits of 'court business' he could find to get by, had yet been waiting, nudging and cajoling Carr to help him. Meanwhile his in-laws had been clamouring at him to more actively seek court preferment; Donne wrote to his brother-in-law that he would go to court 'if I find it necessary to go', but to follow its train without obvious purpose would be 'a treason against myself'. There was a tenacity in his desire to reach the Church; though it was not straightforward, it had grit in it.

What changed, and pushed Donne to navigate the last steps to the pulpit? In part, the deaths of two of his children, Mary aged three in May 1614, and Francis aged seven in November, acted as a knife and a spur all at once. They galvanised him into both misery and more urgent action. And, simultaneously, Carr's star began to decline; first slowly, throughout 1614, and then it crashed out of the sky altogether. In August 1614, a beautiful young gallant caught James's eye during a hunt – George Villiers, the Duke of Buckingham, 'the handsomest-bodied man in all of England'. James gradually became enamoured; later, he would write to him, 'I desire only to live in the world for your sake.' Carr was shunted to second place, and as his power waned, he became vulnerable to staggering new accusations: Carr and Frances, the whispers hissed, had murdered Thomas Overbury. The gossips gathered to spread the word: they had sent him sweet tarts and jellies laced with poison.

A poem went round the city, very different from Donne's strained epithalamion:

A page, a Knight, a Viscount and an Earl
All those did love a lustful English girl
A match well made, for she was likewise four:
A wife, a witch, a poisoner and a whore.

The two would, eventually, be tried and found guilty of murder. It was a constellation of circumstance that proved enough to propel Donne forward. On 3 December, we find Donne on his way to Newmarket to discuss his 'purpose' with the King in person; there he met with 'as good allowance, and encouragement' as he could have longed for. Donne promptly gave up an unspecified piece of 'business' (probably a clerkship) he was engaged upon, and began to prepare for priesthood: he had already been working hard, he wrote, 'in the search of the eastern tongues'. He must have known the decision would shake everything in his life into a new and daunting shape – what it was not, though, was a repudiation of his bone-deep love of the strange ways that language works upon us.

We have so many brilliantly drawn images of priests in British literature – Austen, Oliver Goldsmith, Chaucer – but they tend to skew towards the comedic, the meek, the venal or the po-faced. To be a priest in seventeenth-century England, though, was to be part of a system of power and performance. A priest was charged with a vast task – both a political and spiritual marshalling – and was expected to use every weapon in his arsenal to carry it out. Donne would be expected not to tone down his rhetorical alchemy, but rather to feed it. He had always been in search of stark, fresh ways to tell the things he knew and believed; in that sense, the priesthood made perfect sense for him. It demanded of him both his gifts – for distillation and contraction ('my face in thine eye, thine in mine appears') and for unpredictable expansion and connection. It was a leap into a land at once brand new and familiar. He took it: he sent out a budget of letters to friends announcing the news.

He was greeted by no standing ovations. Lucy, Countess of Bedford, he said, 'was somewhat more startling, than I looked for from her'. He was dismayed to find she did not take his decision wholly at face value: 'she had more suspicion of my calling, a better memory of my past life, than I had thought her nobility could have admitted.' Wotton, though, wrote to congratulate him. Donne thanked him, rather defensively: that 'though better than any other you know my infirmity, yet you are not scandalized with my change of habit.'

Once he had decided on his purpose, it was easy enough to navigate. He did not need to undertake training, having so amply demonstrated his grasp of theology with his *Pseudo-Martyr*. In the bleak middle of winter, 23 January 1615, Donne went quietly to St Paul's Cathedral to be ordained by John King, the Bishop of London. He was forty-two. To mark the change in his life, he took on a new seal: his previous one, a knot of snakes, was cast aside, and replaced with Christ crucified on an anchor; he wrote, 'a sheaf of snakes used heretofore to be/My seal, the crest of our poor family' – and now, 'the cross (my seal at baptism) spread below/Does, by that form into an anchor grow.' Very swiftly, he was appointed to be a chaplain-in-ordinary to the King. James was in comparison to Elizabeth an addict of the pulpit, and had doubled the number of sermons the monarch heard preached every week. He cajoled the Vice-chancellor of Cambridge – apparently against the latter's better judgement: he refused at first, perhaps remembering Donne's Catholic beginnings, or perhaps having read some of the more vivid sex imagery – to award Donne an honorary doctorate of divinity.

When Donne did change his mind, Walton tells us, he changed it hard. He met his new calling with the energy and determination of someone who had previously lived in the relentless watchfulness of uncertainty and now cast it aside with relief: 'now all his studies, which had been occasionally diffused, were all concentred in divinity. Now he had a new calling, new thoughts, and a new employment for his wit and eloquence.' For someone without solid work for so long, the singleness of purpose would have been a gift. It's what Hamlet wanted; it's what Donne was to thrive on. He had written that letter to Goodere, 'I would fain do something; but that I cannot tell what, is no wonder.' The irrevocability of the 'something' he had picked must have had the same appeal as a sea after the weedy lakes.

Walton, though, as ever, pushes it too far: 'now, all his earthly affections were changed into divine love; and all the faculties of his own soul were engaged in the conversion of others.' Walton's version of Donne as a stained-glass saint is exactly what he wasn't. The 160 extant sermons show he was far more interesting than that. Roughly, his preaching was in step with religious orthodoxy of the early seventeenth century, and his careful political nuance showed him to be a man who had no interest in starting revolutions. But he was to become a sermoniser who spoke openly about his own failures, would enfranchise his audience in startling ways, and would offer imagery of sufficient sharp clarity that you could hook a faith upon it.

¶

Renaissance sermons were long: often upwards of an hour, some up to three. The villagers of Shadwell once rebelled and took their rector before the ecclesiastical court to complain: 'with a long extemporary prayer before and another very long prayer after them, many of which sermons and prayers have been ended so late in the evening that some of the parishioners have called for candle and lantern to go home,' and it was too late for the congregation to properly tend to their cattle. People couldn't sit or stand still for so long, so there was moving, rustling, eating. Rowdy episodes could break out: it was recorded that one of the aldermen of Norwich Cathedral suffered when 'somebody most beastly did conspurcate and shit upon his gown from the galleries above . . . some from the galleries let fall a shoe which narrowly missed the mayor's head.' But generally sermons, in Donne's day, were heard hungrily: they had breaking news in them, politics, entertainment, theatre; people gossiped about them and picked over in the week that followed. For that reason Donne would often repeat a point over and over in slightly different wording, because people took notes: they were not ephemera, but something to be carried out into the city more widely. A school system which hinged on colossal amounts of memorisation had built a population with the kind of mammoth recall which is, in retrospect, breathtaking – so listeners went home and argued over them, plagiarised them, fell out over them, made them part of the fabric of their days.

Donne's sermons almost all follow the same structure, as was common to the vast majority of preachers. He would begin by laying out what was to follow, which usually was formed in two or three parts, and each part would have branches running out from it, and each branch further branches. Donne preached without a text in front of him; he would write the sermon out in full, take notes, and memorise it. He used the classical trick, employed by orators for thousands of years, of imagining a speech as a physical structure – a memory palace, a temple – through which he could move in his imagination. He was explicit about it: he compares the sermon to a 'goodly palace' through which he guides his audience. Partway through, they will 'rest a little, in an outward Court, upon consideration of prayer in general; and then draw near the view of the palace, in a second court'.

For all their length, his sermons were never sombre or staid: they were passionate performances, attempts to strike a match against the rough walls of the listeners' chest cavities. It was a moral duty: the most popular preacher's manual at the time dictated that 'the preacher . . . standeth of no one thing more in need' than 'moving the affections'. Donne unleashed his charisma, for the first time, upon live, reactive audiences who could eat it in full and demand more: he was:

> a preacher in earnest; weeping sometimes for his auditory, sometimes with them; always preaching to himself, like an angel from a cloud, but in none; carrying some, as St. Paul was, to heaven in holy raptures . . . here picturing a vice so as to make it ugly to those that practised it, and a virtue so as to make it beloved even by those that loved it not; and all this with a most particular grace and an unexpressible addition of comeliness.

He made a speciality of conjuring infinity for his listeners: 'there shall be no cloud nor sun, no darkness nor dazzling, but one equal light; no noise nor silence, but one equal music; no fears nor hopes, but one equal possession; no foes nor friends, but an equal communion and identity; no ends nor beginnings; but one equal eternity.'

His fame spread fast. In the summer of 1616 he was made priest in charge of Sevenoaks in Kent, a sinecure in the gift of Egerton, worth perhaps £80; it was expected that he would take the money and install other priests to do the actual preaching and shepherding – although in fact he did preach there at least once. Most clerics treated the smaller parishes as something between a collectible and a cash cow, and Donne was not above following suit, gathering up smaller benefices. Within a year of his ordination, the man who had struggled so hard to extract a few pounds out of his patrons and patronesses was offered fourteen different clerical positions. In October 1616, he was made Divinity Reader of Lincoln's Inn, at £60 per annum; a good sum, for which he was to preach fifty sermons a year. The money would have been especially helpful, as that same summer his newest daughter, Elizabeth, was born. At last his prosperity was growing fast enough to meet the needs of his family.

At Lincoln's Inn, where he had once been Master of the Revels and a hunter of pleasure, Donne became not just preacher but arbiter of law. He entered into it without leaving much leeway for mercy. Perhaps his Catholic contemporaries hoped that some memory of his past would make him more gentle to anyone who sought to diverge from the Protestant path: if so, they were to be disappointed. One Anthony Hunt, refusing to attend Holy Communion at the Inns, was told 'to bring a Certificate from Mr Doctor Donne of his conformity in religion and thereupon order was made to be taken for his expulsion or continuance in the house'. Donne did not grant the certificate, and the man was expelled; his ruthless streak in vivid evidence.

THE WIDOWER

It happened quickly: as his fortunes rose, tragedy rose alongside. Anne died, and it was a baby that killed her. On 10 August 1617, she gave birth to a stillborn child. The labour – her twelfth – was too long and too hard. She survived less than a week before mother and child were buried in the same grave. They lie in the graveyard of St Clement Danes, amid the rush of buses going down the Strand towards the West End's theatres. Seven of her children lived to mourn her, aged from fourteen-year-old Constance to little Elizabeth, just reaching her first birthday.

It was, for Donne, an irreversible end. He would not take another lover: she was his last. He wrote in a poem: 'my good is dead.' If pain takes the precise shape of the love you have for the dead, then his heart in those days must have been complicated and terrible.

Walton said he was crucified to the world. He preached her funeral sermon, and his tears, Walton wrote, worked on 'the affections of his hearers, as melted and moulded them into a companionable sadness'. Amid the horror, he could not resist getting in a little flourish about Donne's superiority to everyone: it was such a love and such a loss 'as common people are not capable of'.

Out of all the verse that Donne wrote, there are many

lines that are surely about Anne – 'she all States, and all Princes I' – but there is only one poem that he acknowledged unequivocally was written for her and about her: her epitaph. The epitaph is in Latin, and Donne chose words that can be translated in a multitude of ways, so that behind each Latin word there's a queue of English possibilities. For this, the end of her life, he chose words for her that unfurl. This is an attempt at giving as many terms as possible for the original:

Anne
Daughter of George More, of Loseley, Gilt/Golden Knight,
     Sister of Robert More,
Granddaughter of William More,
Great-granddaughter of Christopher More:
A woman most choice/select/read, most beloved/loving/well
     read;
A spouse most dear, most chaste/pure;
A mother most loving/merciful/pious/dutiful, most self-
     sacrificing/indulgent/tender; Fifteen years in union/covenant
     completed,
Seven days after bearing the twelfth of her children (of whom
     seven survive)
(Wherefore this stone to speak he commanded,
Himself by/beyond grief [made] speechless/infant)
Her husband (most miserable/wretched to say) once dear to
     the dear
His own ashes to these ashes pledges/weds
[in a] new marriage (may God assent) in this place joining
     together,
John Donne,

Doctor of Theology.

She withdrew in the thirty-third year of age, hers and Jesus's
1617/In the year of her Saviour
1617,
on 15 August.

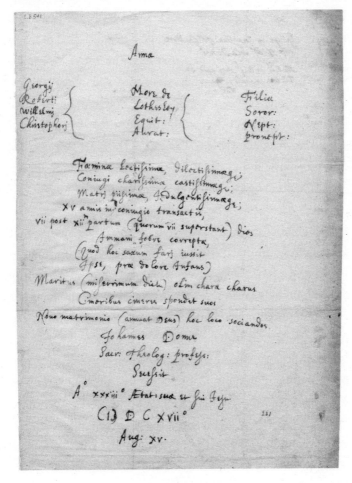

Donne's epitaph to Anne

The Latin, in Donne's handwritten version, forms, loosely, the shape of a cross. The epitaph is both a hymn and a promise: a vow never to marry again. In the Latin she is '*Faeminae lectissimae dilectissimaeque*': the words are drafted to do double work, in the Latin *lector*, so that Anne becomes Donne's best reader *and* best text. She is both well read, and read hungrily by Donne: he has studied her and tried to know her. But the Latin of the first part has a harmony which the second half abandons. It grows awkward and uneven in syntax and scansion when it talks about time, decay and loss; he broke the form of the epitaph to salute the breakdown of the heart. He had written, 'Language, thou art too narrow, and too weak/To ease us now; great sorrow cannot speak.' Words, belonging to the living, struggled to tell of death.

And for her: had it been worth it? Worth that great shining leap that she made as a teenage girl? The shame that immediately followed their marriage must have been agonising: one moment she was the beloved child of a wealthy man, dancing gavottes with boys in London, the next the wife of a jailed husband, with a disgusted father, knowing you're whispered about across the city. Then the poverty, isolation, the slow clawing back of respectability; her husband's elongated visits to London, and glowing letters to other women; the pain of relentless childbirth and of so much death. The poems suggest that they remained, at first, wildly enamoured: but the poems tapered off in the end. Anne More married the finest love poet England has ever known: but love was not, after all, enough.

THE (UNSUCCESSFUL) DIPLOMAT

The wound of Anne's loss was still sharp, and the new ordering of daily life was still in chaos. Who was to look after the children? Not him, for he surely would not have known how to care for a baby: they were probably largely in the charge of Constance, who was old enough to act as housekeeper, and the servants, with help from whichever kinswomen he could convince to come to help. Anne's sister, Lady Margaret Grymes, had a large family of her own with at least four boys, and could sometimes be persuaded to take some of his children into her home, but the disorder must have been enormous. And then, still in the middle of the hurricane of grief, Donne was finally offered a job of the kind that he had, as a young man, dreamed about.

Europe was striding towards disaster. Tensions were mounting between the citizens of Bohemia (loosely the modern-day Czech Republic and part of Poland) and the Holy Roman Empire (which, as Voltaire said, was 'neither holy, nor Roman, nor an empire': it was a Catholic, largely German-speaking patchwork of federations in western and central Europe, stretching from Hungary to Flanders and Geneva, its borders shifting like a kaleidoscope with time and war). The population of Bohemia was majority Protestant, but it was ruled by a succession of Catholic

Habsburg kings with enormous jaws and close friendships with the Pope.

In 1617, a new monarch, Ferdinand, was installed in Bohemia, much to the disgust of the Protestant masses, who knew that his fondness for the Catholic Counter-reformation wouldn't bode well for their freedoms. In May 1618, during a conflict over Protestant rights, two Catholic lords regent and one servant were turfed out of a third-floor window, in the famous 'Defenestration of Prague'. They landed on a dungheap (or at least so you were told, if you were a Protestant) or were saved by angels (if you were Catholic) and survived, but the line had been crossed. Protestant territories and the Catholic Habsburgs began to gather allies for war.

This was made more complicated for England by the fact that Frederick V of the Palatinate, who ruled over the Rhine, was James I's son-in-law. Frederick had married James's daughter Elizabeth in a political union of enormous pomp and flourish: in Heidelberg, in the grounds of the castle, there still stands an arch that Frederick was said to have had built overnight to surprise his bride in the morning. Frederick was Protestant, and it was to him that the citizens of Bohemia turned. Frederick, they said, should be their new king. The prospect horrified the Catholic Habsburgs, for whoever was King of Bohemia got one of the seven votes for the new Holy Roman Emperor. Chosen, not born, the Holy Roman Emperor was reckoned *primus inter pares* – first among equals – of the Catholic monarchs of Europe.

Into the turmoil stepped James I. James believed his own motto, appropriated from the Sermon on the Mount, '*Beati pacifici*': blessed are the peacemakers. He desperately did not want a war. He hoped he could formally mediate between his son-in-law Frederick, who was loudly calling for aid and arms from England, and the Habsburgs: and he planned to do this all while maintaining civil relations with Catholic Spain, so that he could marry his son Charles to a Spanish princess. James landed upon the charming courtier James Hay, Viscount Doncaster, as the man for the diplomatic job. Hay – whom young Elizabeth Stuart addressed as 'camel face', in part because she hoped it would deter him from passing her letters around, and in part for reasons which are obvious if you find a painting of him – knew Donne a little, and had tried to help him in his youthful job-questing days. Now, James decreed, Donne was to be his chaplain. They were to go to Germany, on a mission to stop the spread of the Bohemian troubles across the whole continent.

Considering whether or not to accept James's mediation, the King of Spain asked the advice of his ex-ambassador, who replied with unflattering candour:

The vanity of the present King of England is so great that he will always think it of great importance that peace should be made by his means, so that his authority may be increased . . . [nonetheless] it is possible and fitting to accept this mediation, since it cannot do any harm, or make things worse than they would be without it.

It was a delicate mission, and probably impossibly ambitious for anyone. But at the time Doncaster was full of hope, and planned to travel with opulence (his motto was 'Spare Nothing'); they were to have an allowance of £6 a day, and he was taking 'a great many noblemen's sons, and other personages of quality, that the Germans might admire the glory of the English'.

The chaplaincy was the kind of post that, if all went well, would inevitably lead to ecclesiastical promotion. Travel, authority, the chance to serve God, King and country: it was all Donne had been striving for during his Mitcham years, and yet now it was offered, he passionately did not want to go. His wife was dead, his children reeling, and he was in fear for his health and his safety, as the lifelong physical weaknesses that dogged him had flared again: he wrote to Goodere, 'I leave a scattered flock of wretched children and I carry an infirm and valetudinary body, and I go into the mouth of such adversaries as I cannot blame for hating me, the Jesuits, and yet I go.' He wrote a poem, while he waited, 'A Hymn to Christ, at the Author's last going into Germany', in which he bleakly resurrects the ship imagery of his youth.

In what torn ship soever I embark,
That ship shall be my emblem of Thy Ark;
What sea soever swallow me, that flood
Shall be to me an emblem of Thy blood.

In May 1619 they set off with great ceremony – and then had to halt when Doncaster realised he had left a vital letter on a window seat in Prince Charles's room (inauspicious beginnings: a theme of Donne's life). When Donne, the ambassador and his train – spending munificently wherever they went in a bid to curry favour with the locals – reached Heidelberg, the seat of Frederick V, they found he was away. Instead, his wife Elizabeth was waiting to greet her old friend with the dromedarian face. Doncaster was wary of the protocol of kissing Elizabeth's hand without the presence of her husband, and tried to make Donne and his companions lurk in the town until Frederick returned, which Elizabeth effectively scotched by forbidding anyone in the town to feed them unless they came to stay at the castle. The meeting with Frederick, when he finally arrived a few days later, went well, with Doncaster urging on him both friendship and caution – but it was to be the last of their successes. They went on to Salzburg, to seek out Ferdinand, the deposed King of Bohemia, and to press on him James's offer to negotiate a peace with the Bohemians. Ferdinand was impeccably courtly, but refused to say anything other than polite nothings to Doncaster's questions; no, he would not accept James's help; and no, thank you, he had no desire of any English interference.

Bruised and thwarted, they left, beginning a long and roundabout journey while they awaited further instructions: they swerved plague in Venice, went on to Vienna, Graz, the Hague. They arrived in the immediate aftermath of the

James Hay, Viscount Doncaster, 1st Earl of Carlisle,
alias Camel Face

Synod of Dort, a clash between the Calvinist and Arminian wings of the Dutch Church. Were some, as Calvinists argued, elected before their birth to receive salvation, while others, irrespective of their actions, were born predestined to eternal damnation? Or, as the Arminians on the liberal side of Reformed theology argued, had God foreseen which individuals would have faith in Christ, and elected all those who did? Donne would have watched with eager interest. He had always carefully refused to be drawn on predestination, but he had, once, lashed out against men who speak of 'decrees of condemnation before decrees of creation', and he would have been both unsurprised and undelighted when the Dutch Church came down on the Calvinist side.

The whole endeavour of the embassy, so visibly hopeless, must have been exhausting work – but there were moments in which Donne was able to snatch excitement from the route. In Linz, he broke free from Doncaster and made a pilgrimage to the home of Johannes Kepler.

Johannes Kepler was one of the finest astronomers of all time, a man with a revolutionary understanding of the movement of the planets, obsessed with the stars since the age of six. Their meeting was polite and formal: Kepler wanted Donne's advice on how best to get a book he had dedicated to James I into the King's hands – but it wouldn't have been polite at all, had Kepler known more about Donne's life and work.

Kepler had written a book called *Somnium* ('The Dream') in 1608, a strange, allegorical text which depicts a trip to the moon. He became fixated on the idea that malicious gossip about this book had implicated his own mother, Katharina Kepler, in a trial for witchcraft – the narrator's mother in Kepler's book summons a demon, and Kepler worried it had been taken literally. (His mother was imprisoned for fourteen months, but, though threatened with torture, refused to ever confess to witchcraft – which seems entirely reasonable, given the worst she was guilty of was, according to her son, being 'small, thin, swarthy, gossiping and quarrelsome': i.e. unpopular.) Kepler wrote, after the trial, that 'the spreading abroad of [Somnium] seems to have been . . . ominous for my domestic affairs . . . There issued slanderous talk about me, which, taken up by foolish minds, became blazing rumour, fanned by ignorance and superstition.' Among these rumour-mongers, he included the unnamed author of *Ignatius His Conclave*: he wrote in a footnote to *Somnium*, 'I suspect that the author of that impudent satire, the Conclave of Ignatius, had got hold of a copy of this little work, for he pricks me by name in the very beginning.'

Very few people on the continent knew that Donne was *Ignatius*'s creator; the book had been published anonymously, and so he was safe from Kepler making the association. In fact, Kepler gave Donne's text too much credit: he probably hadn't had a chance to read *Somnium* at all. The actual reference to Kepler in *Ignatius His Conclave* is very slight: the narrator claims the power to travel to other planets, but won't go into detail because he doesn't want to insult 'Keppler [*sic*], who (as himself testifies of himself) . . . hath received it into his care that no new thing should be done in heaven without his knowledge'. At worst, it's rather heavy-handed teasing; not enough to start bringing mothers into it.

Meanwhile, the embassy was turning into a palpable failure. While they loitered at Spa, there was a sudden rush of action: James's son-in-law, Frederick, was crowned King of Bohemia, and Ferdinand, who had been so elegantly dismissive of the English, was elected the new Holy Roman Emperor. War now looked inevitable, and Donne and Doncaster had managed to please a sum total of nobody. On the one hand, the Spaniards blamed the English embassy for helping Frederick secure the Bohemian crown; on the other side, European Protestants believed the Catholics had used the diplomatic mission as a distraction while they gathered their forces. An English diplomat at the time wrote waspishly that such 'are the inscrutable depths of his Majesty's incomparable wisdom, to amuse his son's enemies'. Doncaster and Donne returned home in a hot blaze of embarrassment, and Donne was not employed again on foreign diplomatic missions.

§

But that stop that Donne made is tantalising: what did he and Kepler talk about? Donne had some German, and they both had impeccable Latin, so language was no barrier to speech. There's one letter that Kepler sent his sister-in-law about their meeting, but it's dry as sand, entirely about the logistics of asking Donne to 'convey and commend' his book to the King. Did Donne ask about Kepler's discoveries? It's likely – because Donne had long been fascinated and troubled by the stars.

Donne's lifetime spanned a period of astronomical discovery; every year chipped away at old assumptions. Donne's parents' generation would have been taught Ptolemy's model of the universe, which had been devised in the second century AD and had remained the standard model into the sixteenth century. In his theory, the Earth was stationary at the centre of the universe, the Sun was one of the Seven Ancient Planets, and everything was encased in a shell of stars, beyond which was the Prime Mover: God, essentially. In 1543 the Polish Nicolaus Copernicus published his model – which is, in many of its essentials, the one we use today – in which the Earth, with its crystalline sphere of stars, rotates on its axis once a day and is one of several planets that revolve about the Sun; but it was still controversial in Donne's day. (Incidentally, nobody had thought the world was flat for hundreds of years. Columbus knew it was round; the scientific arguments of the day were centred on the extent of its size and, in a few of the more vivid religious circles, whether it was going to explode.)

Some writers embraced the new order with gusto. At the end of *Cymbeline* (1611 or thereabouts) one of the most beautiful and most lunatic of Shakespeare's plays, Jupiter descends and a stage direction calls for four ghosts to dance in a circle; a reference to the planet's quartet of newly discovered moons, as described by Galileo in 1610. But Galileo's discoveries – in a world in which heliocentrism had been declared heretical in 1616 – shook Donne. Just a year after Galileo saw the moons rotate around Jupiter, and not around the Earth, Donne wrote:

And new Philosophy calls all in doubt:
The Element of fire is quite put out,
The Sun is lost, and th'Earth, and no man's wit
Can well direct him where to look for it.

It was harder to stretch the imagination wide enough, now that the universe was no longer thought to rotate around mankind.

And freely men confess that this world's spent,
When in the planets, and the firmament
They seek so many new; they see that this
Is crumbled out again t'his atomies.
'Tis all in pieces, all coherence gone.

It was part thrill and part anxiety: a tussle between two parts of Donne's imagination. It's part of the riddle of Donne's personality that he was at once wary of innovation and one of the greatest innovators in the English language. 'God', he wrote in a sermon, 'loves not innovations', and in *Ignatius*, the text which had made Kepler so furious, one of the main thrusts is a mockery of innovation. The place nearest Lucifer's throne in hell is reserved for whichever innovator's works have caused most confusion in the world – among the candidates are Machiavelli, Columbus, Copernicus and Paracelsus, the father of toxicology. Whoever 'gave an affront to all antiquity, and induced doubts and anxieties' should be rewarded with the devil's favour. Copernicus prides himself on rearranging the heavens: he is 'thereby almost a new Creator'.

Donne's anxiety about innovation, though, was closely bound up with a sense of the splendour of the world: the Earth, as he saw it, had been created flawless, and we could only make it worse. 'In the beginning of the world,' he told his congregation, 'we presume all things to have been produced in their best state; all was perfect.' Humans, he believed, were capable of many things: genius, but also destruction. 'For knowledge kindles calentures [burning zeal] in some,/ And is to others icy opium'. The same imagination which had tried to wrest control over the sun in his poetry also believed that we could not be trusted not to lay waste to the world: which turned out, of course, to be true. There was a dry-edged wit to it: his reckoning with our extraordinary capacities for invention, and our ability to break things. His love for the power of mankind's mind did not extend to blindness about the amount of chaos we can cause.

THE DEAN

Donne returned from Germany in January 1620, sped home to his children and waited to see what would be the results of his work in the embassy. Though the mission had been an embarrassment and a failure, Donne himself had not been; he had preached a warmly received sermon at the Hague, and was given a gold medal to mark the occasion, etched with images of disputing men. Back home, he gave sermons at Lincoln's Inn in the winter and three times at court in the spring, where the King watched him with careful eyes. He had Donne in mind for something more exacting and remarkable than chaplain; but there were delays in the usual progress of the Church. In July 1621 George Abbot, the Archbishop of Canterbury, went out hunting, aimed at a deer, missed and hit a keeper. (Lord Zouch, whose land they had been shooting on, insisted the man had been standing directly behind the deer at the time, and the animal had leapt away at the last moment. This was greeted with scepticism: it was reckoned more likely that a cleric would wreak accidental havoc with a crossbow than that a professional gamekeeper would loiter among a herd, mid-hunt.) Manslaughter was not something in which God's servants were supposed to partake, and a number of churchmen who were due to be made bishops refused to receive the consecration from his hands. The workings of the Church, therefore, were even slower than usual. But in August, when the Bishop of Exeter died, the hearts of priests around the country must have quickened with hope: for Valentine Cary, the current Dean of St Paul's, was to take his post, leaving behind him a fantastically desirable vacancy.

In 1621, according to Walton, the King sent for the forty-nine-year-old Donne and asked him to arrive at dinnertime the next day.

> When his Majesty sat down, before he had eat any meat, he said after his pleasant manner, 'Dr. Donne, I have invited you to dinner; and, though you sit not down with me, yet I will carve to you of a dish that I know you love well; for, knowing you love London, I do therefore make you Dean of St. Paul's; and, when I have dined, then do you take your beloved dish home to your study, say grace there to yourself, and much good may it do you.'

This story may or may not be true: it sounds suspiciously like an almost identical anecdote told about Bishop Andrewes. If it is true, though, Donne would have had to put up with dribbles. A much-repeated report of the King told: '(His tongue) was too large for his mouth, which ever made him speak full of mouth, and made him drink very uncomely, as if eating his drink, which came out into the cup of each side of his mouth.'

How did Donne come to be given one of the most distinguished positions in the English Church? It must have been in part because he was remarkable: his sermons had a rhetorical punch that was rarely achieved by the other men, however gifted, who mounted the pulpit before the King. But there was also Donne's canny, politic side at work: he had been, for some time, putting himself in the good graces of the King's new favourite.

King James I of England and VI of Scotland

Carr and his wife were fully out of favour, though their death sentences for Overbury's murder were commuted to imprisonment, and eventually they retired to live quietly in the countryside. In Carr's place stood the Duke of Buckingham, in all his fine-limbed beauty. Donne wrote to Buckingham, offering himself up for any work that the duke might find acceptable: 'all that I mean in using this boldness, of putting myself into your Lordship's presence by this rag of paper is to tell your Lordship that I lie in a corner, as a clod of clay, attending what kind of vessel it shall please you to make of Your Lordship's humblest and thankfullest and devotedest servant.'

Buckingham may well have seen a use for Donne. The buildings of the cathedral were beginning to crumble dangerously as Donne took office as dean, and a large batch of expensive Portland stone had been bought to restore them; stone which disappeared and reappeared, quietly, in the hands of the Duke of Buckingham for use in the restoration of his own town house.

The deanship was a heavy responsibility, carrying with it the imperative to stir the hearts and mind the souls of the whole of London – but it was also a fantastic piñata of a job: hit it, and perks and favours and new connections came pouring out. Even before the deanship was made official, the riches began to come in; he wrote to Goodere, 'Though be I not Dean of Paul's yet, my Lord of Warwick hath gone so low, as to command of me the office of being Master of my game, in our wood about him in Essex.' He had to give

George Villiers, 1st Duke of Buckingham

The stained-glass window in Lincoln's Inn

up his post at Lincoln's Inn: but the minutes noted that he would 'be no stranger there'. (There survives today, on the west side of the church nearest the pulpit, a tiny shard of stained glass that commemorates him.) His popularity in that quarter remained enormous, almost deadly: it was there that the crush to see his sermons had nearly killed three men.

As soon as he was able, he moved his family to the Deanery, bidding farewell to those of the Drurys who still lived, for Robert Drury had since joined his daughter in death. He invited his ageing mother to move in with them. Despite her adherence to the old faith, he wrote,

> though the poorness of my fortune and greatness of my charge hath not suffered me to express my duty towards you as became me, yet I protest to you before Almighty God and his Angels and Saints in Heaven that I do and ever shall esteem myself to be as strongly bound to look to you and provide for your relief as for my own poor wife and children.

This, and the letter he sent on the death of his sister Anne, are both very formal, even for him: his new position necessitated caution. On her part, it must have been thorny – did she believe as some Catholics did, when she moved in with her rosaries and relics, that he was damned eternally?

The installation finally took place on 22 November 1621. The act-books which would tell us the details of his incumbency have vanished, but the process for becoming dean would have had an elaborate protocol. The members of the chapter of the cathedral met in person and passed their vote (a pure formality: the King had sent his letter, and Donne was waiting in a house nearby, presumably with his beard at its finest and most pointed). They gave word, whereupon Donne was ushered in like a bride, presented to the bishop and processed up into the cathedral and to the altar. A *Te Deum* was sung under the high echoing ceiling: Donne prostrated himself upon the stone ground. He kissed the altar, and rose to stand in the church that was now his own.

To picture the cathedral in which he stood in as akin to how it is now – all roped-off solemnity and Quiet Please – would be to give the wrong idea, in part because the original building burned in the Great Fire, but largely because of the noise and the smell. There were no hushed voices; rather, the church's paperwork noted, 'the boys and maids and children of the adjoining parishes . . . after dinner come into church and play as children used to till dark night.' Boys peed on the floor and used the slippery surface as an ice rink, adults scattered food or turned up drunk. If hot young gallants strode into the church still wearing their spurs, which rang out noisily against the stone floors, choirboys were allowed to chase them down and fine them 'spur-money'. One of the aisles was known as Duke Humphrey's walk, and was the place to be seen;

all the diseased horses in a tedious siege cannot show so many fashions, as are to be seen for nothing, every day, in Duke Humphrey's walk. If therefore you determine to enter into a new suit, warn your tailor to attend you in Paul's, who with his hat in his hand shall like a spy discover the stuff, colour and fashion of any doublet or hose that dare be seen there and stepping behind a pillar to fill his tablebooks with those notes, will presently send you into the world an accomplished man; by which means you shall wear your clothes in print with the first edition.

Visitors could pay to climb up to the tower and carve their names – 'or, for want of a name, the mark which you clap on your sheep' – into the leaded roof; 'and indeed the top of Paul's contains more names than Stow's Chronicle.'

The cathedral came with a large cast of churchmen over whom Donne presided: five archdeacons, a precentor to take care of the musical services, a treasurer, a chancellor, at least a dozen minor canons, six vicars choral, a host of choirboys. There were also the vergers, whose unenviable job it was to keep order in the cathedral. It was Donne's job, now, to wrangle with their personalities and their jostling for power; it was he, now, who had to decide to whom to grant the benefices in the gift of the cathedral, how to keep order: duties for which paperwork and tact were required.

He was expected, too, to entertain. He wrote to Robert Ker of how he had tried to rise to it – to the new pomp and circumstance of the dinner table: 'I have obeyed the forms of our church of Paul's so much as to have been a solemn Christmas man, and tried conclusions upon my self how I could sit out the siege of new faces, every dinner.' He asked Ker to come and see him, alone, for something more intimate – 'choose your day, and either to suffer the solitude of this place, or to change it, by such company, as shall wait upon you, and come as a visitor and overseer of this hospital of mine, and dine or sup at this miserable chezmey.' ('Chezmey' is not in the dictionary: it must be his own, joking version of chez moi. It's one of those moments that reminds us how his letters must be full of in-jokes and hark-backs and warm hat-tips to past conversations that sail straight over our heads.)

Most of all, though, he preached. Technically, Donne was bound to preach only three times a year: Christmas, Easter and Ascension Day. But he was a man who preached like others eat meat: hungrily. The Dean of St Paul's was expected to preach in multiple places: inside the church, of course, and for the King at court, but, too, in the spot outside the cathedral known as the Paul's Cross pulpit. This was where enormous crowds could gather. It was the place to be, for everyone up to and including assassins; Mary I's pet Bishop Bourne had had a knife thrown at his head while preaching at the Cross: it missed and hit the wooden pole next to him. Benches, stored in the cathedral and hauled out for the sermon days, were available to rent, seating up to about 250; servants would be sent ahead to snag a place. Everyone else had to stand or lean, and try not to be pickpocketed. There are accounts of crowds at Paul's reaching six thousand.

A question to which we still do not wholly know the answer: how did they hear him? Did they telegraph his words backwards, like a game of whispers? Recently a group of academics staged a re-enactment of the preaching conditions to test what, exactly, the crowds of thousands would have been able to hear, and discovered that the courtyard was designed to allow sound to reverberate, so Donne would have been heard relatively well by at least the nearest five hundred to a thousand people. He would only have had to go slowly, so as not to tangle with his own

A sermon preached from St Paul's Cross in 1614, by John Gipkyn

echo. It wouldn't, though, have been comfortable for his listeners: Paul's Cross sermons were held, on and off, year round, unless severe weather drove everyone inside. (One of Donne's sermons is listed as 'Intended for Paul's Cross, but by reason of the weather, preached in the Church'.) London

253

was colder back then – the Thames froze over in 1608, and a Frost Fair was held, with nine-pin bowling and pubs on the ice. It would have been often ice-bound and windy; the coal that Londoners preferred, known as seacoal, produced great vats of sulphurous smoke which hung perpetually over the most populous parts of the city. There would, too, have been the scents of London: vegetables rotting, human waste, manure from passing horses and dogs, the stink of the Thames. It was over this never-quiet, always-moving world that Donne prepared to send his words flying.

To read the full text of a Donne sermon is a little like mounting a horse only to discover that it is an elephant: large and unfamiliar. To modern ears, they are winding, elongated, perambulating things; a pleasure that is also work. If you are a scholar, they offer notes to an A–Z of Renaissance religious flashpoints: Aquinas, bishops, casuistry, Divine Right of Kings, Erastianism, Foxe, Gnostics, heresy, incarnation, Judaism, Koran, Laudian ceremonialism, Manicheans, numerology, oaths, Plots (Gunpowder), Queen Henrietta Maria (for speaking clumsily of whom he was reprimanded), recusancy, scholasticism, Thirty-Nine Articles, utopianism, vanitas, Worms (Diet of), Xenophon, York, Zoroaster. But they can also be mined by those reading for other, less erudite and more unpindownable reasons.

You could turn to Donne's sermons for meditations on the Gospel as the bedrock of faith: less so if you are a fan of Mark (who only gets two sermons) or Luke (three), but there are sixteen on Matthew and sixteen on John; and it's

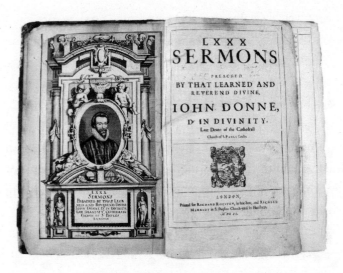

The frontispiece of Donne's *LXXX Sermons*

John, the man who trafficked in such powerful metaphors – Christ as True Light, Christ as the Word – whom Donne loves best. That, and, wholly unsurprisingly, the Psalms – of the 160 sermons, thirty-four took their text from the Book of Psalms: 'The whole frame of the poem', he wrote of one, is akin to 'a beating out of a piece of gold'.

You could turn to him for condemnations of divisions-among-allies within the Church:

> Lying at Aix . . . I found myself in a house which was divided into many families, and indeed so large as it might have been a little parish, or at least, a great limb of a great one; but it was of no parish: for when I asked who lay over my head, they told me a family of Anabaptists;

and who over theirs? – another family of Anabaptists; and another family of Anabaptists over theirs; and the whole house was a nest of these boxes; several artificers, all Anabaptists; I asked in what room they met, for the exercise of their religion; I was told they never met: for, though they were all Anabaptists, yet for some collateral differences, they detested one another, and, though many of them were near in blood, and alliance to one another, yet the son would excommunicate the father, in the room above him, and the nephew the uncle.

Even if you have to have strong feelings about Anabaptists to really relish the humour, the thrust of his argument holds fast: that division is absurd and destructive, and very little that is destructive, he believed, is of God.

You can also find him, in the sermons, at his most authoritarian. There are places where he is harsh where his audience would have expected joy. At the wedding of the daughter of his dearest friend Henry, Lucy Goodere, to the supremely handsome diplomat Francis Nethersole, he declared, 'marriage is but a continual fornication sealed with an oath.' Sex, he bemoaned, had overtaken all else in marriage: 'few pray for the gift of continency; few are content with that incontinency which they have, but are sorry they can express no more incontinency.' His preaching left his audience in no doubt of where they stood: 'we rise poorer, ignobler, weaker, for every night's sin, than we lay down . . . We sin, and sin, and sin.' It's a long way from the gleeful rakery of his youth;

Anne was dead, he was older and in physical pain, and his thinking about sex had taken on a flinty quality. What Lucy and Francis thought of being sent in such funereal tones to their marriage bed is not, alas, recorded.

Those condemnations which ring through so many of the sermons, though, are not surprising – he always had a streak of fury in him. It is the same Donne whom we had glimpses of years earlier, when in *Biathanatos*, he condemned the practice of pulling on the feet of those who are being hanged 'to hasten their end': 'in my understanding, such an act either by an executioner or a bystander is in no way justifiable.' He had always been capable of sounding grotesque: he ordains that the death must be as agonising as possible, because it is an affront 'to the judge, who has appointed a painful death to deter others from the crime'. This, from a man whose great-uncle had been hanged in front of an eager crowd.

You could also, though, find a radical spark in his sermons. At a time in which the idea of an individual desiring an entirely unmediated relationship with God could cause riots, he speaks a bold promise of individual spiritual enfranchisement: 'at the sacrament every man is a priest . . . consider then, that to come to the communion table, is to take orders . . . There thou art a priest.'

But Donne is at his most remarkable when he speaks about how very hard it is to seek God at all. More than anyone else, he acknowledged the way that the human heart darts about like a rat. His body, he found, so readily present in desire for other humans, betrayed him when he sought

257

the same intensity in prayer. Donne was a man so in control of his poetry that he could layer it with ten dozen references; he could write a twelve-line sonnet that would take you a week to read, but he was not in control of his mind:

> I throw myself down in my chamber, and I call in and invite God and his angels thither; and when they are there, I ignore God and his angels for the noise of a fly, for the rattling of a coach, for the whining of a door; I talk on . . . sometimes I find that I forgot what I was about, but when I began to forget it, I cannot tell. A memory of yesterday's pleasures, a fear of tomorrow's dangers, a straw under my knee, a noise in mine ear, a light in mine eye, an any thing, a nothing, a fancy, a chimera in my brain, troubles me in my prayer.

It is his lifelong quest and lifelong disappointment: that we cannot be struck daily by lightning. This is the same Donne who, in the Holy Sonnets (impossible to date for sure, but perhaps written around 1610), seeks a force so great that it will sweep away doubt, exhaustion, distraction, and leave something stripped back and certain: 'And burn me, O Lord, with a fiery zeal/Of Thee and Thy house, which doth in eating heal.' Both verse and sermons are the voice of a man seeking to have doubt torn away. In Holy Sonnet X:

> Batter my heart, three-personed God, for you
> As yet but knock, breathe, shine, and seek to mend;

That I may rise and stand, o'erthrow me, and bend
Your force to break, blow, burn, and make me new.

It is not possible, of course. It doesn't happen for him.
He remains relentlessly embodied, and therefore relentlessly
distractible, limping. But the hope remained:

We ask our daily bread, and God never says you should
have come yesterday. He never says you must again tomorrow, but *to-day if ye will hear His voice*, to-day He
will hear you . . . He brought light out of darkness, not
out of a lesser light; He can bring thy summer out of
winter, though thou have no spring; though in the ways
of fortune, or understanding, or conscience, thou have
been benighted till now, wintered and frozen, clouded
and eclipsed, damped and benumbed, smothered and
stupefied till now, now God comes to thee, not as in the
dawning of the day, not as in the bud of the spring, but as
the sun at noon, to illustrate all shadows, as the sheaves
in harvest, to fill all penuries, all occasions invite His
mercies, and all times are His seasons.

For those haltingly seeking the divine, there's no sense
in looking to those with unshakeable faith. It's no good,
for those who long for angels but also for sex, jokes, skin,
doubt, good clothes, oceans and huge appetites, looking to
the saints. Donne might be the person to turn to, if you
desired to seek God but cannot leap into the infinite. He is

the writer and the preacher for those who make their way there in gestures, symbols, flickers, errors.

And for all his bitterness and furies, he was insistent on joy. He quotes St Basil the Great, one of the Church's top ten least cheerful saints: '"But how far may we carry this joy? To what outward declarations! To laughing?" St Basil makes a round answer to a short question . . . "May a man laugh in no case."' But Donne turns on Basil:

> It is a dangerous weakness, to forbear outward declarations of our sense of God's goodness, for fear of misinterpretations . . . When David danced and leaped, and shouted before the ark; if he laughed too, it misbecame him not . . . not to show that joy, is an argument against thankfulness of the heart: that is a stupidity, this is a contempt.

The idea resonated through his life: he had written years before to Goodere, 'Our nature is meteoric . . . we respect (because we partake so) both earth and heaven; for as our bodies glorified shall be capable of spiritual joy, so our souls demerged into those bodies, are allowed to partake earthly pleasure.' We do wrong if we deliberately 'bury ourselves' in 'dull monastic sadness'. 'Heaven is expressed by singing, hell by weeping.' He knew, as Dante did, that there is a special place in hell for those who, when they could laugh, chose instead to sigh.

It is in his sermons, as it was in all his work. Donne was

able to hold two conflicting truths ever in front of him: a kind of duck-rabbit of the human condition. Humanity, as he saw it, was rotten with corruption and weakness and failure – and even so it was the great light of the universe. He gloried in mankind: if the inner world of each human was extended outwards, 'Man would be the giant, and the world the dwarf.' Few people would turn to Donne's poetry or prose, with its twisting logic and deliberate difficulty, for solace – but you might turn to him to be reminded that for all its horror, the human animal is worth your attention, your awe, your love.

THE MONIED

Donne was finally rich; if not rich enough for the kind of living he would have seen at court – where live birds erupted from pies, metre-high sugar statues decorated feasts, and roast pigs would be brought to the table mounted by little roast chickens dressed up like jockeys in paper reins and spurs – still he was rich enough to breathe easy. He could afford to stable his own horses; at some point around this time, he purchased a painting by Titian. He had enough to be extravagant in his generosity; to send £100 to an anonymous impecunious friend, and to seek out those imprisoned for debts and 'lay for their fees or small debts' (perhaps remembering his own time in the debtor's prison, and the view from the windows over the Fleet). Walton clambers into view, telling us that he was 'a continual giver to poor scholars', sending out bounty via his servants across London.

Donne's work is full of loving, semi-erotic metaphors about money. He relished puns on women and angels and the angel coin, a piece of gold worth about ten shillings and embossed with an image of an impressively muscular and topless Archangel Michael slaying a dragon. When he mounted the pulpit, the fondness remained: coinage gave him a way to talk about salvation which had the tactile, textured reality of daily life. In particular, he conjured up the imagery of salvation as purchase, over and over. Donne knew that there were merchants in his congregation, and he used their language: 'there is a trade driven, a staple established between heaven and earth . . . Thither have we sent our flesh, and hither hath [God] sent his spirit.' Christ had to be 'the nature and flesh of man; for man had sinned, and man must pay'. Money was his best way to point to value that lay beyond money: Christ was 'money coined even with the image of God; man was made according to his image: that image being defaced, in a new mint, in the womb of the blessed Virgin, there was new money coined.' Money was the perfect metaphor, being itself at once concrete and metaphysical: metal and human:

I, when I value gold, may think upon
The ductileness, the application,
The wholesomeness, the ingenuity,
From rust, from soil, from fire ever free;
But if I love it, 'tis because 'tis made
By our new nature, use, the soul of trade.

In contrast to his love for a golden metaphor, though, Donne had always claimed – before he had any – to hate the business of real-life money. He wrote to a friend, probably Wotton, in around 1607 that he loathed the strain of stumbling after cash: 'only the observation of others is my preservation from extreme idleness, else I profess, that I hate business so much, as I am sometimes glad to remember that the *Roman Church* reads that verse *A negotio perambulante in tenebris*'. He's punning: *negotium* can mean both 'business' and 'pestilence', and so, Donne writes, 'equal to me do the plague and business deserve avoiding.'

But Donne, as he grew older, had grown sharper about money. Having known the grind of relative poverty, he was determined not to return there, and he became well able to play the unshining games of money that took place among the elite. In 1623, he was looking to find a match for Constance, who was turning twenty. Marriage was a market in the most bluntly literal sense. Daughters and sons were both expensive to get rid of – an ordinary gentleman might ask for several hundred pounds, while an earl could demand many thousands be settled on his bride-to-be. Earlier, Donne had wondered about sending his girls off to be nuns, as a last-ditch desperate way to balance the books:

> My daughters (who are capable of such considerations) cannot but see my desire to accommodate them in this world, so I think they will not murmur if heaven must be their nunnery, and they associated to the B[lessed] virgins there; I know they would be content to pass their lives in a prison, rather then I should macerate my self for them.

The deanship made the nunnery unnecessary; but once you were in the market, there was bidding, haggling, and occasionally bargains escaped you. There was at least one missed chance: Donne wrote to Goodere:

Tell both your daughters a piece of a story of my Con. which may accustom them to endure disappointments in this world. An honourable person (whose name I give you in a schedule to burn, lest this letter should be mislaid) had an intention to give her one of his sons, and had told it me, and would have been content to accept what I, by my friends, could have begged for her; but he intended that son to my profession, and had provided him already £300 a year, of his own gift in Church livings, and hath estimated £300 more of inheritance for their children: and now the youth (who yet knows nothing of his fathers intention nor mine) flies from his resolutions for that calling, and importunes his Father to let him travel. The girl knows not her loss, for I never told her of it: but truly, it is a great disappointment to me.

Donne's eye roved with careful intent – he wanted, as George More had wanted so many years before, a match that would secure for his daughter safety and prosperity in a hard world – and lit on fifty-seven-year-old Edward Alleyn. Alleyn: the greatest actor of the age, the man who made Faustus his own, Master of the King's Bears, and possessed, in the etchings, of a beard that looks like he cut it with a rusty ice skate.

Alleyn came round to dine and they talked terms: he wrote to Donne,

after dinner in your parlour you declared your intention
to bestow with your daughter Con all the benefits of your
prime lease . . . worth £500 at the least, and whensoever
it should rise to more, it should wholly be hers. My offer
was to do as much for her as yourself, and add to that
at my death £500 more . . . this gave not content and Sir
Thomas persuaded me to do somewhat more, which I
did, and promised to leave her at my death 2000 marks.
This was accepted, and security demanded.

The marriage, which was planned as a grand and celebratory affair, instead took place in a rush on 3 December
1623, because Donne was suddenly struck with another
sickness: perhaps with his recurring fever, or with the typhus
which was sweeping London that winter. The doctor visited,
and was apparently bad at disguising his feelings; Donne
wrote; 'I see he fears, and I fear with him; I overtake him, I
overrun him, in his fear, and I go the faster, because he makes
his pace slow; I fear the more, because he disguises his fear,
and I see it with the more sharpness, because he would not
have me see it.'

Donne was convinced he was dying. In the depths of it,
from 3 to 6 December, he was very close: so close that he was
even, he said, 'barred of my ordinary diet, which is reading'.
But even in the thick of illness, Donne began to write. He
knew that readers give special weight to the words of those
who are at the edge of life. He wrote to Robert Ker: 'though
I have left my bed, I have not left my bedside';

EDWARD ALLEYN Esqr

Founder of Dulwich College

Edward Alleyn

I sit there still, and as a prisoner discharged sits at the prison door to beg fees, so I sit here to gather crumbs. I have used this leisure, to put the meditations I had in my sickness into some such order as may minister some holy delight. They arise to so many sheets (perchance 20) as that without staying for that furniture of an epistle, that my friends importun'd me to print them, I importune my friends to receive them printed.

The book that came from it, *Devotions upon Emergent Occasions*, moved from inception to publication in a staggeringly short period of time; it was entered into the Stationer's Register on 9 January 1624 and was published almost immediately after. The writing itself took barely more than a few days: his illness had not eroded the speed of his mind.

He organised the book into a series of numbered meditations: a record of the knowledge he had gleaned, and an urgent list of what he most wanted others to know. He wrote of the isolation of illness: he had so often sought out seclusion to work, yet the inflicted loneliness of pain paralysed him. 'As sickness is the greatest misery, so the greatest misery of sickness is solitude . . . Solitude is a torment which is not threatened in hell itself . . . it is an outlawry.'

He put down, from his bed, his sharpest words about illness: on its ruthless capriciousness. He knew that bodily safety is an illusion and a fiction – a clarity that was the necessary flipside of his celebration of the bodily astonishment and urgency of sex. He looked with pitiless clear-sightedness at our precarity:

We study health, and we deliberate upon our meats, and drink, and air, and exercises; and we hew, and we polish every stone, that goes to that building; and so our health is a long and regular work. But in a minute a cannon batters all, overthrows all, demolishes all; a sickness unprevented for all our diligence, unsuspected for all our curiosity; nay, undeserved if we consider only disorder, summons us, seizes us, possesses us, destroys us in an instant.

The book burns with pain – but it is not sad. Donne's work rarely is: full of calm terror and sardonic horror, but only very rarely tears. Looking towards death, he saw the glory of what he had been: 'I am more than dust and ashes: I am my best part, I am my soul.'

§

To read the *Devotions* is to expect that the man who emerged from his sickness would be one purified in the fire, whose moral vision was razor-sharp. But no; Donne at this point in his life is such vivid proof, if ever you find yourself in need of it, that you can be an excavator of the human soul, perceptive to the very bone marrow, and also capable of thoughtlessness and cruelty.

No sooner was he out of his sick bed than relations with Constance began to sour. Donne had promised his girl 'a little nag' which he rarely rode, but then he changed his mind without warning and sent it to Oxford, to John junior. He took from Constance a diamond ring, on the promise of replacing it with a better one which he himself wore, and then kept both. (This was particularly egregious, in that Constance as a married woman could not own property independently from her husband, but jewels and 'paraphernalia' could be hers alone.) Donne also offered to pay Alleyn a loan, which he then partially reneged on, and, according to Alleyn's furious letter, he'd promised to throw open the doors of the Deanery whenever Alleyn was in London: except, every time Alleyn attempted to take him up on his offer, Donne turned regal and told the actor that it wasn't an ideal time. Words grew heated: the revered Donne was accused of acting with 'unkind, unexpected and undeserved denial of the common courtesy afforded to a friend', and of using language more 'fitting you 30 years ago when you might be question[ed] for them, than now under so reverent a calling as you are'. Donne does not, in his reckonings with his girl, come off very magnificently, striding up to the pulpit with his daughter's ring on his finger.

(His children did not turn out much of a credit to him: John, Donne's editor after his death, without whom so much of his father's work would be lost, committed manslaughter: an eight-year-old child startled his horse, and John killed him by hitting him on the head with a riding crop. He was an incorrigible drinker who was arrested at least twice, and in 1629 was accused of having 'had about' with a young maidservant called Sara, leaving her pregnant and abandoned. The seventeenth-century antiquarian Anthony à Wood wrote, about John Donne junior, 'His nature being vile, he proved no better all his lifetime than an atheistical buffoon, a banterer, and a person of over-free thoughts.' George, like father like son, served in a spectacularly unsuccessful British siege in 1627, the Siege of Saint-Martin-de-Ré, and spent several years imprisoned at Cadiz.)

In 1624, Donne added another source of income to his slate; he became vicar of St Dunstan in the West, the tithes of which alone were worth at least £240 a year. This, added to a very tentative reckoning of his various revenues from his parishes in Sevenoaks and three other absentee benefices he held, plus the far greater sum from St Paul's, puts his annual income at close to £2,000. (For comparison: at around the same time a Norfolk knight was paying his dairy maid £2 a year, and his scullery maid £1 10s, while in Kent the yearly wage bill for a smart household of twelve servants came to £55 13s 10d.) Donne had to pay his curates' salaries out of it, but even so he was now among London's elite. St Dunstan was on Fleet Street, just along from the prison in which Donne had once been shackled. It was the same church in which William Tyndale, the great translator of the English Bible, had lectured and prayed: a church which has known more than its fair share of men who knew how to make their words grip hold of the heart. It was then that Donne met Izaak Walton; Walton, son of an innkeeper, had a linen draper's shop on Fleet Street, so St Dunstan was his local church. It was Donne who married Walton to Rachel Floud, great-grandniece of Archbishop Thomas Cranmer; it's likely to have been Donne who buried the couple's five sons, none of whom lived past four years old.

James I died in March 1625. If Donne quaked at the thought of the upheaval, and wondered if he would need to begin his careful politicking again with the new king, his tremors were unnecessary. James's son Charles I waited a week after his accession before appearing in public, when he sent out word that he wanted to hear a sermon in the chapel at St James's Palace, and that the preacher should be Dr Donne. It was testament to how securely Donne was established as the star preacher of the age; a compliment and a relief. He was at once gratified and surprisingly flustered: he wrote to Ker, asking for the loan of his rooms in the palace 'at one after noon' before he preached, so as to have enough time, like an actor, to compose himself before he made his entrance. He went to his pulpit fasting: 'I do not eat before, nor can after, till I have been at home'; nothing distracted him from focusing the full force of his mind on the sermon to come. He preached a sermon full of the nation's grief: 'The Almighty hand of God hath shed and spread a text of mortification over the land'; it was a careful compliment to the Stuart family, and Charles was sufficiently gratified that he ordered for the sermon to be published.

In 1626, there was another sermon to mark a death. This one, though, was of a very different kind of man, and it stands as some of the best evidence we have of Donne's willingness to occasionally put expediencies over moral exigencies. He was asked to give the funeral sermon of Sir William Cokayne; one-time Lord Mayor, and a man rich beyond the dreams of almost any other merchant of the time.

Cokayne had ordered, for his funeral, lavish mourning cloth and a great procession: it was one of the more elaborate death-spectacles of the year. He was also the man who had, ten years before, almost brought about the collapse of the entire English economy. It would have been not unlike being asked to preach the funeral sermon for Richard Fuld, the 'Gorilla of Wall Street' and 2008 CEO of Lehman Brothers.

In 1614 Cokayne had bribed commissioners for Treasure Affairs to prohibit the export of undyed cloth. At the time, the Dutch and Germans bought vast quantities of undyed and undressed cloth from England; some years it consti-tuted ninety per cent of all of England's exports. The idea, Cokayne claimed, was that it would foster the English dye-ing trade. The scheme went explosively badly: the Dutch, outraged, simply forbade the importing of dyed cloth and bought their undyed cloth from other countries. Customs revenues fell £6,000 in three months. The value of undyed cloth plummeted. Unemployment doubled. But Cokayne was untroubled – he simply started buying up the cloth at the reduced prices, which, when the law was (inevitably) reversed, he was able to sell on at a colossal profit: not unlike short-selling. Cokayne then cemented his position by giving James a gold basin filled with £1,000 in gold: not a million miles from those who donate selflessly to their preferred English political party, and miraculously end up in the House of Lords. He seems to have been a prototype for the destructive City boy; he also left his wife, a close friend of Donne's, in the middle of the financial chaos, and

endowed his verse with his own peculiar, fervent relish –
but it did require squinting at the passage in the Gospels
about the rich man, the camel and the eye of the needle.
Despite his ecclesiastical cap and cope, Donne never was the
scourge of the rich.

DONNE AND DEATH

The world is made up entirely of things that can kill you. Scarcely anything exists, Donne wrote with relish in the *Devotions*, which has not caused the death of someone once: 'a pin, a comb, a hair pulled, hath gangrened and killed.' A grim truth, and one which makes our modern attempts to avoid the topic of death look malarially unhinged. Donne lived in a time more familiar with the details and look of death than we; almost every adult was likely to have seen a dead body. They prepared intensively for it, contemplated it; Donne discussed it in letters that were otherwise about horses and dentistry. Donne had a *memento mori*, lest he forget even briefly that we are born astride the grave – he left it to a friend in his will, 'the picture called The Skeleton which hangs in the hall'.

Artists and writers especially were expected to contemplate death: there were rumours (probably mad and unfounded) that Michelangelo murdered a man and watched him die in order to be able to paint the agonies of Christ more accurately. Poets and playwrights, meanwhile, were killed and killing at a far greater rate of frequency than their percentage of the population seems to merit: Thomas Wyatt killed a man in an affray, Ben Jonson stabbed a man in a duel, Christopher Marlowe was murdered, probably in a tavern brawl, though possibly in an elaborate intrigue.

When Donne wrote about suicide there was urgent pain: but when he wrote about death *in itself*, there is great serious joy, and occasional rampant glee. Spiritually speaking, many of us confronted with the thought of death perform the psychological equivalence of hiding in a box with our knees under our chin: Donne hunted death, battled it, killed it, saluted it, threw it parties. His poetry explicitly about death is rarely sad: it thrums with strange images of living.

Death! be not proud, though some have called thee
Mighty and dreadful, for thou art not so;
For those whom thou think'st thou dost overthrow
Die not, poor Death, nor yet canst thou kill me.
From rest and sleep, which but thy pictures be,
Much pleasure, then from thee much more must flow,
And soonest our best men with thee do go,
Rest of their bones, and souls' delivery.

As a young man he had imagined his death in extravagantly sexual terms. 'The Relic' had imagined a gravedigger coming across the bodies of himself and his lover, buried together.

When my grave is broke up again
Some second guest to entertain . . .
And he that digs it spies
A bracelet of bright hair about the bone

He took tradition of the *memento mori* – a reminder of death – and injected hot desire into it. Donne's imagination was fundamentally alive, and on the side of life, on both sides of the grave. 'Death,' he wrote, 'thou shalt die.'

When Donne was talking about death he did not, unlike most of his contemporaries, yearn for the silence and stillness of the tomb. No: death was to be explosive, multicoloured, transmogrifying. He wanted ravishment: 'I would not that death should take me asleep. I would not have him merely seize me, and only declare me to be dead, but win me, and overcome me.' Donne wanted, ideally, to be struck down mid-sermon and topple down, an abrupt corpse, onto the congregation below: 'it hath been my desire (and God may be pleased to grant it me) that I might die in the pulpit.' It's telling that none of the love poems are sonnets: he kept that form for death, his other, permanent love. In Holy Sonnet VIII, Donne dared to imagine the end of all time, loud and very much awake:

At the round Earth's imagined corners, blow
Your trumpets, angels! and arise, arise
From death, you numberless infinities
Of souls, and to your scattered bodies go!
All whom the Flood did and fire shall o'erthrow,
All whom war, dearth, age, agues, tyrannies,
Despair, law, chance hath slain, and you whose eyes
Shall behold God, and never taste death's woe.

¶

He loved death in theory, and for himself: less so for others. In the very early winter days of 1627, his Lucy, nineteen and just old enough to be beginning her life as a woman, was on a visit away, probably with her sister Constance who had been widowed the year before. Donne was at home for the new year, ploughing his way ruefully through the necessary entertaining, when the message came to his door. Lucy was dead. She died with no warning, like lightning out of a blue sky – just five days before, Donne's letters had been full of amiable gripes about his social calendar. She was buried swiftly, in Camberwell on 9 January. If he wrote to tell Goodere and Wotton, the letters don't survive, but the weight of her loss leaked into his work. That Easter, he preached, and it is clear that he is preaching about her: 'If I had fixed a son in court, or married a daughter into a plentiful fortune, I were satisfied for that son and that daughter. Shall I not be so, when the King of Heaven hath taken that son to himself, and married himself to that daughter, forever?' You can hear the fixed set of his jaw in his words: 'I shall have my dead raised to life again.' It reads like a man wringing consolation by force from beliefs that had been already agonisingly hard-wrung.

His friends began dying: it must have felt like the end was setting in. Goodere went in March 1627, impoverished and untriumphant. Goodere's only son was already dead, and he left three daughters unmarriageable because of his impecuniousness: he couldn't give them dowries, and a woman without a dowry would have to be spectacularly beautiful or lucky. Goodere had loved the old chivalric code of the Henrican court, and had been beloved by Elizabeth I for his gallantry; under the more Machiavellian, less code-bound norms of the Jacobean court, he floundered, fell into debt, stumbled. Donne had told him: 'make . . . to yourself some mark, and go towards it alegrement'; but he had never been able to do it. It was almost certainly he to whom Donne gave that £100 that Walton mentions, the 'old friend'. Goodere refused it, but Donne knew very well how to be importunate; he had had long practice. He sent it back again with a note: 'my desire is, that you who in the days of your plenty have cheered and raised the hearts of so many of your dejected friends, will now receive this from me, and use it as a cordial for the cheering of your own.'

Possibly the shock of the deaths made him take his eye off the ball. His sermons had been so full of insistence on Death as liberator and translator, and yet the reality of it must have been a punch to the chest. The double loss blurred his precision, and he paid for it. On 1 April he preached a sermon for the new King Charles I. It included, as so very many of Donne's sermons had done, a long-drawn-out metaphor about the Church. Just, he said, as 'very religious Kings may have wives, that may have retained some tincture, some impressions of error, which they may have sucked in their infancy from another church,' and yet 'should not be publicly traduced to be heretics', just so the church 'may lack something of exact perfection'. Charles I's hackles rose. Word

came from Robert Ker to be on the lookout for royal fury –
and then, fast on its heels, a letter from Bishop Laud, asking
for a copy of the sermons in the name of the King. Donne
darted out instantly to visit Laud, agitated and bewildered.
His political prudence and his care around kings had been
such a fundamental feature of his rise. He had never made
a habit of being daringly inflammatory, and it must have
been alarming to face the possibility he had been so by accident. Laud would not explain what, exactly, had offended
the King, and Donne was thrown into a panic. He wrote to
Ker, 'I have cribrated [i.e. sifted: a word he himself invented,
when none other in his arsenal would do], and re-cribrated,
and post-cribrated the sermon' – and could find nothing in
it that did not 'conduce to [the King's] service'. Laud took it
upon himself to read over the text and report to the King, and
Donne was summoned into the presence to throw himself to
the ground before Charles and ask pardon. Laud wrote in
his diary, 'his Majesty King Charles forgave Doctor Donne
certain slips in a sermon.' Donne was never told exactly what
those 'certain slips' were for which he had so humbly apologised. It seems likely that Charles had bristled at the possible
aspersions Donne's simile had cast on his bride, Henrietta
Maria – daughter of the King of France – who was an ardent
Roman Catholic. Metaphors, Donne was reminded, are slippery beasts: they can escape out of your hands and bite you.

The bodies kept piling up. In May, Lucy Bedford died,
and was followed in June by his patroness Magdalen Herbert, over whose body he preached his super-infinite sermon.

he would be spoken of after his departure. 'A man would almost be content to die . . . to hear of so much sorrow and so much good testimony from good men as I (God be blessed for it) did upon the report of my death.'

Death came closer, and he thought incessantly about infinity. There would be no end, he decided. Even the demons in Hell, he wrote, cannot long for annihilation; he wanted to see in death the most living form of life. 'I shall not live till I see God; and when I have seen him I shall never die.' Exactly how the soul and body are anchored together teased him his entire life. He owned a library of books debating the soul's status: whether, at the start, it was formed inside the body of the mother or injected into the foetus individually by God before birth; 'whole Christian Churches', he noted testily, 'arrest themselves upon propagation from parents, and other whole Christian Churches allow only infusion from God.' He never decided: but he insisted that, whatever the beginning, there is no conclusion. We are a maze with no end.

Perhaps his love for writing about death was an attempt to transform fear into longing. He had known the dread of death: it's in Holy Sonnet I, 'I dare not move my dim eyes any way,/Despair behind, and death before, doth cast/Such terror.' Perhaps it was an attempt to convince himself when he said: 'who can fear the darkness of death, that hath the light of this world, and of the next too?' But perhaps he was, sometimes, as confident as he sounds: 'In the agonies of death, in the anguish of that dissolution, in the sorrows of the valediction, in the irreversibleness of that transmigration, I shall have a joy which shall no more evaporate than my soul shall evaporate: a joy that shall pass up and put on a more glorious garment above, and be joy super-invested in glory.' 'Invested in glory' would be enough for most of us, but not him: *super-invested*.

§

In December of 1630, Donne knew that his body was collapsing, and he made his will. He wrote it out in his own hand, having no need of a lawyer: he had, after all, been one himself long ago. To his servants he left £5 apiece to buy mourning rings; to his friends, he left a list of paintings. Their descriptions reveal a glimpse of his artistic taste, which ran unsurprisingly religious, and of what he must have seen daily as he walked through his London home: one was of the Virgin, another of the Entombment, another of Adam and Eve, plus one of King James. The oil painting of himself in his twenties, 'the picture of mine which is taken in the shadows', all pout and hat, he left to Robert Ker, the man to whom he had trusted his *Biathanatos* all those years ago, and who had repaid his trust by keeping it safe and out of sight. His money was split evenly between his six surviving children, irrespective of gender – and provision was made for his mother, who was, like him, just clinging on to life.

As he grew weaker, he grew skeletally thin. He consulted his London doctor, Simeon Foxe – son of Foxe of the *Book of Martyrs* – who, alarmed at his swift decline, insisted that he should build his strength and gain weight. Foxe told him 'that by cordials, and drinking milk twenty days together, there was a probability of his restoration to health'. Donne loathed milk 'passionately' – to humour Foxe, he drank it for ten days, but stopped in disgust, declaring 'he would not drink it ten days longer upon the best moral assurance of having twenty years added to his life.' Donne had reached such an intimacy with death that milk held more terrors for him. His fear was not death, but slow entropy. It was his last terror, as all the other possible terrors fell away. He wrote in his final letter, to Cokayne's widow: 'I am afraid that Death will play with me so long, as he will forget to kill me, and suffer me to live in a languishing and useless age.'

¶

Donne did not get his wish; he didn't die in his pulpit – but he came close. On 25 February 1631 he preached his final sermon in the full knowledge that he was dying. Men and women who came to see him preach in London, and saw his 'decayed body, and a dying face', wondered if he might in truth be a corpse. They 'saw his tears, and heard his faint and hollow voice, professing they thought the text prophetically chosen, and that Dr Donne had preached his own funeral sermon'. He was fifty-nine: the national average life expectancy for those who made it into adulthood.

The sermon, published posthumously as *Death's Duel*, is dark as pitch, until almost the very end. Donne, standing like an ambulant *memento mori* in his church, told the listeners that their whole life was merely a movement from death to death. 'Our very birth and entrance into this life is *exitus à morte*, an issue from death': 'in our mother's womb we are dead,' he writes, or as if dead, because 'we have eyes and see not, ears and hear not,' and 'we have a winding sheet in our Mother's womb . . . for we come to seek a grave.' His own mother had died weeks before, and the grief infects the sermon: the womb from which he came was in the grave.

Worse, we can be murderers before we draw breath: if a child dies in its mother's womb it 'kills the mother that conceived it, and is a murderer, nay, a parricide, even after it is dead'. It is impossible not to think of Anne, and her childbirth death. 'There in the womb we are taught cruelty, by being fed with blood.' No other sermon by Donne is so resolutely sad.

Its ending, though, is not sad. What a person decides on matters unprovable is the surest way to know their imagination, and Donne could not write his final word without saluting the beginning.

The end of the sermon is a litany of images of life: of life 'blessed and glorious', 'that shall last as long as the Lord of Life himself'. Death would not just give life: it would give life free from his constant, relentless questing, finally solidify him and define him. Montaigne called it 'a death united in itself . . . wholly mine'. Certainty, never once available in life, is what death promised him. Donne's desire for death was a desire to see himself.

The sermon's last words – and the last Donne spoke to his congregation – were these: 'There we leave you . . . suck at [Christ's] wounds, and lie down in peace in his grave, till he vouchsafe you a resurrection.' Who is that 'we' that comes down from the pulpit: 'there we leave you'? Preachers did often use the royal 'we', but Donne in all the rest of the sermon had used 'I'.

One option: *we* is all the dozens of Donnes. He was a man constantly transforming. He was a one-man procession: John Donne the persecuted, the rake, the lawyer, the bereaved, the lover, the jailbird, the desperate, the striver, the pious, John Donne the almost dead and reporting from the front line of the grave.

Donne, though, will have meant another we. He had written years before, in another sermon, of his longing for the interlinking of God and man: 'God hath made himself one body with me.' So that 'we' is Donne imagining himself as having already made that final leap, stepped across the barrier and made a final transformation: John Donne, Jack Donne, Dr Donne, and now, finally, *we*. The 'we' is Donne and the God he has been summoning and summoning.

§

His death came daily closer, and Donne prepared for it as others prepare for great theatrical debuts. His fascination with the dramatic silent gestures that we can make with the clothes we put on our backs lasted to the very end. In his home in London he set about designing his monument that would stand in the cathedral after his death. First he ordered a wooden urn to be carved, and a shroud to be made. He stripped naked in his study and wrapped himself in his shroud, with the knots at his feet and atop his head; then he pushed back the cloth so that only his face was showing.

The artist sketched his dying body life-size, onto a wooden plank; and the plank was set by Donne's bedside. It was entirely characteristic of him: that he forced from the fact of his dying body a final piece of art. He, of all people, was liable to insist on a *memento mori* of the most bespoke kind.

The drawing was used as the model for the stone monument that stands upright in an alcove in St Paul's Cathedral. Henry Wotton, by now the distinguished old Provost of Eton, said of it: 'It seems to breathe faintly, and posterity shall look upon it as a kind of artificial miracle.' It would be one of the only statues in the cathedral to survive the Fire of London, standing intact amid the rubble.

Donne died in his own home on 31 March 1631. Walton was close by, and ecstatic to the last:

> His speech, which had long been his ready and faithful
> servant, left him not till the last minute of his life, and
> then forsook him not to serve another Master (for who
> speaks like him) but died before him, for that it was then
> become useless to him that now conversed with God
> on earth, as Angels are said to do in heaven, only by
> thoughts and looks.

Nicholas Stone's effigy, St Paul's Cathedral

As Donne felt death reach him, 'he closed his own eyes; and then disposed his hands and body into such a posture as required not the least alteration by those that came to shroud him.' Donne made himself ready; part, perhaps, of a desire to have things done exactly as he had imagined them – an artist of ferocious precision, dying precisely.

His last words – 'I were miserable if I might not die.'

The frontispiece of *Death's Duel*

SUPER-INFINITE

Donne had wanted to be buried, he said in his will, 'in the most private manner that may be': but nothing could keep the crowds away. He was buried in St Paul's, and an anonymous poet wrote on charcoal across the wall over his grave:

Reader! I am to let thee know
Donne's body only lies below
For, could the grave his soul comprise
Earth would be richer than the skies.

The bishop Henry King wrote Donne a more formal elegy, in ink and paper. It mourned that Donne couldn't have gone beyond making his own monument, and written his own epitaph: 'since but thine own/no pen could do thee justice.' King had all of a bishop's tendency to be excessively polite about the dead, but he was right. Donne, more than any other of his lifetime, understood that flair is its own kind of truth: if you want to make your point, make it so vivid and strange that it cuts straight through your interlocutor's complacent inattention. To read his verse is to hear him insist, across the gap of hundreds of years: *for God's sake, will you listen.*

¶

He was dead, but his poetry and his sermons were alive, spreading exponentially as they were copied and recopied. John Donne junior had a keen eye to a commercial endeavour, and in 1633 he produced the first printed collected works of Donne's poetry. It opened with a preface, headed 'The Printer to the Understanders': a nod to the fact that Donne was a man who required all your focus and ingenuity to untangle. For those who persevered, though, the preface said, 'a scattered limb of this author hath more amiableness in it, in the eye of a discerner, than a whole body of some other.'

Soon, those outside the literary elite were able to buy it in the marketplace outside St Paul's. Other poets and playwrights of his generation loved his work enough to lift it wholesale: Francis Beaumont, Thomas Carew, Francis Quarles and John Webster all took lines from Donne and included them, unattributed, in their own work; outright theft as the highest form of flattery. Dryden, for all his carping on Donne's scansion, stole lines from two of his obsequies and inserted them into his poem 'Eleonora'. But people wanted more. They were ravenous enough for his work to make it worth faking it, and within two decades of Donne's death, 'new' work by him began appearing.

The phenomenon – pseudepigraphy, the attribution of work to an author who didn't write it – was nothing new. People had been doing it to Shakespeare for decades; the market mushroomed with work by 'W.S.' or 'W.Sh.' – as many as ten between 1595 and 1622. In the mid-seventeenth century poems began to crop up in printed miscellanies, aping Donne's style and ascribed to a just-about-plausibly deniable 'J.D.' or 'Dr Dun'. The fakeries range from comically bad to mediocre: but all are useful, in that they revealed exactly what the forgers were thinking of as typically Donnean.

For instance: in 1654 an opportunistic young royalist called Robert Chamberlain produced *The Harmony of the Muses*, a miscellany of verses which included some real Donne poetry alongside three fakes. They show how far the idea of the glamorously woman-conquering Donne had entered the popular imagination in the twenty years after his death: 'Dun's Answer to a Lady' takes bedrooms and wordplay as Donne's hallmark.

Lady:

Say not you love unless you do,
For lying will not honour you.

Answer of the Doctor's:

Lady I love, and love to do,
And will not love unless be you.
You say I lie, I say you lie, choose whether,
But if we both lie, let us lie together.

Another, 'The Rapture', by one 'J.D.', remembers that Donne liked suns:

Just as the Sun, methinks I see her face,
Which I may gaze upon, but not imbrace:
For 'tis heavens pleasure sure she should be sent
As pure to heaven again, as she was lent
To us.

What's so telling is that although the fakers thought they knew basically what Donne was about – he liked sex, he loved a metaphor – the pastiches don't ring even slightly true. They could not step into his voice, because his voice was so constantly in motion: turbulent, shifting between triumph and anxiety, bravado and dread, irony and humility.

The other reason they don't ring true is that they're just too easy. Donne would have scoffed. It was very deliberately that he wrote poems that take all your sustained focus to untangle them. The pleasure of reading a Donne poem is akin to that of cracking a locked safe, and he meant it to be so. He demanded hugely of us, and the demands of his poetry are a mirror to that demanding. The poetry stands to ask: why should everything be easy, rhythmical, pleasant? He is at times almost impossible to understand, but, in repayment for your work, he reveals images that stick under your skin until you die. Donne suggests that you look at the world with both more awe and more scepticism: that you weep for it and that you gasp for it. In order to do so, you shake yourself out of cliché and out of the constraints of what the world would sell you. Your love is almost certainly not like a flower, nor a dove. Why would it be? It may be like a pair of compasses. It may be like a flea. His startling timelessness is down to the fact that he had the power of unforeseeability: you don't see him coming.

The difficulty of Donne's work had in it a stark moral imperative: pay attention. It was what Donne most demanded of his audience: attention. It was, he knew, the world's most mercurial resource. The command is in a passage in Donne's sermon: 'Now was there ever any man seen to sleep in the cart, between Newgate and Tyburn? Between the prison, and the place of execution, does any man sleep? And we sleep all the way; from the womb to the grave we are never thoroughly awake.' Awake, is Donne's cry. Attention, for Donne, was everything: attention paid to our mortality, and to the precise ways in which beauty cuts through us, attention to the softness of skin and the majesty of hands and feet and mouths. Attention to attention itself, in order to fully appreciate its power: 'Our creatures are our thoughts,' he wrote, 'creatures that are born Giants: that reach from East to West, from earth to Heaven, that do not only bestride all the sea and land, but span the sun and firmament at once: my thoughts reach all, comprehend all.' We exceed ourselves: it's thus that a human is super-infinite.

Most of all, for Donne, our attention is owed to one another. Donne's most famous image comes not from his poetry, but from the words he set down in extremis, in *Devotions upon Emergent Occasions*:

When one man dies, one chapter is not torn out of the book, but translated into a better language; and every chapter must be so translated; God employs several translators; some pieces are translated by age, some by sickness, some by war, some by justice; but God's hand is in every translation, and his hand shall bind up all our scattered leaves again, for that library where every book shall lie open to one another.

On his deathbed, facing down what he imagined to be the end of everything he had known, this was what he most urgently wanted to tell. We, slapdash chaotic humanity, persistently underestimate our effect on other people: it is our necessary lie, but he refused to tell it. In a world so harsh and beautiful, it is from each other that we must find purpose, else there is none to be had:

No man is an island, entire of itself; every man is a piece of the continent, a part of the main; if a clod be washed away by the sea, Europe is the less, as well as if a promontory were, as well as if a manor of thy friend's or of thine own were; any man's death diminishes me, because I am involved in mankind, and therefore never send to know for whom the bell tolls; it tolls for thee.

There's a characteristic bite in the passage, which stands as both promise and warning: death is coming for *you*. But they are glorious words. If we could believe them, they would upend the world. They cast our interconnectedness not as a burden but as a great project: our interwoven lives draw their meaning only from each other.

In his hardest days Donne wrote that his mind was a 'sullen weedy lake'. But it was fertile water: in it, things were born. From his prodigious learning, from his lust, from his fear, came work strong enough to ring through the barricade of time. Donne was honest about horror and its place in the task of living, and honest too in his insistence: joy is also a truth. Who else of his peers had been able to hold grotesqueries and delights, death and life so tightly in the same hand?

There's a scientific term, autapomorphic, which denotes a unique characteristic that has evolved in only one species or subspecies. That was him: there are ways of reckoning with the grimly and majestically improbable problem of being alive that exist only because four hundred years ago a boy was born on Bread Street to Elizabeth Donne. John Donne was super-autapomorphic.

ACKNOWLEDGEMENTS

I have built up a colossal debt, to so many for such kindness, in the long writing of this book. If you are one, please consider this a lifelong promissory note.

My first thanks are to the Warden and Fellows of All Souls College, Oxford, where this book was written – and especially to Colin Burrow, for his kindness and ruthless eradication of extraneous adjectives.

I owe a great debt to the scholars who gave their time to talk over and read this text. To John Carey, whose *John Donne: Life, Mind and Art* was the most electric piece of literary criticism I read as a teen and thereby set me on the road to Donne, and who read and commented on this text with formidable generosity. To Daniel Starza Smith, whose scholarly insight changed this book, and whose friendship spurred me on. (Good*ere*, forever.) To A. N. Wilson, who, with great kindness, read an early draft. I owe an enormous amount, too, to those who gave their expertise and time during my doctoral thesis: especially Norma Aubertin-Potter and Gaye Morgan at All Souls college library, Dennis Flynn, Arthur Marotti, Peter McCullough, Jeanne Shami and Jo Wisdom, the librarian of St Paul's Cathedral.

I owe thanks to my two wonderful editors, Alex Bowler and Mitzi Angel, and everyone at RCW: Zoe Waldie, Claire

Wilson, Peter Straus and Safae El-Ouahabi. Nic Liney expertly wrangled my dates as an independent fact-checker.

This book took more than half a decade to write, and my greatest luck is in my friends, who have put up with my talking about Donne solidly for the last ten years – especially to Susie Atwood, Chanya Button, Abi Elphinstone, Lavinia Harrington, Tom Hodgson, Ellen Holgate, Anna James, Daisy Johnson, Jessica Lazar, Kiran Millwood Hargrave, Daniel Morgan, Simon Murphy, Gerard Rundell, Adélia Sabatini, Julie Scrase, Sophie Smith, Alice Spawls, Lauren St John, Issy Sutton, Piers Torday, Katie Webber and Fred Wilmot Smith. To Mary Wellesley and Miranda Vane, donkey wardens, comrades in PhDs, joy women. To Alex Cole, for such glorious talk. To Amia Srinivasan, for such rich wisdom, about this book and so much else. Most of all to Liz Chatterjee, my most brilliant and incomparable twin, who was with me and Donne from the very start.

To Barbara and Peter Rundell I owe absolutely everything, but especially, in the context of this book, gratitude for pinning Donne poetry next to the bathroom sink when we were small.

To Charles Collier, the best and boldest editor I've ever had: it is because of you that the love poetry makes sense to me.

Finally, I have had such life-shaping good fortune in my teachers. To Professor Bart van Es, my undergraduate tutor, doctoral thesis supervisor and colleague, I owe gratitude for more than a decade of generosity and erudition: thank you.

FURTHER READING

For those seeking a wider sense of how the world has received Donne over time, the Critical Heritage series is an understated delight: a compendium of some of the many – often scathing and furious – things that have been said about Donne's work in the last four hundred years: A. J. Smith, *John Donne: The Critical Heritage* (2010).

For more on Donne and his circle of friends, and the ways in which they passed poems and jokes and knowledge between themselves: Arthur Marotti, John Donne: Coterie Poet (1986).

For the text of the letters that Donne and his in-laws exchanged during the tumultuous months of the marriage, and the four letters that are probably his love letters to Anne: M. Thomas Hester, Robert Parker Sorlien and Dennis Flynn (eds), *John Donne's Marriage Letters in the Folger Shakespeare Library* (2005).

For more on Donne's writing for Anne: M. Thomas Hester (ed.), *John Donne's 'Desire of More': The Subject of Anne More Donne in His Poetry* (1997).

For more on how Early Modern patronage functioned, as well as more on Henry Goodere: Daniel Starza Smith, *John Donne and the Conway Papers: Patronage and Manuscript Circulation in the Early Seventeenth Century* (2014).

For more on the sermons – on their structural innovations, their politics and their nuance: Peter McCullough, *Sermons at Court: Politics and Religion in Elizabethan and Jacobean Preaching* (1998) and Jeanne Shami, *John Donne and Conformity in Crisis in the Late Jacobean Pulpit* (2003).

For more on Donne's working life, and his navigation of the court and Church, David Colclough (ed.), *John Donne's Professional Lives* (2003).

For more on Donne's obsessing over the binding between the body and the soul: Ramie Targoff, *John Donne: Body and Soul* (2008).

For an electric analysis of Donne's life and work together: John Carey, *John Donne: Life, Mind and Art* (1981, revised 1990).

For those in search of where to begin with Donne's prose – the *Devotions upon Emergent Occasions* (the 1999 edition prints them with *Death's Duel* and Izaak Walton's *Life of Donne*) are relentlessly beautiful, and *Ignatius His Conclave* (ed. T. S. Healy (1969)) is genuinely funny, in ways that are revealing about the spiky, elaborate humour of the seventeenth century. For those searching for warnings against the place not to begin: for all the powerful astonishments to be found in Donne's work, it's difficult to recommend that anybody read *Pseudo-Martyr*, except under duress.

Key Manuscripts

Bodl. Rawl. poet. 117: mid-seventeenth-century quarto verse miscellany, English and Latin, including thirty-seven poems by Donne, in several hands, compiled in part by the Oxford printer Christopher Wase

BL Egerton MS 2421: mid-seventeenth-century verse miscellany, containing copy of *The Tempest*'s 'full fathoms five' alongside verse by Donne and Jonson

BL Harley MS 5110: independent quire, seven folio leaves containing three satires by Donne, in two hands, headed 'Jhon Dunne his Satires Anno Domini 1593'

BL Harley MS 6931: seventeenth-century octavo miscellany, chiefly verse in two italic hands, religious verse and prose at the reverse end in another hand, verse by Carew and Donne

The Burley manuscript, DG. 7/Lit. 2: 616 items over 373 folios, including poems, legal reports and letters, three or four of which may be Donne's love letters. The manuscript was believed lost in the devastating 1908 fire at Burley-on-the-Hill, until it was rediscovered in 1960 by I. A. Shapiro in the National Register of Archives. It then disappeared again in a series of administrative muddles, turning up sixteen years later at the University Library of Birmingham, and is now in the Leicestershire Record Office. It is also printed in facsimile by Peter Redford (ed.), *The Burley Manuscript* (2017), and so is safe for posterity for now.

Cambridge University Library MS Add. 29: verse miscellany, in multiple hands, containing thirty-five Donne poems

Folger MS V.a.125: composite headed 'a book of verses collected by mee R Dungaravane', including Donne verse and a number of recipes for wine

Folger MS V.a.245: quarto verse miscellany, single secretary hand, probably associated with Oxford and afterwards with the Inns of Court

Folger MS V.a.262 : quarto verse miscellany, in English and Latin, multiple hands, title 'Divers Sonnets & Poems compiled by certaine gentil Clarks and Ryme-Wrightes', probably associated with Oxford University and the Inns of Court

Heneage MS (private collection): early seventeenth-century quarto miscellany, eleven texts in verse and prose, in several hands, including seven poems by Donne in a single hand with ornamentation

Westminster MS 41: octavo verse miscellany, including thirteen poems by Donne, in several hands over an extended period, associated with Christ Church, Oxford, 1620–40s

The Westmoreland Manuscript, Berg Collection, New York Public Library, NY3: perhaps the 'canonically purest' of Donne manuscripts, it is written in the hand of Donne's friend Rowland Woodward and contains seventy-nine of Donne's poems, ten prose paradoxes, and a prose letter addressed by Donne to Woodward. Many editions of Donne's poetry have used this manuscript as their textual starting point.

NOTES

Introduction

1 **carrying paper and ink** Francis Russell, the Earl of Bedford, filled multiple notebooks with listening notes from Donne's sermons. S. Verweij, 'Sermon Notes from John Donne in the Manuscripts of Francis Russell, Fourth Earl of Bedford', *English Literary Renaissance* 46:2 (2016), pp. 278–313.

– **charm the soul** Henry Valentine, 'An Elegy upon the Incomparable Doctor Donne', in Donne, *Poems* (1633), p. 379.

– **There was a great concourse.** Thomas E. Tomlins (ed.), *Walton's Lives, with Notes* (1852), p. 79.

3 **raw vapours** There is not yet a modern edition of Donne's letters, though *The Oxford Edition of the Letters of John Donne* is forthcoming, and has been in progress for more than fifty years. Therefore all quotations from Donne's letters, unless otherwise stated, come from the collection his son John put together and published after his death: *Letters to Severall Persons of Honour* (1651). p. 31

– **'O Lady, lighten our darkness'** In the Latin Bible, Psalm 17 reads: 'O Lord, lighten my darkness.'

4 **License my roving hands** 'To His Mistress Going to Bed', lines 25–8. All quotations of Donne's poetry are from Robin Robbins' brilliant edition, *The Complete Poems of John Donne* (2014). Poems are usually identified in the text of the book, but where they are not they are noted here in the endnotes, as well as in the index.

5 **But O, self-traitor** 'Twickenham Garden', lines 6–8.

– **Us she informed** 'To the Countess of Huntingdon', line 26.

7 **Nothing but man** 'An Elegy upon the Death of Lady Markham', lines 13–14.

– **one might almost say** 'The Second Anniversary', line 246.

– **it is too little.** John Donne, *Devotions upon Emergent Occasions* (1624), Meditation IV.

– **be thine own palace** 'To Mr Henry Wotton', line 52.

10 **just over 9,100 lines** Gary Stringer, 'The Composition and Dissemination of Donne's Writings', in *The Oxford Handbook of John Donne*, ed. Jeanne Shami, Dennis Flynn and M. Thomas Hester (2016), p. 13.

– **Donne seems to have used the form** Margaret Maurer, 'The Verse Letter', in *The Oxford Handbook of John Donne*, p. 207.

13 **twenty-four ten-syllable lines** Julia M. Walker, 'Donne's Words Taught in Numbers', *Studies in Philology* 84 (1987), pp. 44–60, 51.

14 **dwell bodily** All sermon quotations are from *The Sermons of John Donne*, ed. George R. Potter and Evelyn M. Simpson, 10 vols (1953–62). *Sermons*, Vol. VI, p. 363.

– **super-edifications, super-exaltation** All these examples are collected by John Carey, *John Donne: Life, Mind and Art* (2014), 113.

15 **more extravagant rendering** Thomas Docherty, *John Donne, Undone* (1986), p. 54.

16 **Donne seems to deserve** Robbins, *The Complete Poems of John Donne*, p. 355.

17 **akin to sacrament** Robbins notes Donne's love of words that evoke sacrament in *The Complete Poems of John Donne*, p. 355. 'The Canonisation', lines 26–7.

– **All measure, and all language** 'The Relic', lines 32–3.

19 **Dark texts** 'To the Countess of Bedford', line 11.

The Prodigious Child

20 **whispered (erroneously)** Colin Burrow, 'Recribrations', *London Review of Books*, 5 October 2006.

– **The family had once owned** M. Thomas Hester, Robert Parker

Sorlien and Dennis Flynn (eds), *John Donne's Marriage Letters in the Folger Shakespeare Library* (2005), p. 11.

22 **Though [Donne's] own learning** Izaak Walton, *The Lives of Dr John Donne, Sir Henry Wotton, Mr Richard Hooker, Mr George Herbert* (1670), p. 11. All quotations from Walton's life are from this text, unless otherwise stated.

– **I have seen women** John Heywood, *The Play Called the Four PP: A new and a very merry interlude of a palmer, a pardoner, a potycary, a pedler* (1545), unpaginated.

23 **If thou beest born** 'Go and Catch a Falling Star', lines 10–18.

– **His grandfather became famous** C. S. Lewis (ed.), *English Literature in the Sixteenth Century: Excluding Drama* (1954), p. 146.

24 **divers Latin books** John Stow, *Annales*, cited in William Bernard MacCabe, *A Catholic History of England* (1847), Vol. I, p. 322.

25 **suffered with great constancy** William E. Andrews, *Review of Fox's Book of Martyrs* (1826), Vol. III, p. 337.

– **I went out to Charing Cross** Samuel Pepys, *The Shorter Pepys*, ed. Robert Latham (1985), p. 86.

– **tradition holds** Dennis Flynn, *John Donne and the Ancient Catholic Nobility* (1995), p. 70.

– **fell asunder** ibid., p. 21.

27 **I pray you** William Roper, *The Life of Sir Thomas More, Knight*, ed. E. V. Hitchcock (1935), p. 103.

– **Pluck up thy spirits** ibid.

– **I cannot tell** Flynn, *John Donne and the Ancient Catholic Nobility*, p. 21.

– **the pretended Queen** Alec Ryrie, *The Age of Reformation: The Tudor and Stewart Realms 1485–1603* (2017), p. 228.

28 **some bystanders, leaving** John Donne, *Pseudo-Martyr* (1610), p. 222.

29 **I accompanied her** Flynn, *John Donne and the Ancient Catholic Nobility*, p. 129.

– **a Consultation of Jesuits** ibid., pp. 123–30.

30 **I have been ever kept awake** *Pseudo-Martyr*, foreword, sig 1r.

The Hungry Scholar

31 **read the Bible thorough** Katherine Philips, *The Collected Works of Katherine Philips*, Vol. I: *The Poems*, ed. Patrick Thomas (1990), p. x.

– **another Picus Mirandula** Walton, *Lives*, p. 13.

32 **unto their urine** Liza Picard, *Elizabeth's London: Everyday Life in Elizabethan London* (2013), p. 195.

– **when a schoolmaster** Richard Burn, *Justice of the Peace*, cited in Jonathan Gathorne-Hardy, *The Public School Phenomenon 597–1977* (2014), p. 97.

– **Donne learned that later** R. C. Bald, *John Donne: A Life* (revised edition, 1986), p. 40. Robert Cecil Bald's biography of Donne forms the bedrock of this book, and of every other account of Donne's life since its first publication in 1970; it's a piece of spectacularly detailed scholarship, and though many new documents have since come to light which nuance and adjust his telling, his work remains central to Donne scholarship.

33 **mean men's children** Lawrence Stone, *The Crisis of the Aristocracy, 1558–1641* (1965), p. 687.

– **in the most unsettled days** Walton, *Lives*, p. 62.

34 **I exercise my pen** James McConica and T. H. Aston (eds), *The History of the University of Oxford*, Vol. III (1986), p. 41.

– **'The Oxford Scholar'** Cambridge University Library, MS Add. 29.

35 **once of New College** Alan Davidson, 'An Oxford Family: A Footnote to the Life of John Donne', *Recusant History* 13:4 (1976), pp. 299–300.

– **not dissolute** Sir Richard Baker in Bald, *John Donne: A Life*, p. 72.

36 **Sir, more than kisses** 'To Mr Henry Wotton', line 1.

– **Izaak Walton's son** This fact has been hiding in the footnotes on page 32 of Jonquil Bevan's edition of Izaak Walton's *The Compleat Angler* (1988).

– **most heterogeneous ideas** Samuel Johnson, *Lives of the Poets*, ed. George Birkbeck Hill (1905), p. 20.

– **first recorded use** Peter McCullough notes the 'commonplacer' coinage in his Oxford edition of Donne's sermons; cited in Piers Brown, 'Donne, Rhapsody, and Textual Order', in Joshua Eckhardt and Daniel Starza Smith (eds), *Manuscript Miscellanies in Early Modern England* (2016), p. 48.

37 **make himself as full a list** Ann Moss, 'Locating Knowledge', in Karl Enenkel and Wolfgang Neuber (eds), *Cognition and the Book: Typologies of Formal Organisation of Knowledge* (2005), p. 36.

– **whatever you come across** ibid.

38 *Academia* and *Tedium* The commonplace book of Robert Southwell, Beinecke MS Osborn b112, pp. 470–1. Southwell was a fan of Donne's: under *Vita*, he lists 'Lives of persons written', including 'Dr. Donne, Sr. Henry Wotton, & Mr. Hooker by Mr. Isaac Walton'.

– **When a poet's mind** T. S. Eliot, *Selected Essays* (3rd edn, London, 1951), p. 287.

40 **goes twitching and hopping** Cited in *The Complete Poems of Joseph Hall*, ed. Alexander B. Grosart (1879), Vol. VIII, p. xvi.

41 **made a bolt for Europe** Dennis Flynn, 'Donne's Education', in *The Oxford Handbook of John Donne*, p. 411.

– **swear the Oath of Supremacy** Heywood to Acquaviva, n.d., ARSI, Anglia 30/I, fo. 118v, cited in Flynn, *John Donne and the Ancient Catholic Nobility*, pp. 131–2.

– **school hostages** Flynn, 'Donne's Education', p. 411.

– **He shuttled twenty students** Allen to Agazzari, 5 November 1582 and 8 August 1583, *Catholic Record Society* IV (1907), pp. 73 and 115; Flynn, 'Donne's Education', p. 412.

42 **perpetual aqueducts** ibid.

– **gentleman, dwelling in Southwark** Bald, *John Donne: A Life*, p. 50.

– **Mistress Symones** ibid.

43 **When Donne arrived** ibid., p. 55.

– **concerns noblemen and gentlemen** Stone, *The Crisis of the Aristocracy*, p. 691.

44 **it shall be lawful** Picard, *Elizabeth's London*, p. 73.

- **fined 13s 4d** ibid., p. 207.
- **found fault with his study** ibid.
45 **For my purpose** *Letters*, p. 238.
- **my best entertainment** ibid.
46 **six or seven galliards** Suzanne Lord and David Brinkman, *Music from the Age of Shakespeare: A Cultural History* (2003), p. 9.
- **If any man will sue** *Sermons*, Vol. VIII, p. 145.
- **Away, thou changeling** Satire I, lines 1–4.
48 **written all his best pieces** 'Certain Informations and Manners of Jonson to W. Drummond', in *Notes of Ben Jonson's Conversations at Hawthornden*, cited in Gary A. Stringer (ed.), *The Variorum Edition of the Poetry of John Donne*, Vol. II: *The Elegies*, p. xciv.
49 **If love could find** Walter Raleigh, 'Now We Have a Present Made', lines 25–8; *Selected Writings*, ed. Gerald Hammond (1986), p. 50.
- **Donne, whose muse** Samuel Taylor Coleridge, 'On Donne's Poetry', cited in A. J. Smith, *John Donne: The Critical Heritage* (2010), p. 264.
- **Would not Donne's satires** John Dryden, 'Of the Original and Progress of Satire' (1693); *Of Dramatic Poesy and Other Essays*, ed. George Watson (1962), Vol. II, p. 144.
51 **produced by a voluntary deviation** Samuel Johnson, *Lives of the Poets*, ed. Robina Napier (1890), p. 42.
52 **And they're his own** Satire II, lines 25–30.

The Exquisitely Clothed Theoriser on Fashion

55 **his apparel pretend no lightness** William Dugdale, *Origines Juridiciales or Historical Memorials of the English Laws, Courts of Justice, Forms of Tryal* (1671), p. 197.
56 **of stature moderately tall** Walton, *Lives*, p. 80.
57 **his beard well brushed** Simion Grahame, *The Anatomy of Humours* (1609), p. 30.
- **snotty nosed gentlemen** ibid.

Brother to a Dead Man

61 **Oh happy people** George Deaux, *The Black Death* (1969), p. 94.

62 **If you fell ill** Picard, *Elizabeth's London*, p. 92.

– **What an unmatchable torment** *The Plague Pamphlets of Thomas Dekker*, ed. F. P. Wilson (1925), p. 160.

– **dine with his friends** Ernest B. Gilman, *Plague Writing in Early Modern England* (2009), p. 33.

– **felt a pricking** *The Plague Pamphlets of Thomas Dekker*, p. 160.

– **The brothels emptied** Antoine Joseph, *English Professional Theatre, 1530–1660* (2000), p. 84.

63 **whimpring sonnets** Everard Guilpin, *Skialetheia* (1598, 1958 facsimile reprint), sig B8.

– **in this lamentable calamity** *Sermons*, Vol. VI, p. 362.

64 **every puff of wind** ibid.

– **Fair London** John Taylor, *The Fearful Summer, or London's Calamity* (1636), sig A3r.

– **not only incurable** *Sermons*, Vol. VII, p. 80.

65 **said he was a priest** F. P. Wilson, 'Notes on the Early Life of John Donne', *Review of English Studies* 3:11 (1927), pp. 272–9.

66 **eaten of lice** Thomas Boys, *Notes and Queries*, 19 February 1859, p. 159.

– **drawn from Newgate** Stow, cited in Bald, *John Donne: A Life*, p. 58.

– **proofs of unusual constancy** Richard Simpson, *Under the Penal Laws: Instances of Sufferings of Catholics* (1930), p. 82.

67 **A contemporary Catholic claimed** See Wilson, 'Notes on the Early Life of John Donne', p. 275.

– **have favour shown them** Tom Cain, 'Elegy and Autobiography: "The Bracelet" and the Death of Henry Donne', *John Donne Journal* 23 (2004), pp. 25–57.

– **Donne did not visit** ibid., p. 33.

– **He was nineteen** Some sources have him as twenty years old; Cain, 'Elegy and Autobiography', p. 33.

68 **at least ten per cent of deaths** A. Lloyd Moote and Dorothy C.

Moote, *The Great Plague: the Story of London's Most Deadly Year* (2004), p. 10, and Paul Slack, *The Impact of Plague in Tudor and Stuart England* (1985), p. 145.

- **killed up to seventy per cent** Gilman, *Plague Writing in Early Modern England*, p. 192.

69 **I have a sin of fear** 'To Christ', lines 13–14.

- **I am a little world** Divine Meditation VII, lines 1–2.

The Convert (Perhaps)

70 **eleven members** Cain, 'Elegy and Autobiography', p. 29.

- **the art of copying** John Donne, *The Courtier's Library, Or Catalogus Librorum Aulicorum incomparabilium et non vendibilium*, ed. and trans. Evelyn M. Simpson (1930), p. 43.

71 **Grief which did drown me** 'To Mr Rowland Woodward', lines 6–8.

72 **Donne may even have helped** Cain, 'Elegy and Autobiography', p. 32.

- **be then thine own home** 'To Mr Henry Wotton', line 47.

- **answerable to my father's estate** Letter to Lord Keeper Puckering, cited in Cain, 'Elegy and Autobiography', p. 35.

- **Jesuits were in part to blame** Bald, *John Donne: A Life*, p. 67.

- **indirectly . . . cause Priests** William Clark, *A Reply unto a Certain Libel Lately Set Forth by Father Persons* (1603), 18r.

73 **They do not indeed** Christopher Bagshaw, *A True Relation of the Faction Begun at Wisbich* (1601), pp. 73–4.

- **coded reference to Henry** Cain, 'Elegy and Autobiography', p. 42.

74 **image of a dead boy** Carey, *John Donne: Life, Mind and Art*, p. 39.

The (Unsuccessful) Adventurer

75 **dearths and Spaniards** Satire II, line 6.

76 **A Journal of all the particularities** Lambeth Palace MS 250, cited in Bald, *John Donne: A Life*, p. 80.

77 **they are strong enough** R. A. Roberts (ed.), 'Cecil Papers: May 1596, 16–31', in *Calendar of the Cecil Papers in Hatfield House*

(1895), Vol. VI, pp. 183–208. John Stubbs cites George Carew in his description of the sailors setting out: 'three hundred green-headed youths, covered with feathers, gold and silver lace'. John Stubbs, *Donne: The Reformed Soul* (2006), p. 59.

– they all let ship Edward Edwards, *The Life of Sir Walter Raleigh* (1868), Vol. II, p. 152.

– died of grief. Henry Baerlein, *Spain: Yesterday and Tomorrow* (1930), p. 152.

– to march into the market place Cited in J. S. Corbett, *The Successors of Drake* (1900), p. 108.

81 we thought to yield *Calendar of State Papers (Domestic) 1595–1597*, p. 463, cited in Robbins, *The Complete Poems of John Donne*, p. 64.

– Some coffined in their cabins 'The Storm', lines 45–6.

– Memorable accidents. *'Memorable Accidents, and Unheard of Transactions' Published in English by B.B.* (1693), sig A4.

82 at this awful hour *Memoirs of William Hickey* (1921), Vol. II, p. 22.

– it is true that Jonas Edward le Comte, *Grace to a Witty Sinner: A Life of John Donne* (1965), p. 34.

83 We were very much becalmed Sir Arthur Gorges, Captain of the *Warspite*, in *Voyage to the Iles of Azores*, cited in Robbins, *The Complete Poems of John Donne*, p. 65.

85 As West and East 'Hymn to God My God in My Sickness', lines 13–15.

– landmasses took on eyes Noam Flinker, 'John Donne and the "Anthropomorphic Map" Tradition', *Applied Semiotics* 3:8 (1999), pp. 207–15, 208.

86 *venite commiscemini nobiscum* John Block Friedman, *Trade, Travel and Exploration in the Middle Ages* (2000), p. 459.

The Inexperienced Expert of Love

87 history of the handshake Peter Hall and Dee Ann Hall, 'The Handshake as Interaction', *Semiotica* 45 (1983), pp. 249–64;

Keith Thomas, 'Introduction', in Jan Bremmer and Herman Roo-
denburg (eds), *A Cultural History of Gesture* (1991), pp. 1–14.

89 **like place, pre-eminence** 5 Eliz 1 c 18; John Lord Campbell,
*Lives of the Lord Chancellors and Keepers of the Great Seal of
England, from the Earliest Times Till the Reign of King George
IV* (1868), p. 219.

– **I had a desire** Edmund Gosse, *The Life and Letters of John
Donne* (1899, reprinted 2019), Vol. I, p. 114.

– **took him to be** Walton, *Lives*, p. 17.

91 **it is wonderful** Erica Fudge, *Perceiving Animals: Humans and
Beasts in Early Modern English Culture* (2002), p. 11.

– **with biting** Edgar Innes Fripp, *Shakespeare, Man and Artist*
(1964), p. 101.

– **lions so tame** Caroline Grigson, *Menagerie: The History of
Exotic Animals in England, 1100–1837* (2016), p. 7.

92 **Priss Fotheringham** John Garfield, *The Wand'ring Whore*
(1661), in Fergus Linnane, *London, The Wicked City: A
Thousand Years of Prostitution and Vices* (2007), p. 73.

93 **had the running** E. K. Chambers, *William Shakespeare: A Study
of Facts and Problems* (1930), Vol. II, p. 12.

– **The navel must be tied** Jacques Guillemeau, *Child-birth or the
Happy Delivery of Women* (1612), p. 99.

94 **necessary for conception** Deborah Simonton (ed.), *The Routledge
History of Women in Europe Since 1700* (2006), p. 56.

– **almost certainly, not** Arthur Marotti, *John Donne, Coterie Poet*
(1986), passim.

– **proved with child** Gary Fredric Waller, *The Sidney Family
Romance: Mary Wroth, William Herbert, and the Early
Modern Construction of Gender* (1993), p. 78.

– **if it had pleased god** Brian O'Farrell, *Shakespeare's Patron: William
Herbert, Third Earl of Pembroke, 1580–1630* (2011), p. 22.

– **those who risked it** R. V. Schnucker, 'Elizabethan Birth Control
and Puritan Attitudes', *Journal of Interdisciplinary History* 5:4
(1975), pp. 655–67.

95 **brothels lining the river** Gustav Ungerer, 'Prostitution in
 Late Elizabethan London: The Case of Mary Newborough',
 Medieval and Renaissance Drama in England 15 (2003), pp.
 138–223.
 – **the young novice** 'Look on Me London – a Countryman's
 Counsel Given to His Son Going up to Dwell at London'
 (1613) in *Blood and Knavery: A Collection of English
 Renaissance Ballads of Crime and Sin*, ed. Joseph Mashburn
 and Alec R. Velie (1973), p. 164.
98 **thirty-two of Donne's** Carey, *John Donne: Life, Mind and Art*,
 p. 201.
99 **The meaning could be** This is very much debated. See Noralyn
 Masselink, 'Wormseed Revisited: Glossing Line Forty of
 Donne's "Farewell to Love"', *English Language Notes* 30:2
 (December 1992), pp. 11–15.

The Erratic Collector of His Own Talent

101 **your Lordship's secretary** Stephen W. May, 'Donne and
 Egerton', in *The Oxford Handbook of John Donne*, p. 452.
 – **His signature appears** ibid.
102 **cost me more diligence** Gosse, *Life and Letters*, Vol. II, p. 68.
 – **a rag of verses** Carey, *John Donne: Life, Mind and Art*, p. 70.
 – **I know very many** George Puttenham, *The Art of English
 Poesy: A Critical Edition*, ed. Frank Whigham and Wayne
 Rebhorn (2007), p. 112.

The Witness of Disastrous Intrigue

107 **he kept 50 liveries** Bald, *John Donne: A Life*, p. 129.
108 *An Unknown Woman* Dennis Flynn argues that the portrait
 is Anne in an as yet unpublished paper, 'Getting to Know An
 Unknown Woman'.
109 **nor did his Lordship** Walton, *Lives*, p. 17.
 – **he perhaps giveth** John R. Gillis, *For Better, for Worse: British
 Marriages, 1600 to the Present* (1985), p. 35.

110 **numerological joke** Robbins, *The Complete Poems of John Donne*, p. 539.

 – **my lord is at cards** David Loades, *Elizabeth I: A Life* (2006), p. 259.

 – **he spent £40** P. E. J. Hammer, 'Robert Devereux, second earl of Essex (1565–1601), soldier and politician', *Oxford Dictionary of National Biography*.

111 **liked his bumptiousness** Loades, *Elizabeth I: A Life*, p. 260.

112 **he neither could nor would** Carole Levin, *Dreaming the English Renaissance: Politics and Desire in Court and Culture* (2008), p. 131.

 – **she was as crooked** William Oldys, *The Life of Sir Walter Ralegh* (1829), p. 329.

113 **cannot princes err** A. R. Braunmuller, *A Seventeenth Century Letter-Book* (1983), p. 66.

114 **for our wars** L. P. Smith, *The Life and Letters of Sir Henry Wotton* (1907), Vol. I, p. 309.

 – **he never drew sword** Ernest George Atkinson (ed.), *Calendar of the State Papers Relating to Ireland of the Reign of Elizabeth 1599–1600* (1899), p. 260.

115 **removed to a better air** Historical Manuscripts Commission, MSS of Lord de L'Isle and Dudley.

 – **the ladies dance** E. K. Chambers, *The Elizabethan Stage* (2000), Vol. IV, p. 112.

116 **full of jollity** Evelyn M. Simpson, *A Study of the Prose Works of John Donne* (1948), p. 310.

 – **Good Will** Samuel Schoenbaum, *William Shakespeare: A Compact Documentary Life* (1987), p. 200.

 – **A book called Amours** Bald, *John Donne: A Life*, p. 108.

117 **It's possible** ibid., p. 108 n.

 – **My Lord Essex** Simpson, *A Study of the Prose Works of John Donne*, p. 310.

 – **withers still in sickness** Bald, *John Donne: A Life*, p. 108. The attribution of this letter is disputed, but there is a strong case for it being by Donne.

118 **my Lord Keeper** Historical Manuscripts Commission, MSS of Lord de L'Isle and Dudley.

119 **I will have leave** The attribution of this letter is disputed, but Ilona Bell's argument for its being by Donne is persuasive. Ilona Bell, '"Under Ye Rage of a Hott Sonn & Yr Eyes": John Donne's Love Letters to Ann More', in Claude J. Summers and Ted-Larry Pebworth (eds), *The Eagle and the Dove: Reassessing John Donne* (1986), pp. 25–52.

121 **Or as sometimes** 'The Second Anniversary', lines 9–17.

122 **Donne's original plan** *The Works of William Drummond of Hawthornden* (1711), p. 97.

The Paradoxical Quibbler, Taking Aim at Women

125 **I thank God** *Calendar of State Papers: Domestic, 1611–18*, p. 527.

126 **in all that part** Cited in Hester et al. (eds), *John Donne's Marriage Letters*, p. 13.

 – **the sun forsakes us** Bald, *John Donne: A Life*, p. 108.

 – **the twin of his promise** Bell: '"Under Ye Rage of a Hott Sonn & Yr Eyes"', passim.

127 **Take the fresh unspotted** Karen Gordon-Grube, 'Anthropophagy in Post-Renaissance Europe: The Tradition of Medicinal Cannibalism', *American Anthropologist* 90 (June 1988), pp. 405–9.

129 **ate their own belts** Jean de Léry, *Histoire mémorable de la ville de Sancerre* (1574), cited in Robbins, *The Complete Poems of John Donne*, p. 301.

130 **enormous vogue** Peter Platt, *Shakespeare and the Culture of Paradox* (2009), p. 22.

 – **As for those who are offended** Erasmus, *The Praise of Folly*, cited in Platt, *Shakespeare and the Culture of Paradox*, p. 21.

 – **misinterpretation of the work** Cited in Platt, *Shakespeare and the Culture of Paradox*, p. 24.

 – **Oftentimes** Puttenham, *The Art of English Poesy*, p. 311.

131 **a vile man** ibid., introduction passim.
 – **wash made of cabbage stalks** J. L. Heilbron, *Galileo* (2012), p. 86.
 – **Foulness is loathsome** John Donne, *Selected Prose*, ed. Neil Rhodes (1987), p. 38.
132 **That women are inconstant** ibid., p. 48.
 – **Women are like flies** ibid., p. 49.
133 **so many advantages** ibid., p. 53.
 – **we deny souls** ibid.
 – **Valens Acidalius** Michael Nolan, 'The Mysterious Affair at Mâcon: The Bishops and the Souls of Women', *New Blackfriars* 74:876 (November 1993), pp. 501–7.
 – **Perchance because the Devil** *Selected Prose*, p. 54.
134 **Some men** *Sermons*, Vol. I, p. 448.
 – **No author of gravity** ibid.
 – **He chose to level** Meg Lota Brown, *Donne and the Politics of Conscience in Early Modern England* (1994), p. 70.
 – **in a letter** Simpson, *A Study of the Prose Works*, p. 216.

Anne

137 **that fair and learned hand** This is still much debated: Janet E. Halley, 'Textual Intercourse: Anne Donne, John Donne, and the Sexual Poetics of Textual Exchange' in Sheila Fisher and Janet E. Halley (eds), *Seeking the Woman in Late Medieval and Renaissance Writings: Essays in Feminist Contextual Criticism* (1989), pp. 187–206, calls Anne 'functionally illiterate'. I believe Wotton's comment, along with George More's wealth and Donne's epitaph, are sufficient to think she was educated, but the point isn't universally agreed upon.
 – **passionate treatises** Lawrence Stone, *The Family, Sex and Marriage in England 1500–1800* (1977), p. 142.
 – **Do we not see** Richard Mulcaster, *Positions Wherein Those Primitive Circumstances Be Examined, Which Are Necessarie for the Training Up of Children, Either for Skill in their Booke, or Health in their Bodie* (1561), p. 168.

– **Women, in Castiglione's world** Stone, *The Family, Sex and Marriage in England*, p. 143.

138 **Plato in petticoats** ibid.

– **this humour in both sexes** ibid.

– **too quickly won** *Romeo and Juliet*, Act II, Scene 2, lines 96–7.

– **The richer you were** Stone, *The Family, Sex and Marriage in England*, p. 130.

– **beaten once in the week** ibid.

The Daring of the Lover, and the Imprisoned Groom

141 **Donne could be as metaphysical** Wayne K. Chapman, *Yeats and English Renaissance Literature* (1991), p. 144.

142 **Pierre de Ronsard** Hugh Richmond, *Puritans and Libertines: Anglo-French Literary Relationships in the Reformation* (1981), p. 246.

– **worst voluptuousness** *Letters*, p. 51.

– **the lazy seeds** Thomas Carew, 'An Elegy upon the Death of the Dean of Paul's, Dr John Donne', lines 26–8.

143 **about three weeks** Folger MS L.b. 526.

– **the Savoy** John Schofield, 'The Construction of Medieval and Tudor Houses in London', *Construction History* 7 (1991), pp. 3–28.

145 **I knew my present estate** Gosse, *Life and Letters*, Vol. I, p. 101.

146 **employed lawyers** Hester et al. (eds), *John Donne's Marriage Letters*, p. 16.

147 **that fault which was laid** Folger MS L.b.529.

– **it is not safe** *The Works of Francis Osborne* (1701), p. 66.

148 **disgusting and expensive** Walter Thornbury, 'The Fleet Prison', in *Old and New London: Volume 2* (1878), pp. 404–6.

149 **accusing the deputy warden** ibid., p. 406.

– **And though perchance** Gosse, *Life and Letters*, Vol. I, p. 104.

150 **all my endeavours** ibid., p. 106.

– **whom I leave no humble way** ibid.

– **be pleased to lessen** ibid.

151 **My conscience** ibid., p. 107.

  – **neither gave rest** Walton, *Lives*, p. 20.

152 **and pardon me** Izaak Walton, *The Life of John Donne, with some original notes by an antiquary*, ed. T. E. Tomlins (1865), p. 29.

  – **elegant irresistible art** Walton, *Lives*, p. 21.

  – **I was four years** Gosse, *Life and Letters*, Vol. I, p. 114.

153 **To seek preferment** ibid.

  – **unfeignedly sorry** Walton, *Lives*, p. 21.

  – **unambiguous victory** Hester et al. (eds), *John Donne's Marriage Letters*, p. 18.

  – **A true and pure marriage** ibid., p. 19.

154 **possible the pun was never Donne's** Ernest W. Sullivan, 'Donne's Epithalamium for Anne', in Hester (ed.), *John Donne's 'Desire of More'*, pp. 36–8.

  – **Immediately after his dismission** Walton, *Lives*, pp. 17–18.

  – **the remarkable error** ibid., p. 53.

  – **In the time of Master Donne's** Sullivan, 'Donne's Epithalamium for Anne', p. 37.

155 **Doctor Donne after he was married** ibid.

The Anticlimactically Married Man

156 **adorned with paintings** Bald, *John Donne: A Life*, p. 140.

157 **George More had published** Bald first gestured to this link; *John Donne: A Life*, p. 129, which was also noted in Alistair Cameron Crombie and Michael Hoskin (eds), *History of Science* (1968), p. 35, but first rigorously expanded by John Stubbs in *Donne: The Reformed Soul*, p. 178.

  – **England, my dear country** George More, *A Demonstration of God in His Workes* (1597), p. 1.

158 **We can die by it** 'The Canonisation', line 28.

  – **I died at a blow** *Letters*, p. 51.

  – **Your friends are sorry** Bald, *John Donne: A Life*, p. 144.

159 **When Octavio Baldi came** Walton, *The Life of Henry Wotton*, *Lives*, p. 26.

160 **he departed as true** ibid.

– **such a one as I** Cited in Bald, *John Donne: A Life*, p. 146.

– *For me.* This letter to Wotton, and the logistics of their friendship, are discussed in Bald, *John Donne: A Life*, p. 146.

162 **I accompany** *Letters*, p. 88.

163 **Sometimes when I find** ibid., p. 71.

The Ambivalent Father

164 **Gentlemen of thirty** John Aubrey, *Brief Lives: And Other Selected Writings*, ed. Anthony Powell (1949), p. 11.

165 **kneel to ask blessing** *Sermons*, Vol. IX, p. 59.

– **I have not been out** *Letters*, pp. 137–8.

– **When I must shipwreck** ibid., pp. 50–1.

– **I write not to you** ibid., p. 137.

166 **Thou hast delivered** John Donne, *Essays in Divinity: Being Several Disquisitions Interwoven with Meditations and Prayers*, ed. Anthony Raspa (2003), p. 83.

– **unlikely to lie** Carey, *John Donne: Life, Mind and Art*, p. 73.

167 **spectacularly off** This assessment – that the poem would fail as a piece of indirect compliment, and is more likely to have been a paradox composed by Donne to send among his male coterie – is indebted to Robin Robbins, *Poems*, p. 733.

– **a world alone** Walton, *Lives*, p. 101.

168 **the incommodity** Bald, *John Donne: A Life*, p. 158.

– **closer to London** ibid.

– **ordinary forges of letters** *Letters*, p. 137.

169 **Anne's sisters** Bald, *John Donne: A Life*, p. 158.

– **I am a Father** *Letters*, p. 119.

– **I must beg of you** ibid., p. 232.

– **The newest thing** ibid., p. 154.

170 **I stand like a tree** ibid., p. 233.

– **I have already lost** ibid., p. 153.

– **of one of which** ibid.

171 **Because I loved it** ibid., p. 273.

- **Infant mortality** A. Wrigley and R. S. Davies et al. (eds), *English Population History from Family Reconstitution 1580–1837* (1997), p. 207.
- **stone effigies** Stone, *The Crisis of the Aristocracy*, p. 595.

172 **Rest in soft peace** *The Cambridge Edition of the Works of Ben Jonson: 1601–1606*, ed. Ian Donaldson et al. (2012). 'On My First Son', lines 9–10.
- **the Lord hath taken** Raymond Anselment, *The Realms of Apollo: Literature and Healing in Seventeenth-century England* (1995), p. 82.
- **Dear infant** Pamela S. Hammons, *Despised Creatures: The Illusion of Maternal Self-Effacement in Seventeenth-Century Child Loss Poetry* (2002), 30.
- **Nor can I think** ibid., p. 29.
- **people of bygone ages** Marcel Proust, *In Search of Lost Time*, Vol. III, *The Guermantes Way*, trans. C. K. Scott Moncrieff, ed. William Carter (2018), p. 460.

173 **Two days after** Gosse, *Life and Letters*, Vol. I, p. 280.

174 **the same day** Bald, *John Donne: A Life*, p. 252.

How to Pretend to Have Read More than You Have

175 **Must!** J. R. Green, *A Short History of the English People* (1874), ch. 7.
- **children of the chapel** James Basire II after William Camden, *The funeral procession of Queen Elizabeth I on 27 numbered sheets* (1791).
- **In the death of that Queen** *Sermons*, Vol. I, p. 217.

176 **indeed made up of two** James Spedding, *Evenings with a Reviewer* (1848), p. 229.
- **The new king** *Calendar of State Papers (Venetian) 1603–1607*, p. 70, cited in Robbins, *The Complete Poems of John Donne*, p. 247.

177 **he was the most honest** Walton, *Lives, The Life of Sir Henry Wotton*, p. 113.

178 **satirical list of books** Daniel Starza Smith, Matthew Payne and Melanie Marshall, 'Rediscovering John Donne's *Catalogus librorum satyricus*', *Review of English Studies* 69:290 (June 2018), p. 455.

179 **Sir Edward Hoby's Afternoon Belchings** *The Courtier's Library*, ed. and trans. Simpson, p. 50.

– **What Not?** ibid., p. 52.

– **itself a joke** Starza Smith et al., 'Rediscovering John Donne's *Catalogus librorum satyricus*', p. 455.

180 **a Latin letter** The first ever English translation of this letter is offered by Melanie Marshall in Starza Smith et al., 'Rediscovering John Donne's *Catalogus librorum satyricus*', Appendix III

181 **Donne implied** This reading is wholly indebted to conversations with Daniel Starza Smith, and his blog with Melanie Marshall, 'John Donne and the Jacobean Fake Media', 15 August 2018, blogs.kcl.ac.uk/english/2018/08/15/john-donne-and-the-jacobean-fake-media.

– **jabs of disapprobation** ibid.

The Suicidal Man

183 **The pleasantness of the season** *Letters*, p. 78.

– **I have contracted** ibid., p. 32.

– **The day before** ibid., p. 34.

184 **conclude two things** John Donne, *Biathanatos* (1644), p. 183.

185 **Successful suicides** Carey, *John Donne: Life, Mind and Art*, p. 206.

– **And Nicephorus** *Biathanatos*, p. 186.

186 **many martyrs having hanged** ibid., p. 189.

– **other than His own will** ibid.

– **utterly defeated** Cited in Jeremy Bernstein, 'Heaven's Net: The Meeting of John Donne and Johannes Kepler', *The American Scholar* 66:2 (1997), pp. 175–195, 185.

– **because I had my first breeding** *Biathanatos*, p. 17.

187 **whensoever any affliction** ibid., p. 18.

– It was written by me *Letters*, p. 22.

188 a stomach colic ibid., p. 57.

– it hath pleased God ibid., p. 168.

– I have passed ten days ibid.

189 this advantage ibid., p. 242.

– I am not alive ibid., p. 317.

190 Anthony Tuckney Carey, *John Donne: Life, Mind and Art*, p. 209.

– Thomas Creech ibid.

– Charle Blount wrote approvingly Lucio Biasiori, 'The Exception as Norm: Casuistry of Suicide in John Donne's Biathanatos', in Carlo Ginzburg and Lucio Biasiori (eds), *A Historical Approach to Casuistry* (2020), p. 168.

191 found that self-preservation ibid.

The Flatterer

192 I may not accept Walton, *Lives*, p. 26.

193 your going away *Letters*, p. 1.

– they are disfigured Allen Barry Cameron, 'Donne's Deliberative Verse Epistles', *English Literary Renaissance* 6:3 (1976), pp. 369–403, 370.

– I am not come out *Letters*, p. 244.

197 that favour ibid., p. 104.

– I have learned Preparatory letter, 'Obsequies to the Lord Harington, Brother to the Countess of Bedford'.

198 I confess to you *Letters*, p. 219.

– tell you truly Peter Redford, *The Burley Manuscript* (2017), p. 210.

199 A man may flatter *Sermons*, Vol. V, p. 58.

200 The influence of those *Pseudo-Martyr*, dedicatory letter, 'To the high and mighty Prince James, by the Grace of God, King of Great Britain, France and Ireland, defender of the faith'.

201 who but a monomaniac Simpson, *A Study of the Prose Works*, p. 179.

– apprehending it Walton, *Lives*, p. 34.

- **Ignatius rushed out** John Donne, *Ignatius His Conclave*, ed. T. S. Healy (1969), p. 31.
- **whosoever flatters** ibid., p. 33.

202 **(at the best) instructs** ibid.
- **Whoe'er is raised** Jonson, 'To My Muse', Epigram 65.
- **not worth/The least** *Works of William Drummond of Hawthornden*, p. 225.

203 **had her ears boxed** Le Comte, *Grace to a Witty Sinner*, p. 129.

204 **descend[ed] to print** *Letters*, p. 74.
- **if he had written it** Ben Jonson, *Selected Works*, ed. Ian Donaldson (1985), p. 596.
- **if any of those ladies** *Letters*, p. 239.
- **For since I never saw** ibid.

205 **An exercise in testing** As argued by John Carey, *John Donne: Life, Mind and Art*, p. 103.

The Clergyman

207 **at every corner** Thomas Dekker, *The Seven Deadly Sins of London*, ed. H. F. B. Brett-Smith (1922), p. 37.
- **The inhabitants** Charles Dudley Warner, *The People for Whom Shakespeare Wrote* (2018), p. 41.

208 **they care little for foreigners** ibid.
- **give up his horse** Bald, *John Donne: A Life*, p. 280.
- **expectation of a state-employment** Walton, *Lives*, p. 25.

210 **still charm[ed]** A. J. Smith, *John Donne: The Critical Heritage*, Vol. II, p. 153.

211 **Donne had to fight** This reading is indebted to Jeanne Shami, 'Donne's Decision to Take Orders', in *The Oxford Handbook of John Donne*, who lays out the newest evidence for re-dating the Carr letters in a way that suggests Donne pushed for ordination for significantly more than a year, before he was able to take orders. The forthcoming *Oxford Edition of the Letters of John Donne*, ed. Daniel Starza Smith, Lara Crowley et al., will take the same stance.

- a new reading has emerged Most notably Jeanne Shami's reading.
- if any mischance Robert Chambers, *The Life of King James the First: In Two Volumes* (1830), Vol. II, p. 181.
212 *Rex fuit Elizabeth* John Lockman, *The History of England, by Question and Answer* (1811), p. 140.
- constantly leaneth Alan Stewart, *The Cradle King: A Life of James VI & I* (2011), p. 258.
213 that men had had David Lindley, *The Trials of Frances Howard: Fact and Fiction at the Court of King James* (2013), p. 97.
214 all the ladies about the Court ibid., p. 55.
- immoderately given up ibid.
- Carr was the route Daniel Starza Smith, *John Donne and the Conway Papers: Patronage and Manuscript Circulation in the Early Seventeenth Century* (2014), p. 258.
215 For, having obeyed Gosse, *Life and Letters*, Vol. II, p. 20.
- perchance this business *Letters*, p. 270.
216 by my troth ibid., p. 180. The Oxford *Letters*, the first modern edition of Donne's letters, will date this letter to 19 January: almost a full month after the wedding, Donne had not yet started the poem, though he dates it, once it is finally completed, 26 December. Starza Smith, *John Donne and the Conway Papers*, p. 258.
217 the implication in his letter Shami, 'Donne's Decision to Take Orders', p. 531.
- surprised that my ancestors John P. Kenyon, *The Stuarts: A Study in English Kingship* (1959), p. 56.
- pursue my first purpose Shami, 'Donne's Decision to Take Orders', p. 532.
218 a treason against myself ibid., p. 534, citing the Donne marriage letters, a collection of letters between Donne and his in-laws which were not available to earlier scholars.
- the handsomest-bodied man Angus Stroud, *Stuart England* (2002), p. 35.
- I desire only David Bergeron, *King James and Letters of Homoerotic Desire* (2002), p. 138.

219 **A page, a Knight** Lindley, *The Trials of Frances Howard*, p. 178.

– **as good allowance** Shami, 'Donne's Decision to Take Orders,' p. 535.

– **in the search of the Eastern tongues** Gosse, *Life and Letters*, Vol. II, p. 16.

220 **she had more suspicion** *Letters*, p. 218.

– **though better than any other** Bald, *John Donne: A Life*, p. 305.

221 **a sheaf of snakes** 'To Mr George Herbert with My Seal of the Anchor and Christ', lines 22–4 and 27–8.

– **now all his studies** Walton, *Lives*, p. 37.

– **I would fain do** *Letters*, p. 50.

222 **now, all his earthly affections** Walton, *Lives*, p. 37.

– **villagers of Shadwell** W. G. Hoskins, *Provincial England: Essays in Social and Economic History* (2015), p. 179.

– **somebody most beastly** Kevin Sharpe, *The Personal Rule of Charles I* (1992), p. 398.

223 **rest a little** Peter McCullough, 'Donne as Preacher', in Achsah Guibbory (ed.), *The Cambridge Companion to John Donne* (2006), p. 172.

224 **the preacher . . . standeth** Andreas Hyperius, *The Practise of Preaching*, trans. John Ludham (1577), p. 70, cited by McCullough, 'Donne as Preacher', p. 175.

– **a preacher in earnest** Walton, *Lives*, p. 38.

– **there shall be no cloud** *Sermons*, Vol. VIII, p. 19.

225 **he did preach there** Bald, *John Donne: A Life*, p. 426.

226 **I would gladly see** Cited ibid., p. 323.

The Widower

227 **my good is dead** 'Since She Whom I Loved', line 12.

– **the affections of his hearers** Walton, *Lives*, p. 42.

– **as common people are not** ibid.

228 **words for her that unfurl** M. Thomas Hester, 'Faeminae Lectissimae: Reading Anne Donne', in *John Donne's 'Desire of More'*, p. 18.

230 **shape of a cross** Loseley manuscript collection, Folger
      Shakespeare Library, MS L.b.541.

   – **well read, and read hungrily** Hester, 'Faeminae Lectissimae',
      p. 23.

   – **awkward and uneven** ibid.

   – **Language, thou art** 'Elegy upon the Death of Mistress
      Bulstrode', lines 1–2.

The (Unsuccessful) Diplomat

232 **to surprise his bride** John Carey, *The Unexpected Professor: An
      Oxford Life in Books* (2014), p. 277.

233 **The vanity of the present King** Bernstein, 'Heaven's Net', p. 192.

234 **a great many noblemen's sons** Cited in Bald, *John Donne: A
      Life*, p. 343.

   – **I leave a scattered flock** *Letters*, p. 174.

235 **had to halt** Stubbs, *Donne: The Reformed Soul*, p. 343.

237 **decrees of condemnation** *Sermons*, Vol. VIII, p. 246.

238 **small, thin, swarthy** Rocky Kolb, *Blind Watchers of the Sky:
      The People and Ideas That Shaped Our View of the Universe*
      (1999), p. 44.

   – **the spreading abroad** Cited in Marjorie Nicolson, 'Kepler, the
      Somnium and John Donne', *Journal of the History of Ideas* 1
      (1940), pp. 259–80, 268.

   – **I suspect that the author** Cited ibid., p. 269.

   – **too much credit** Johannes Kepler, *Kepler's Somnium: The
      Dream or Posthumous Work on Lunar Astronomy*, trans. with
      commentary by Edward Rosen (1967), pp. 212–13.

   – **The actual reference to Kepler** ibid., p. 212.

239 **the inscrutable depths** Francis Nethersole, cited in Bald, *John
      Donne: A Life*, p. 365.

240 **convey and commend** Bernstein, 'Heaven's Net', p. 192.

241 **a reference to the planet's quartet** David Levy, *The Starlight
      Night: The Sky in the Writings of Shakespeare, Tennyson and
      Hopkins* (2016), p. 73.

- **And new Philosophy** 'The First Anniversary', lines 205–13.
- **loves not innovations** *Sermons*, Vol. II, p. 305.
242 **gave an affront** *Ignatius*, p. 9.
- **thereby almost a new Creator** ibid., p. 15.
- **In the beginning** *Sermons*, Vol. IV, p. 136, cited in Achsah Guibbory, *Returning to John Donne* (2016), p. 25.
- **For knowledge kindles** 'To Sir Edward Herbert at Juliers', lines 43–4.

The Dean

243 **refused to receive the consecration** Bald, *John Donne: A Life*, p. 372.
244 **When his Majesty sat down** Walton, *Lives*, p. 46.
- **His tongue** It's a fact about James that's much loved by scholars: cited in Stubbs, *Donne: The Reformed Soul*, p. 368, and Derek Parker, *John Donne and His World* (1975), p. 82.
246 **all that I mean** Gosse, *Life and Letters*, Vol. II, p. 140.
- **Portland stone** Carey, *John Donne: Life, Mind and Art*, p. 90.
- **Though be I not Dean** *Letters*, p. 227: cited in Bald, *John Donne: A Life*, p. 381.
248 **be no stranger there** Bald, *John Donne: A Life*, p. 383.
249 **though the poorness of my fortune** Sir Tobie Matthew (ed.), *A Collection of Letters* (1660), p. 326.
250 **the boys and maids** *Calendar of State Papers, Domestic, 1631–1633*, cited in William Longman, *A History of the Three Cathedrals Dedicated to St Paul in London* (1873), p. 54.
- **spur-money** Roze Hentschell, '"Our Children Made Enterluders": Choristers, Actors, and Students in St Paul's Cathedral Precinct', *Early Theatre* 19:2 (2016), pp. 179–95, 184.
- **all the diseased horses** *The Non-Dramatic Works of Thomas Dekker: In Five Volumes*, ed. Fredson Bowers (1884), Vol. II, p. 234.
251 **or, for want of a name** ibid., p. 236.
- **I have obeyed the forms** *Letters*, p. 316.

– **choose your day** ibid.

252 **a re-enactment** John N. Wall., Principal Investigator, *Virtual Paul's Cross Project: A Digital Re-creation of John Donne's Gunpowder Day Sermon.*

255 **Donne loves best** *John Donne's Sermons on the Psalms and Gospels: With a Selection of Prayers and Meditations*, ed. Evelyn M. Simpson (2003), p. 11.

– **The whole frame of the poem** ibid., p. 4.

– **Lying at Aix** *Sermons*, Vol. I, p. 112.

256 **we rise poorer** ibid., Vol. VIII, p. 101.

257 **to hasten their end** *Biathanatos*, p. 137.

– **at the sacrament** *Sermons*, Vol. X, p. 18.

258 **I throw myself down** ibid., Vol. I, p. 95.

259 **We ask our daily bread** ibid., Vol. VI, p. 172.

260 **But how far** ibid., Vol. X, p. 216.

– **It is a dangerous weakness** ibid.

– **Our nature is meteoric** *Letters*, p. 46.

261 **Man would be the giant** *Devotions upon Emergent Occasions*, Meditation IV.

The Monied

262 **lay for their fees** Walton, *Lives*, p. 65.

– **a continual giver** ibid.

263 **there is a trade** *Sermons*, Vol. IV, p. 62.

– **I, when I value** 'Love's Progress', lines 11–16.

– **only the observation of others** *Letters*, p. 142.

264 **My daughters** ibid., p. 117.

265 **Tell both your daughters** ibid., p. 187.

266 **after dinner in your parlour** Some renderings of this letter have 'gave you not content', others 'gave content', as George Hosking, *The Life and Times of Edward Alleyn* (1970), p. 331. From the context, 'not' seems more likely.

– **I see he fears** Gosse, *Life and Letters*, Vol. II, p. 184.

– **barred of my ordinary diet** ibid., p. 208.

- **though I have left my bed** ibid., p. 189.
268 **As sickness is the greatest** *Devotions upon Emergent Occasions*, Meditation V.
- **We study health** ibid., Meditation I.
269 **I am more than dust** ibid., Expostulation I.
- **a little nag** Gosse, *Life and Letters*, Vol. II, p. 218.
270 **unkind, unexpected and undeserved** Bald, *John Donne: A Life*, pp. 464–5.
- **a young maidservant** Daniel Starza Smith, 'Busy Young Fool, Unruly Son? New Light on John Donne Junior', *Review of English Studies*, 62: 256 (2011), pp. 538–56, p. 540. Sara's employer Robert Bedingfield publicly accused John junior, who in turn sued Bedingfield for slander. John junior was acquitted, and the slander action successful, but the balance of evidence suggests John junior was fully guilty.
- **His nature being vile** Anthony à Wood, *Athenae Oxonienses*, ed. Philip Bliss (1813, repr. 1967), Vol. I, p. 503.
271 **his annual income** Bald, *John Donne: A Life*, p. 426.
- **yearly wage bill** Jane Whittle, 'Servants in Rural England 1560–1650: Kussmaul Revisited', Exeter University Working Paper (2015), p. 4.
272 **at one after noon** *Letters*, p. 311.
- **William Cokayne** Coburn Freer, 'John Donne and Elizabethan Economic Theory', *Criticism* 38:4 (1996), pp. 497–520.
273 **The scheme went explosively badly** ibid., p. 509.
274 **did his part diligently** *Sermons*, Vol. VII, p. 274.

Donne and Death

276 **a pin, a comb** *Devotions upon Emergent Occasions*, Meditation XII – as noted by Carey, *John Donne: Life, Mind and Art*, p. 203.
- **the picture called The Skeleton** Donne's Will and Testament, reprinted in Gosse, *Life and Letters*, Vol. II, p. 360.
- **there were rumours** N. E. Land, 'Michelangelo, Giotto, and

Murder', *Explorations in Renaissance Culture* 32:2 (2006), pp. 204–24.

277 **thrums with strange images** Carey, *John Donne: Life, Mind and Art*, p. 201.

– **Death! Be not proud** Holy Sonnet VI, lines 1–2.

278 **I would not that death** *Letters*, p. 50.

– **it hath been my desire** ibid., p. 209.

– **his other, permanent love** Holy Sonnet XI: 'Death be not proud'.

279 **If I had fixed** *Sermons*, Vol. VII, pp. 25–6, cited in Bald, *John Donne: A Life*, p. 491.

– **I shall have my dead** ibid.

280 **he floundered** This sense of Goodere's struggles with the evolving world of the court is wholly indebted to Starza Smith, *John Donne and the Conway Papers*, passim.

– **make . . . to yourself some mark** *Letters*, p. 52.

– **my desire is** Walton, *Lives*, p. 66.

281 **I have cribrated** Bald, *John Donne: A Life*, p. 493.

– **his Majesty King Charles** *The History of the Troubles and Trial of William Laud*, cited in Bald, *John Donne: A Life*, p. 494.

282 **I should be sorry** Cited in the introduction to *Sermons*, Vol. VIII, p. 25.

283 **A man would almost be content** *Letters*, p. 242.

– **he wanted to see in death** Carey, *John Donne: Life, Mind and Art*, p. 202.

– **whole Christian Churches** Ramie Targoff, *John Donne, Body and Soul* (2008), p. 26.

– **who can fear** *Sermons*, Vol. VII, p. 298.

– **In the agonies** ibid., pp. 70–1.

284 **list of paintings** Bald, *John Donne: A Life*, p. 523.

285 **that by cordials** Cited ibid., p. 526.

– **he would not drink** ibid., p. 526.

– **I am afraid** Gosse, *Life and Letters*, Vol. II, p. 269.

– **decayed body** Walton, *Lives*, p. 71.

– **saw his tears** ibid.

286 **Our very birth** John Donne, *Devotions upon Emergent Occasions and Death's Duel* (facsimile edition, 2010), p. 170.

  – **a death united** Michel de Montaigne, *The Living Thoughts of Montaigne*, ed. André Gide, based on translation by John Florio (1946), p. 22.

287 **There we leave you** *Devotions upon Emergent Occasions and Death's Duel*, p. 189.

  – **Who is that 'we'** This shift between I and we in Donne's final work is explored by Ramie Targoff, 'Facing Death', in *The Cambridge Companion to John Donne*, p. 230.

  – **God hath made himself** *Sermons*, Vol. X, p. 117.

288 **It seems to breathe** Walton, *Lives*, p. 80.

  – **His speech** ibid., p. 78.

290 **he closed his own eyes** ibid.

  – **I were miserable** ibid.

Super-infinite

291 **since but thine own** Alison Shell, 'The Death of Donne', in *The Oxford Handbook of John Donne*, p. 651.

292 **a scattered limb** John Donne, *Poems* (1633), sig. A1r.

  – **stole lines** Ernest W. Sullivan II, 'John Donne's Seventeenth Century Readers', in *The Oxford Handbook of John Donne*, p. 30.

  – **doing it to Shakespeare** Lukas Erne, *Shakespeare and the Book Trade* (2013), p. xx.

293 **'Dun's Answer to a Lady'** Robert Chamberlain, *The Harmony of the Muses* (1654), p. 72.

  – **'The Rapture'** ibid., 7.

295 **Now was there ever any man** *Sermons*, Vol. I, p. 197.

  – **Attention** *Letters*, p. 94.

  – **Our creatures** *Selected Prose*, p. 105.

296 **When one man dies** *Devotions upon Emergent Occasions*, Meditation XVII.

  – **No man is an island** ibid.

PICTURE CREDITS

108 'An Unknown Woman', attributed to Nicholas Hilliard, 1602. © *Victoria & Albert Museum, London*

111 Robert Devereux, 2nd Earl of Essex, print by Thomas Cockson, 1599/1600. © *The Trustees of the British Museum*

118 Loseley Park. *Graham Prentice / Alamy Stock Photo*

123 The First Parliament of James I, engraving *c*.1610. © *British Library Board. All Rights Reserved / Bridgeman Images*

147 Sir George More, date and artist unknown. *By kind permission of the More-Molyneux Family*

149 The Fleet Prison, after Hogarth *c*.1735. © *The Trustees of the British Museum*

161 Sir Henry Wotton, date and artist unknown. © *National Portrait Gallery, London*

176–7 The funeral procession of Queen Elizabeth to Westminster Abbey, possibly by William Camden, 1603. © *British Library Board. All Rights Reserved / Bridgeman Images*

196 Lucy Russell, Countess of Bedford, engraved by Simon de Passe, *c*.1599–1618. © *National Portrait Gallery, London*

213 Robert Carr, 1st Earl of Somerset, and Frances, Countess of Somerset, attributed to Renold or Reginold Elstrack, *c*.1615. © *National Portrait Gallery, London*

229 John Donne's epitaph for Anne Donne, 1601/1602. © *Call #: L.b.541. Used by permission of the Folger Shakespeare Library under a Creative Commons Attribution-ShareAlike 4.0 International License.*

236 James Hay, Viscount Doncaster, by an unknown artist, 1628. © *National Portrait Gallery, London*

245 James I of England and VI of Scotland, engraved by Crispijn de Passe the Elder, 1598. © *National Portrait Gallery, London*

247 George Villiers, 1st Duke of Buckingham, attributed to William Larkin, and studio of William Larkin, 1616. © *National Portrait Gallery, London*

248 Stained-glass window in Lincoln's Inn. *The Honourable Society of Lincoln's Inn and York Glaziers Trust*

INDEX